Septem...

by Mary E. Best

Seventy Septembers

by Mary E. Best

Dedication

This book is lovingly dedicated to Sister Marilyn Dobberstein, who had the foresight to request that it be written; to Sister Priscilla Burke, who had the persistency to see that it be completed; and to all the Holy Spirit Missionary Sisters and dedicated lay teachers who have worked in Mississippi and Arkansas.

ACKNOWLEDGEMENT

In 1969 when Sister Marilyn Dobberstein asked me to write a history of the work of the Holy Spirit Missionary Sisters in Mississippi and Arkansas, I was reluctant to do so. I wondered what there could be to write about. From the humble attitude of the sisters whom I had known, I had the impression that their work had been far from exciting and was scarcely newsworthy.

Shortly after I began the research, however, I quickly changed my mind. I realized that the history was, indeed, worth writing; in fact, had to be written if the history of Mississippi was to be complete.

I began the research in early 1969, completing it in 1975. The notes lay idle for almost six years while I adjusted to a new lifestyle. Then in October 1981 Sister Priscilla Burke, with her gentle persuasive manner, prevailed upon me to complete it.

Looking back over a span of fourteen years—from the year 1969, when I began the research, until 1983, when I completed the book—many memories warm my heart: the graciousness with which the Most Rev. Oliver O. Gerow opened the archives of the Natchez-Jackson Diocese to me; the kindness of Rev. John Bowman, the Provincial of the Society of the Divine Word, who opened his society's archives to me; the candor of Bishop Gerow's successor, Most

Rev. Joseph Brunini, who assisted me in every way; the hundreds and hundreds of people of both races, especially the former students, lay teachers and parents of the children in the sisters' schools, who shared their thoughts and feelings; the sisters who spent hours recounting what they remembered of the past, and sisters who translated the early German chronicles into English.

My research took me to many places: to Torresdale, Pennsylvania, where the Sisters of the Blessed Sacrament shared the areas of their archives which pertained to the history of the Holy Spirit Missionary Sisters; to the archives of the Chicago Archdiocese in Mundelein, Illinois; to the Wisconsin State Historical Society in Madison, Wisconsin, and the Chicago Historical Society; to Xavier University in New Orleans, Louisiana; as well as to the cities where the sisters had their schools.

Everywhere people were most kind and helpful. Without their assistance the manuscript could never have been written. The Holy Spirit Missionary Sisters owe these people a debt of gratitude since their own archives, except for the day to day house and school chronicles in each station, were often sparse.

I am grateful to Sisters Kathleen Kane and Priscilla Burke for proofing the manuscript and offering their critique, as well as helping track down last minute elusive details.

Lastly, I'm grateful to my parents, Elmer and Angeline, who taught me by personal example that hard work can be fun. Thus, I was able to enjoy every minute of the research and discover that organizing and writing a book can be a rewarding and satisfying experience.

CONTENTS

Acknowledgement

Key to Abbreviations

BHC   Bay House Chronicle

BS   Archives of the Sisters of the Blessed Sacrament

CAN   Catholicity Among Negroes

CRC   Civil Rights Collection

DAH   Mississippi Department of Archives and History

DEO   Diocesan Education Office

GHC   Greenville House Chronicle

JHSC   Jackson House/School Chronicle

MHC   Meridian House Chronicles

MW   *Master's Work*

NJ   Archives of the Natchez-Jackson Diocese

PP   Archives of the Paraclete Province

SHR   Sacred Heart Rectory

SMR   St. Mary's Rectory

SSpSG   Archives of the Holy Spirit Missionary Sisters in Rome

SVD   Archives of the Society of the Divine Word, Bay St. Louis

VHC   Vicksburg House Chronicle

WSHS   Wisconsin State Historical Society

CHAPTER I
The First September

It was the evening of September 17, 1906. In Chicago, Illinois, four Holy Spirit Missionary Sisters, immaculate in their cream-colored veils and sky-blue habits, almost concealed under a long, heavy mantle of darker blue, boarded the Illinois Central train bound for Vicksburg, Mississippi. They were going to Vicksburg to open a Catholic elementary school for blacks, the only one of its kind in an area of over 27,000 square miles.

Vicksburg had not been the first choice for the school. The missionaries had attempted to open a school in the frontier town of Merigold on the Mississippi Delta the September before, but the idea had met with such strong opposition from the townspeople that the children were dismissed and the project abandoned. Even Bishop Thomas Heslin, in whose diocese of Natchez the school was located, was surprised when he learned that the missionaries' efforts to teach the black children in Merigold had ended in failure and near tragedy.[1]

Certainly the schools were needed. The Catholic Church in Mississippi was conducting only five elementary schools for blacks with a total enrollment of 250 pupils. All the schools but one were along the Gulf Coast, and all but one were adjuncts to schools for white children.[2] The state's record wasn't much better. It was spending an average of $4.56 a year for each black child in school, and political leaders in the state were saying that even that was a waste.

The Jackson *Clarion-Ledger* quoted Governor James K. Vardaman on July 30, 1903:

When I speak of educating the people, I mean the white people. The Negro is necessary in the economy of the world, but designed for a burden bearer. Then why squander money on his education when the only effect is to spoil a good field hand and make an insolent cook?[3]

If schools for blacks were needed in Mississippi, so also were religious teachers needed to staff them. In 1906 the entire United States was a mission territory of the Roman Catholic Church, depending upon personnel and money from Europe for its very existence and growth.

The four sisters on the coach were members of a German community established across the border in Steyl, Holland, because the climate in Germany under the reigning chancellor, Prince Otto von Bismarck, was unfavorable to the Church. The founder, Father Arnold Janssen, established two societies of religious missionaries: the Society of the Divine Word for priests and brothers in 1875, and the Missionary Sisters Servants of the Holy Spirit for religious women in 1889. The priests had made their first settlement in the United States on a farm south of

2

Shermerville, now Techny, Illinois, 20 miles north of Chicago, and had started a technical school for boys. On May 11, 1901, the first five sisters, led by Sister Leonarda Lentrup, came from Steyl to assist the priests and brothers with the work. By 1906 over forty sisters had made the voyage across the Atlantic.[4]

If the Church in the United States looked to overseas personnel for its existence and growth, this was even more true of Mississippi, where Catholics numbered fewer than 16,000 in a total population of one and a half million. Among the 908,000 black Mississippians, the Church scarcely figured at all. There were a few thousand black Catholics along the Gulf Coast under the care of the Josephite Fathers, but in the entire central and northern part of the state there were fewer than fifty, and four-fifths of these were in Vicksburg.[5] By responding to the educational needs of the blacks, the missionaries hoped to win entrance into their hearts and lead them to the Catholic faith.

Once outside the Chicago city limits, the train picked up speed. Lush cornfields came into view, were replaced by inviting farms and apple-laden orchards that bowed in turn to fields of grain and cattle grazing on the prairie grasses.[6] The directress for the school, Sister Maria Heinemnn, 24, sat quietly, statue-like in the high-back seat of the coach, absentmindedly fingering her gleaming, new profession crucifix which hung from a narrow red ribbon just visible below her white starched collar. She had been the community's first American vocation and was the only one of the four who was an American citizen. Born in Geis, Germany, she had come to the United States with her parents when she was nine and had grown up in an Atlantic seaboard commu-

3

nity where she learned to speak fluent English. These factors influenced her superiors to choose her as the directress for the new school despite her youth and inexperience in the classroom.[7]

Sister Bertranda Berning, the superior of the new mission, was a native of Essen and was one of seven sisters who had come to the United States from Steyl in 1903. Although she had studied English for several years, she had continual difficulty with the language, often mixing English and German in the same sentence, adding umlauts to English dipthongs so that they were almost unrecognizable. *Coat* was pronounced *katie*, and the listener would have to think before deciphering her sentence: *Haben Sie zwei katie?* Sister Leonarda hoped the short, chubby sister's lovable disposition would offset her language difficulties. So good-natured was she that even when she was serious, her face seemed poised for a laugh.[8]

The third sister was Sister Alexia Gerhards, who had been one of the first sisters to come to the United States with Sister Leonarda. The two sisters had graduated from a four-year Teachers' Training School at the mother house in Steyl. After coming to the United States, they had lived for a time with the Franciscan Sisters in Joliet, Illinois, and the Dominican Sisters in Sinsinawa, Wisconsin, to become more acquainted with American culture and perfect their English.[9]

In the fall of 1901 the two sisters taught the neighborhood children of Shermerville in a two-room school near the convent. To prepare Sister Maria for her new position as directress of the school in Vicksburg, Sister Leonarda had taken the young sister into the classroom with her during the past spring to give her firsthand lessons in the basics of discipline and pedagogy. Not satisfied with this bare bones preparation, Sister Leonarda had freed Sister Alexia from her duties at the school so she could go with the sisters to Vicksburg and help them make a start.[10]

The fourth sister was Sister Sebastiana Saar who, born in Bergweiler, Germany, was in the U.S.A. less than a year.[1][11] She was to be the cook and homemaker for the small community and was excited about learning how to cook the Southern dishes she had heard so much about. A parishioner in Vicksburg had promised to be her teacher.[12]

During the night the sisters, like many of the other passengers, slept in their seats, while the train lurched and jolted, squeaked and rumbled through the darkness. Bugs and mosquitoes sucked in through the open windows annoyed them; coal dust, belched from the engine's smokestack, peppered their white coifs and blue habits with soot.

When the sun rose, the scenery outside the window had changed, and the train was snaking its way between miles and miles of Mississippi cotton fields, a paradise for the Mexican boll weevil which was wreaking havoc with the state's cotton-based economy.[13]

After their prayers, the sisters breakfasted on apples and wholesome sandwiches of homemade bread and butter filled with meat and cheese from their own farm in Shermerville and felt a twinge of homesickness as they remembered the community they had left behind.

As the morning wore on, it grew hot in the coach despite the open windows and ceiling fan, and perspiration beaded the passenger's faces. The sisters' stiffly-starched collars became wilted and soft. Undisturbed, they kept their rule of silence and let their rosaries slip through their fingers or prayed from their worn community prayer books, asking God's blessing on this new undertaking, praying that it might succeed where the other had failed. When it was time for lunch, they opened the basket again and munched on the remaining sandwiches and apples and thought nothing had ever tasted better.

Five hundred forty miles south of Chicago, the train halted at a small cotton-ginning town in the heart of the Mississippi Delta. From the coaches the tired travelers caught glimpses of frame buildings on both sides of the tracks—general merchandise stores, a doctor's office, several commissaries—and then the train moved on. This was Merigold, the inhospitable town that had closed the doors of what was to be their first school in Mississippi five days after it had opened and had driven the priest out of town.[14]

Merigold was eleven years old in 1906. It had been born out of a movement in the Catholic Church around the turn of the century to colonize rural pockets of the United States with enough Catholics to warrant a church and a resident priest. In 1895 Rev. Thomas F. Cashman of St. Jarlath's Parish, Chicago, together with prominent Chicago businessmen, formed the Marquette Colonization Company and purchased 5000 acres of land in Bolivar County, Mississippi, which included 640 acres of cutover timberland west of Merigold between the Mississippi River and the railroad. That same year Father Cashman persuaded forty Catholic families to settle on the land, and on April 19 of the following year, Bishop

Thomas Heslin dedicated their small frame church and assigned a thin, sandy-haired, genial German, Rev. Andrew H. Gmelch, to offer Mass there twice a month.

Most of the colonists had property along Snake Creek where the land was low and swampy, and they fell easy prey to dysentery and malaria. When it rained, the settlers became prisoners in their own houses, separated from one another by seas of mud; and when the Mississippi River, fourteen miles to the west, overflowed and ruined the cotton crop before the fields could be harvested, the discouraged and homesick colonists fled.[15] David F. Bremner, a member of the colonization company, who had made his money in the cracker and biscuit business, bought the company's 640 acres near Merigold along with other land in the area and scattered lots in the town. "To take it off the hands of the priest," someone said.[16]

Soon 140 black families had moved on to his cotton plantations to work them. Only one, a Catholic, though weak in his faith, was educated.[17]

The Northern landowner wished to give his plantation workers an opportunity for schooling, and in the summer of 1904, at the suggestion of Father Gmelch and with the approval of Bishop Heslin, he approached Archbishop James E. Quigley of Chicago to ask his assistance in finding a religious community who would be interested in the work. The Chicago prelate knew exactly whom to ask—the Divine Word Fathers and Holy Spirit Missionary Sisters in Shermerville. Although the technical school they had started there was a success, both communities were looking for an apostolate that was more in

7

keeping with their missionary character.[18]

Archbishop Quigley and Bremner called on Rev. John Peil, the superior of the priests and brothers in Shermerville, who had already begun communications with Bishop Heslin about the possibility of taking up missionary work in his diocese. The landowner offered the missionaries 320 acres of land near Merigold on which he promised to erect a trade school, a church, a rectory, and a convent. In addition, he would support them for the first five years. After that, he said, the produce from the land would make the mission self-supporting.[19] Father Peil liked what he heard and believed that he had the right man to begin the work—Rev. Aloysius Heick, 41, a Bavarian by birth, wiry, energetic, and five years in the United States.[20]

After a lengthy correspondence with Bishop Heslin in which Father Peil assured the bishop that the mission at Merigold would not be a financial burden to his diocese, the latter gave his half-hearted consent.[21] He wrote that the consultors had agreed to allow the missionaries to come, at least by way of trial, but that they were not enthusiastic about the project. Father Heick set up housekeeping in the four-room shotgun rectory next to St. Mary's Church at the end of June. The bishop intended that he minister to a few white Catholics in the town as well as to the blacks on the Bremner plantation.[22]

Shortly after Father Heick's arrival in Merigold, it began to rain and continued steadily all through July. The land turned to mud so deep that it came halfway up the thighs of the mules. People could not move from their houses. Mosquitoes thrived in the lowland marshes, and people fell prey to malaria. Father

Heick was not spared. Sapped of his strength by illness and prevented from visiting the people by the inclemency of the weather, he was unable to assemble the black leaders for a meeting until the end of August. The six or seven who came received the idea of a school with great enthusiasm and promised to carry the word back to their community. Father Heick said that he would use the old cotton warehouse in town where he offered Mass for them as a classroom. The pupils would sit on the chapel benches, and he himself would build the tables for their books and writing supplies. The pupils were to buy their books.

The leaders did their work well. On the day appointed for the priest to meet with the parents, a veritable procession moved down the street toward the old cotton warehouse, causing a ripple of surprise from the white citizens who watched it curiously to see where it was going.

Twenty-five children enrolled for classes that afternoon, and more were to come after the cotton was in. Father Heick looked forward to the sisters' arrival in Merigold. He had done the groundwork, preparing the soil, and now their work would begin.[23]

Unfortunately for the mission, yellow fever raged in parts of the South during the summer and fall of 1905. At the time the school was to open in Merigold, the entire northern half of Mississippi was under quarantine. Father Heick was beside himself when he realized that the sisters would not be there for the opening day. He had no choice but to stand in for them until the quarantine was lifted.

He began classes on September 20 with twelve pupils. On the next day there were seventeen. On the third day, twenty-eight. If they continued coming he wondered where he would put them all. And when would the sisters come![24]

Before he had time to worry about these problems, however, he found himself facing ones that were far more serious. The white residents of Merigold had decided that the Northern priest and the Yankee landowner had overstepped their bounds: they wanted no school for their black laborers; a little harmless preaching maybe to keep them obedient, but nothing more.

While Bremner was in Chicago, his son, Vincent, and his brother-in-law, George Michie, were running the plantation. On September 27, at the end of the first week of school, they approached Father Heick while class was in session and begged him to dismiss the children immediately.

"The town is in an uproar because you're teaching the children," they said.

"What's wrong about that?"

"The people here don't want it," Michie said. "They don't want white teachers teaching black children. Father, you can't continue. Your life is in danger. They'll kill you if you don't listen to them. They've no respect for either the law of God or the law of the state."

Despite their earnest pleas, Father Heick failed to grasp the seriousness of the situation. "Let them come," he said. "I'm not afraid."

"Don't expect to talk to them," Vincent Bremner pleaded. "We know these people, and they'll shoot in broad daylight when they're opposed." He reminded the priest of a recent shooting in town.

Father Heick finally had to admit that they were

right. With a heavy heart, he dismissed the children at the end of the morning's session, instructing them to take all of their belongings with them. After they were gone, he looked sadly around the empty classroom. How much labor he had put into preparing this room, making the benches, adding more each day as the enrollment increased. Although Vincent Bremner had promised to speak to a few influential people in town to see if anything could be done, the priest knew that the school was finished. How terrible, he thought, if the sisters had been here. What might have happened to them? He blessed God who had protected them.[25]

What Father Heick did not understand was the underlying threat that the school on the Bremner plantation posed to the local peonage system underpinned by the town's commissaries. Indeed, some Mississippians boasted that the commissary system was better than pre-war slavery. On most plantations in and around Merigold, men put on their guns in the morning as they put on their pants and spent their days overseeing some forty to fifty blacks in the cotton fields. Life was cheap, and the guns were not worn for mere decorations: the workers were expected to obey orders or suffer the consequences. Nor could they move out of the area to seek work elsewhere as long as they owed money at the commissary, an easy matter for unscrupulous landlords who managed to see that their illiterate field hands were always in debt. Not only did the school on the Bremner plantation pose serious threats to this system of cheap labor, but it would also stir up discontent among workers on other plantations. It had to be stopped at all costs.[26]

Not even the Bishop was aware of the seriousness of the problem. On October 5 he wrote Father Heick:

I think, if the people are made to understand your object, they will not interfere. They are generally suspicious of strangers or newcomers who try to pay attention to the Negroes. But if you can impress upon them the fact that your Society was instituted for the purpose of educating and Christianizing this race, they may look upon it in a different light.

He continued:

White sisters teach the Negroes here and in some other parts of the diocese, and a white priest is in charge of the congregation.

But should they still oppose or threaten, then appeal to the sheriff of the county for protection. If this will not do, write to the Governor. Although his Excellency does not approve of too much education for the Negroes, he is not opposed to a resonable amount. . . .I think when the people there are made to see things in their true light, they will not bother you. When you show them your chief idea is to make good Christians of those Negroes and industrious and honest laborers, they will not bother you.[27]

The missionary walked the streets of Merigold, baffled and discouraged, weakened from malaria and hemmed in by the quarantine so that he could not even visit his friend, Father Gmelch in Clarksdale, and ask for advice. People cursed him and threw stones at him. When he tried to reason with them, they refused to listen. Finally, they wrote him a letter saying that it was against their time-honored customs to have a white person teach Negroes and they weren't going to allow him to start it now.[28]

Hearing of Father Heick's difficulties from his son,

12

David Bremner obtained a pass to enter the quarantine area and came to Merigold. He saw at a glance that matters were out of hand, that he was powerless to help the missionary, and advised him to leave at once. Old-timers like to recall that Father Heick told friends that he was placed in a piano box and rolled out of town on a horse-drawn wagon because people had planned to kill him that night; but the priest is strangely silent about his exodus in his writings.[29]

Bishop Heslin could offer the missionary little help. He wrote to Father Heick:

It (the opposition) is very unreasonable but reason has nothing to do with it. It is all passion and prejudice.

Then he added that under the circumstances, he didn't think he could use the missionaries in his diocese.[30]

But by December Bishop Heslin had changed his mind. St. Paul's parish in Vicksburg numbering 3,000 members was the largest church in the Natchez Diocese, and its forty black members were asking to have a church of their own. They said that their friends would never worship with them in a church where they had to sit in the last place, be the last to receive communion, be deprived of seeing their sons at the altar and their young people in the choir.[31]

At Bishop Heslin's invitation the dejected and penniless priest arrived in Vicksburg in January, 1906. That month he lived with the pastor of St. Paul's Church, Rev. James J. Mallin, paying him $25 for room and board. By the first of February, his parishioners had raised enough money to rent an unpainted, three-room frame building with a store front at 112 Holly Street across from the Alabama and Vicksburg Railroad station. The women cleaned the rooms and set up a table, and Father Heick offered the first Mass on February 2nd in the presence of thirty parishioners, eleven of whom received communion. He named the mission St. Mary's under the title, Queen of Heaven.[32]

Experiencing the friendly attitude of the white people in Vicksburg that June, Father Heick begged and borrowed money and purchased a lot and four Negro houses on Second North Street. When he told the parishioners that a school would open in September and sisters would come to teach their children, they could hardly contain their joy.

The afternoon sun was already low in the sky when the train bearing the sisters pulled into the Vicksburg station at Holly Street and ground to a stop. For seventy Septembers, trains would pull into the Vicksburg station as well as other Mississippi stations, bringing Holy Spirit Missionary Sisters who were dedicated to the education and spiritual development of the blacks. They would carry out their work quietly in the climate of a political system they did not fully understand or approve without trying to change that system. Only in this way would they be able to serve the black community. This was the lesson that Merigold had taught them, and they never forgot it.

Chapter I Footnotes: The First September

1. Archives of the Society of the Divine Word, Bay St. Louis, Mississippi (Hereafter cited SVD), Bishop Thomas Heslin to Rev. Aloysius Heick, October 17, 1905.

2. Archives of Natchez-Jackson Diocese (hereafter cited NJ) *Parish and Mission Reports 1904*; St. Mary's Rectory Chronicle (hereafter cited SMR), 52.

3. *Journal of Mississippi History*, Volume II, No. 4, August 1940; Richard Aubrey McLemore, ed., *History of Mississippi*, Vol. 1, "The Progressive Era," 29-48 (Hattiesburg, 1973).

4. Frederick M. Lynk, *Life of Arnold Janssen* (Techny, Illinois, 1925), 403 ff; Sister Leonore, SSpS., *Survey of the History of the American Province of the Missionary Sisters Servants of the Holy Ghost* (Popular name used throughout this book is Holy Spirit Missionary Sisters), rough draft, undated.

5. NJ, *Parish and Mission Reports 1905*, op. cit; NJ, File 10: *Negroes*, Calculated from Biennial Reports (Hattiesburg, 1973).

6. These and other descriptions of the trip are constructed from several books and interviews, including Carlton Corliss, *Our Mainline of Middle America*, 1950; Chicago Historical Society, August Mencken, *Railroad Passenger Car*; Newberry Library, Paul W. Gates, *Illinois Central Railroad* (New York, 1968); Interviews with Mrs. Elizabeth Jones, July 12, 1970; Sisters Evangeline Howard, Auxilia Haag, Techny, November 11, 1970; Retired Sisters, 1974.

7. Obituary and vital statistics of Sister Maria Heinemann, Archives of Paraclete Province (hereafter cited PP).

8. PP, Vital statistics of Sister Bertranda Berning; Interview with Sister Liobina Schikora, July 3, 1974.

9. *Paraclete Chronicle*, "Sister Leonarda," Special Number, undated, 8 and 9.

10. Archives of the Generalate of the Holy Spirit Missionary Sisters in Rome (hereafter cited SSpSG), Sister Leonarda Lentrup to M. Theresia, Superior General, May 17, 1906.

11. PP, Vital Statistics of Sister Sebastiana Saar.

12. SSpSG, Sister Bertranda Berning to M. Theresia, October 10, 1906.

13. McLemore, op. cit, 38.

14. SVD, Heick to Peil, October 4, 1905.

15. NJ, Heslin file: M, Rev. Thomas F. Cashman to Bishop
Heslin, St. Jarlath's Church, Chicago, August 1, 1895;
Handwritten Diary of Bishop Janssens, Fr. Meerschaert,
Adm., and Bishop Heslin, April 19, 1896, 175 ff.; Heslin
File: D, Rev. L. A. Dutto to Heslin, December 12, 1897;
Priests, Parishes, Missions, unpublished book, no pagina-
tion; P. H. Keenan, *Extension Magazine*, January 19, 1910;
M. B. Gearon to Heslin, January 13, 1898; Ese Michie to
author, August 6, 1974; Letter, Chancery Clerk's Office,
Bolivar County Court House, Cleveland (MS), to author,
July, 1970; Interview with Ese Michie, January, 1971.

16. Chicago Historical Society, S.S. Schoff, *Industrial Interests
of Chicago* (Chicago, 1873), 166; William Cahn, *Out of the
Cracker Barrel* (New York, 1969), 29 ff.; Michie, op. cit.

17. Michie op. cit.

18. Lynk, op. cit, 183.

19. SVD, D. F. Bremner to Rev. John Peil, December 12, 1904.

20. Interview, Retired Sisters in Paraclete Wing, op cit.; Interview with Rev. Anthony Bourges, June 14, 1971.

21. SVD, folder: *History of Southern Missions*, Rev. John Peil to
Bishop Heslin, December 4, 1904, and April 1, 1905.

22. SVD, Heslin to Rev. John Peil, May 23, 1905.

23. SVD (Techny, Illinois), Letter of Heick to Peil, August 25,
1905; SVD, *Report of Heick on Southern Missions*, September
24, 1905.

24. NJ, Heslin *Diary*, op. cit. 258 ff.

25. SVD, Heick Report, op. cit.

26. Interview with Michie, September 13, 1974.

27. NJ, Heslin to Heick, October 5, 1905.

28. Interview, Sister Desiderata Ramb, November, 1971;
SVD, Heick to Peil, September 17, 1905; Heick's Report,
op. cit.

29. SVD, Bremner to Peil, September 26, 1905; Heick to Peil,
October 4, 1905; Interview with Sister Liobina Schikora,
January 13, 1970; Interview, Bourges, op. cit.; NJ, Bishop
John Gunn, *Diary*, October 11, 1914.

30. NJ, Heslin to Peil, October 17, 1905.

31. NJ, Heslin to Peil, October 28, 1905.

32. NJ, Heick to Heslin, December 31, 1905; SMR, no date.

CHAPTER II
Sunshine in Vicksburg

Father Heick met the sisters at the Holly Street station and directed them to a horse-drawn cab. He was bubbling over with enthusiasm, and his good spirits reassured them that all was going well with the Vicksburg mission.

In 1906 Vicksburg, with a population of almost 15,000 (8,000 of whom were black), was the largest city in Mississippi and an important commercial and industrial center overlooking the junction of the Yazoo River Canal and the Mississippi River.[1] It was a leading railroad center in the area, and sizable repair shops lined Levee street near the water for overhauling railroad cars that came from as far away as Memphis, 220 miles to the north.[2] The Mississippi River added to the industrial importance of the town, but only because of the citizens' ingenuity and determination. In 1876 the River broke through its narrow bed north of Vicksburg and made a new channel for itself, leaving the city high and dry and to all appearances destined to disappear. But the resourceful citizens closed the mouth of the Yazoo River and diverted its waters through a canal into the old Mississippi River bed. When this feat was accomplished on December 22, 1902, just three years before the opening of St. Mary's Mission, Vicksburg once again had a river coursing along its front door.[3]

The city boasted of having the largest sawmill in the entire South. Its mills, fed by the timber resources of the Delta that included cypress, cottonwood, oak, ash, gum and poplar, annually put out 50 to 75 million feet of lumber. Along with the lumber mills, the manufacture of wood products was an important industry.

The city also handled about 100,000 bales of cotton each year and housed three large cottonseed oil mills valued at six million dollars.[4]

The business section was sprawled out along the high bluffs overlooking the river and was served by precipitous streets that ascended sharply from the riverfront. Higher among the bluffs, clinging in scattered clusters to the city's natural terraces, were the homes of the residents.[5]

St. Paul's Catholic Church stood in the heart of the city on the corner of Walnut and Crawford streets. Here in the 57-year-old church, built by slave labor, the Italian and German and Irish descendants of Vicksburg's first citizens gathered to worship.[6] Until St. Mary's Mission was founded in February of that year, some 40 black Catholics also worshiped here,

18

taking their places in the back pews.Many of them worked for the white Catholics of the city and had been converted to the faith through the good example and encouragement of their employers. Love and affection existed between the races as long as the proper distance and protocol were observed, but the relationship was that of parent and child, benefactor and recipient rather than one of equality. That's what the system dictated, and as long as the system was obeyed, all was well.

St. Mary's Mission, located on one of Vicksburg's many hills, was eleven blocks from the river, about a half mile east of St. Paul's. Its location had been approved by Bishop Heslin, who had earlier given the missionaries specific directions for establishing churches for blacks in cities where parishes for whites already existed.

In a letter to Father Peil, dated December 9, 1904, even before the incident at Merigold had occurred, he wrote:

Certain precautions are to be taken into consideration and certain conditions are to be laid down when establishing missions for the Negroes in Vicksburg, Jackson, and the intervening places from along that line to the north of the state. These missions may not interfere with the priests or people of the white parishes. The Fathers of your society must confine themselves exclusively to the Negroes: They must keep aloof as much as possible from the whites; and for this purpose the institutions should be established at a sufficient distance from the church of the whites and with the consent of the respective pastors.[7]

The carriage stopped on Second North Street, and the sisters stepped out into the cool of the evening.

The mission complex was certainly nothing to boast about: four weather-worn, one-story frame houses, resting on blocks of concrete. The property had belonged to a Mrs. Martha E. Perry, a widow. Father Heick had secured a loan at 5% interest from two Vicksburg women, Josephine Genasce and Mary A. Walsh, and had bought the property for $4500 on May 4. Three weeks later, he received a generous sum of $2500 from Mother Katharine Drexel, foundress of the Sisters of the Blessed Sacrament, part of which he applied to the debt, keeping the remainder for current expenses.[8]

The four houses that had once housed black families were now designated as convent, chapel, school, and rectory. The one arranged for the convent was tucked away among fig and persimmon trees and was a welcome sight to the weary, begrimed travelers.[9] The house next to it was the school, then the chapel, and on the far corner, the rectory. Sharing the hill was an impressive two-story colonial house that faced Main Street and belonged to the John Geigers, a white family. Next to the house was a large vegetable garden; the rest of the hilltop was meadow.

Tired though they were after their 24-hour trip, Sister Bertranda directed the sisters to the chapel where they knelt in silent adoration, imploring God's blessing on their new work in Vicksburg. Then according to the custom of their community after completing a long journey, she intoned the Magnificat, the prayer of thanksgiving that Mary, the Mother of Jesus, offered when she reached the home of her cousin Elizabeth: *Hochpreiset meine Seele den Herrn*.

It was a prayer of praise that God had begun a new

work in Vicksburg, that He was visiting His people and would take up His dwelling among them.

Much work had gone into the small house to transform it into a chapel. During the summer one of the brothers of the Society of the Divine Word, Brother Gelatius Frohnatfel, had divided the house into nave, sanctuary and sacristy and papered all the walls.[10] The Sisters of Mercy had given most of the simple furnishings—the altar, pews, candlesticks, ciborium, vestments and linens. After staffing the Vicksburg Charity Hospital for 27 years, the congregation had decided to withdraw their sisters when the state legislature passed a law prohibiting them from offering spiritual ministrations to the sick. The sisters had no further need of the chapel furnishings and were happy to donate them to the mission.[11]

Their thanksgiving over, Sister Bertranda gave the signal to leave and the four of them followed Father Heick to the convent where several women and a child awaited them.

The leader of the congregation was Ellen Cox, a tall, heavy-set, light-skinned woman. Her husband, who was not a Catholic, owned a fashionable barber shop on the corner of Grove and Washington streets that catered to white clientele. The couple had an eight-year-old daughter, Agnes, and lived on Third North. They were probably the most affluent of the congregation, and Ellen was probably the most knowledgeable. The other members looked to her for following the complicated rituals of standing, sitting, and kneeling during Sunday Masses.

Another prominent leader was Mrs. James E. (Lucy) Gilland, a former slave who had the joy of being reunited with her children, Eddie, Carrie and

Inez, after the Civil War. She and her son worked for the Sisters of Mercy.

Like Lucy, many of the blacks in Vicksburg were former slaves or children of slaves who had fled from their plantation owners during the Civil War and had sought refuge in the city after it was captured by the Union Army. When the war ended, they were hired by white people of the city as cooks, laundresses, day laborers, carpenters, porters, and drivers. Nora Comins, a relative of Lucy's, cooked for the Sisters of Mercy at St. Francis Xavier Convent. Mrs. Eliza Campbell, a widow, was a laundress and lived with her son, Thomas, and his wife, Savaue, and child. Thomas was a fireman on the A & V Railroad. Duncan Bowie, whose wife, Fannie, and three children were parishioners, drove for J. Q. Arnold. Many of their employers sent their daughters to St. Francis Xavier Academy, a fashionable day and boarding school run by the Sisters of Mercy, and their sons to St. Aloysius School, conducted by the Brothers of the Sacred Heart. But there was no Catholic school to which they themselves could send their children. They either enrolled them at one of the public schools in the city or at the R. Middleton School, an Episcopalian school at the corner of Third North, where they were taught the 3 R's as well as carpentry and masonry. With the coming of the Holy Spirit Missionary Sisters, this would all change. Now their children could also go to a Catholic school.

Knowing that the sisters would be tired from their long journey, Father Heick had invited only two women and a child, probably Ellen and her daughter and Lucy, or perhaps Hester Winslock (Their names are not given.) to be present to welcome them that evening.[12]

It didn't matter to the women and child that the sisters' habits were soiled and wrinkled; that their veils and collars were wilted. To them they were like angels from heaven.

The sisters responded with joy and curiosity. So rare were blacks in their own country that the German sisters had seen them only in sideshows of traveling circuses.[13] That evening as they exchanged cordial greetings with the women and the child, the missionaries noted the happiness and pride that shone on their faces and they experienced a deep inner peace and joy. As the women served them a light supper, the young girl entertained them with song and poem and that night a lasting bond of love was kindled between the sisters and the blacks they had come to serve.[14]

The next morning in the bright light of day, the sisters appraised their new living quarters. The house was immaculate. The women had scrubbed every corner of it until it shone. The furnishings were simple—a table, six chairs, and four beds. In the kitchen there was a wood stove for cooking; ancient fireplaces that looked almost too dangerous for use were in the other three rooms.[15] The floors were made of rough planks often far enough apart to offer the sisters a view of the weeds growing under the house. Sister Sebastiana would later find this to be an advantage when she washed the floors. She would simply throw a bucket of water over the area and sweep the excess water through the cracks between the planks.[16] Father Heick had made one major outlay for the convent which they had already discovered: In the tiny bathroom stood a shiny new bathtub he had purchased for $23, no small sum in those days. A wide porch on the back, the full length of the house, was another asset. It could be used for so many purposes, especially during the warm weather. The sisters were very pleased with their new dwelling.[17]

After inspecting the convent, they visited the house that had been designated as the school. By adding a partition Brother Gelatius had made two classrooms out of the largest room in the house and had built the children's benches and tables. For blackboards he had painted one wall in each classroom with black paint. There were no elaborate pictorial charts, no library facilities, and few books. But the lack of physical equipment was offset by the dedication of the teachers and the determination of the pupils.[18]

Classes were to begin on the following Monday, September 24, and the prospects were good. Father Francis de Lange, a Dutch priest of the Society of the Divine Word, had been in Vicksburg during the summer and had visited the black households of the city. He reported that 70 parents had promised to send their children to the sisters in September.[19]

The sisters were somewhat disappointed, therefore, when only 26 pupils appeared the first day of school; but they were told that the others were in the fields picking cotton and would come after the harvest was in.[20] They did not accept the report cards that the children brought with them from the public schools, and only after considerable questioning and oral testing did they finally divide them into grades one through five, Sister Bertranda taking the ten older ones and Sister Maria, the sixteen younger ones.[21]

Sister Bertranda had to exercise great patience in the classroom because of her language difficulties. At night, after helping with the household chores, she labored over her lessons for the next day, writing out the questions and asking Sister Maria or Sister Alexia to check them for her. Then she repeated them to herself, over and over again, sometimes falling asleep still mumbling English words and phrases to herself. She was grateful that her number of pupils was small compared to Sister Maria's.[22]

On the other side of the partition, Sister Maria moved quietly about the classroom speaking in a soft, melodious, low-pitched voice under Sister Alexia's watchful eye and diligently applied all she had learned in the classroom from Sister Leonarda during the past spring.[23] Gently, she guided the hands of her youngest pupils to form the letters of the alphabet or helped the older ones through a reading lesson.

Classes were held from 9 to 2, with a half hour off for lunch. After dismissing the children, the sisters returned to the convent for prayers and for recreation, which was spent in conversation while they assisted Sister Sebastiana with household tasks that still needed to be done.

About a week or two after school opened, the sisters began visiting the families of the pupils. Up and down Vicksburg's precipitous streets they walked, two by two, in the later afternoons or on weekends, stopping from time to time to admire the natural beauty of the city, especially the luxuriant wild palms growing along the road. They found some of the homes of their pupils nestled among the

25

more pretentious homes of the white people; others lodged at the bottom of narrow ravines; some perched on top of steep bluffs.[24]

Few of the streets were paved and fewer yet had sidewalks. The main thoroughfares in the business section were garnished with a couple of planks laid side by side that often called for acrobatic skills to prevent the planks from flapping up on the far end like a teeter totter and throwing the pedestrian off balance and into the mud. But for the rest of the city, the streets and sidewalks were dirt which turned into mud after a heavy rain. More than one unhappy pedestrian had to reach down and extricate his or her overshoe from the mire after a downpour, and the missionaries were no exceptions.[25]

By the end of October the missionaries had visited the home of every one of their pupils and were overwhelmed by the poverty they found and saddened to discover how little the blacks were paid for their work. A mother working from dawn to dusk might receive for her wages only $3 a week and food left over from the meals of her white employers; a man putting in the same hours would earn $7.[26] All working-age members of the family pooled their resources to survive, and this was one reason why the children were in the cotton field instead of in the classrooms. More serious still, the sisters were shocked to learn that many white people regarded the blacks as inferior beings, some even doubting that they possessed souls.[27]

It was not in their power to change either the social structure of the South or its beliefs. They were too insignificant and helpless. Merigold had taught them this. What was in their power was the quiet, continuing education of a people who would themselves change what was wrong with their system. Only in this way is change enduring—when it comes from within. The North and South had fought a bitter war in which the North had declared the slaves free; but history has shown that the stroke of a pen did not really free this vast mass of uneducated humanity. Rather, it led them into a greater slavery. Since they were no longer valued as property, they no longer had the protection of their owners, and without an education they were without the means of choosing what to do with their newfound freedom. Education and a deeper knowledge of Christ were the most important benefits the sisters could bring them.

While visiting the homes, the missionaries found fifty- and sixty-year old illiterates hungering for an education in the basics and arranged for them to come to the convent in the evenings for lessons in reading and writing.[28] At the mission everyone was made to feel welcome and invited to attend the services in the chapel. Before long, the little house was filled to the last place for Sunday Mass.[29]

On October 18th Bishop Heslin paid the mission a short visit. He missed nothing as he inspected each of the houses and visited the classrooms in session. He was pleased with the modest beginning and gave the mission his blessing.[30]

During the first few months the sisters wanted for nothing. Parishioners and friends supplied them with fresh vegetables, milk, and bread and the fifty cents monthly tuition from the children took care of their other living expenses.[31] But as winter moved into Mississippi, gifts of fresh vegetables and fruit became fewer, and the sisters, who also cooked for

Father Heick and Brother Gelatius, depended more and more upon the tuition money for food.

At Christmas time, Sister Leonarda visited the small community and Sister Bertranda confided her financial woes to her. There was little that the superior could do but encourage her to trust in the Lord, who would not forsake them. Sister Leonarda remained with them until the fourth of January, and was pleased with the progress of the mission. When she returned to Shermerville, Sister Alexia, her task completed, returned with her. Sad though they were to see her go, Sister Bertranda was relieved to have one less person at the table. She acquired a few chickens, and Sister Sebastiana fed them the scraps from the table, gratefully collecting the eggs almost as soon as they were laid.[32]

That the sisters didn't starve that first bleak winter was partly due to several outstanding benefactors. One of them was the Carl Schumann family who lived on Second North, a few blocks south of the mission in an area known as "Pumpkin Hill" because of all the red-headed girls who lived there. Schumann and his partner operated Sproule's Bakery on Washington Street. Word had reached him that there were German nuns at St. Mary's who didn't have too much to eat, and he asked his wife to visit them and size up the situation. Evidently the sisters made a good impression on Mrs. Schumann. For the next two years, the Schumann children, George, Herman and Hazel, hitched up their goat cart filled with fresh bread, milk and butter and drove it up Second North to the convent. On other days Mr. Schumann sent an employee with large supplies of sugar, flour, smoked ham, jelly, and soap.[33] George Schumann grew especially fond of the sisters, and sometimes his mother had to rescue the last pound of butter in the house from her oldest son as he was slipping off to the convent with it.[34]

One day as a special treat for the sisters George offered them a few stalks of sugar cane he had received. In those days children considered it a great event to receive a piece of sugar cane because money for candy was scarce and sugar cane lasted a long time. They cut the stalk into pieces, then peeled and chewed them to draw out the sweetness. Several days later while visiting the sisters, George was disappointed to see his precious stalks of sugar cane standing in the corner of the kitchen untouched. That evening he complained to his mother that the sisters hadn't used his sugar cane. But the next day George came home doubling over with laughter. Sister Sebastiana had asked him to find out from his mother how she cooked the strange-looking stalk. George had taken a knife, cut off a piece of the cane and demonstrated its use.[35]

Hazel Schumann later joined the Sisters of Mercy, taking the name of Sister Mary Hildegarde, and served her congregation for many years as its provincial superior. She never forgot the Holy Spirit Missionary Sisters and always had a warm spot in her heart for them.

When spring made her appearance in the Delta in 1907, no one was happier to see her than the sisters at St. Mary's. In a letter to superiors in Steyl, Sister Bertranda remarked that the hens were laying better and that she had planted a small vegetable garden which she cared for in addition to her other work.

Toward the end of March, Father Heick brought

them the news that they could expect another important visitor—Mother Katharine Drexel, the foundress of the Sisters of the Blessed Sacrament for Indians and Colored People. In June she had sent Father Heick $2500 to help buy the property in Vicksburg, and she was interested in seeing for herself how the mission was progressing.[36]

Katharine Drexel was the daughter of a wealthy banker who left in his will $14 million dollars to Katharine and her sisters, Louise and Elizabeth—the money to be divided equally among them. Fearful that suitors might marry his daughters for their money, he had prescribed that none of the legacy would go to future husbands, only to heirs. If a daughter died without an heir, her share would be divided between the other two. If the second also died without an heir, her share would be added to the remaining sister's share. If all three died without any living children, the money was to go to the same charitable institutions listed in his will to which he had bequeathed one-tenth of the estate at the time of his death.

Following the example of their parents, the Drexel daughters were generous with their money, each having her favorite charities. Katharine became interested in the Indians and blacks—Americans who, in her opinion, had been and still were being cheated of their rights.

Shortly after her father died, Katharine expressed a desire to join a religious community, but her ecclesiastical superiors persuaded her to found her own congregation so that she could continue the work of her cherished apostolates.

Although Katharine could have contested her

father's will in favor of her congregation, she chose not to do so, maintaining that she wanted her community to be poor and to trust in the Lord for their necessities. She herself practiced personal poverty to a high degree and demanded the same from her sisters, knowing that they would have the use of her inheritance for the apostolate only as long as she lived and after that it would go to her sisters' heirs or to the charities mentioned in her father's will. Eventually, Louise and Elizabeth both died without heirs and Mother Katharine had the entire inheritance for her cherished apostolate; yet she always practiced great caution in dispensing any of the money no matter how large or how small the amount.

Unselfishly she assisted other religious groups working for the Indians and blacks, but being an astute business person like her father, Francis, and her stepmother, Emma, the only mother she had ever known since her own mother died five weeks after giving birth to her, she demanded a full account as to how the money was spent, often visiting the missions she helped to finance.[37] Thus in a letter of 1907 Katharine wrote to her spiritual advisor and lifelong friend, Archbishop Patrick J. Ryan of Philadelphia:

On Monday the first of April, I plan to go to Vicksburg, Mississippi, to see a Colored Mission started there by the Fathers of the Divine Word last year . . . . Their Visitor is now at Lechemy, I mean the priest from their European Mother or Fatherhouse—which is it? If we like their manner of conducting affairs, I can encourage the Visitor that we may probably help them to establish Missions. . . .[38]

The name Techny, resulting from the technical

school in Shermerville, was becoming more and more popular, and in 1909 it became the official name of the village. Mother Katharine was not sure of the spelling in her letter to Archbishop Ryan.

Mother Katharine and her companion, Sister Monica, were to be the guests of the sisters while they were in Vicksburg, an arrangement that was embarrassing to the missionaries since there were only four beds in the house and all were in one room. However, Sister Bertranda did the best she could and offered Mother Katharine her bed while offering the extra one to Sister Monica. But the foundress would not hear of taking Sister Bertranda's bed and insisted on sleeping on the floor herself.

"You need your rest. You have to go to school tomorrow. I'll sleep on the floor. It is quite good enough for one night." And that settled the matter.

The next day Mother Katharine inspected the premises and visited the classrooms. She was visibly impressed by all that she saw.[39] She left the mission with a promise to help the missionaries buy property and erect new buildings in Vicksburg as well as in other cities—if she lived. Her promises always bore this provision—if she lived—since her inheritance would no longer be available on the day of her death.

Shortly after their visitors left, tragedy struck the small community of sisters at St. Mary's. On April 20th Sister Bertranda became critically ill with typhoid fever. Sister Sebastiana attended to her by day while the women of the congregation helped with the cooking, washing and other household tasks. At night, two Sisters of Mercy stayed at her bedside to allow Sister Sebastiana some rest. When Sister Bertranda's condition did not improve, the doctor, who dropped by daily to check on her, suggested to Father Heick that he administer the last sacraments. Courageously, Sister Maria went to the classroom each morning and took all of the pupils into her charge. Relief came a week later when Sister Willibalda Goeke came from Techny to take the older pupils off her hands again. For the next five weeks, the community hoped and prayed as Sister Bertranda languished, so helpless and weak that she continued to require constant care. The doctor dropped by daily to check her condition, and it was with great joy that he announced one day toward the end of May that the fever had left her and she would soon be able to leave her sick bed.[40]

Because of Sister Bertranda's illness and reports of other cases of typhoid in the city, the first school closing exercises were kept very simple.[41] On June 11th, after the children had recited poems and sung songs, Father Heick gave out awards for excellence in Christian Science, conduct, English, arithmetic, and penmanship and presented final report cards to forty-seven pupils.[42] On June 13th the children were treated to a picnic provided by the women of the parish and the Sisters of Mercy.[43]

Three children were baptized into the Catholic church on Pentecost Sunday and one adult on the following Sunday. It had been a good year.[44]

On June 17th Sister Bertranda's health had improved sufficiently for her to return to Techny. It was hard for her to leave Vicksburg. Sister Maria, too, was saddened to see her go; but Sister Leonarda consoled them by telling them that the rest would do her good and give her the opportunity to study and improve her English.[45]

In September the second school year began with double the previous year's enrollment. So many children came for the primary grades that Sister Josepha Delort was sent to Vicksburg.[46] She, like Sister Maria, had been born in Germany and had come to the United States with her parents when she was a child. She had grown up in Chicago and had entered the congregation three months after Sister Maria. They had been novices together and had pronounced their first vows together. It was a time of happy reunion for the two young American sisters.[47]

By now the little schoolhouse was bursting its seams. The convent, too, was overcrowded. It was time for the missionaries to think about building, and the person to take charge of it was on hand, Rev. John Hoenderope, who had arrived in Vicksburg on October 9, 1907. Born of Dutch parents on their ship as it plied German waters, the huge lovable "Father John," as he was called, joked about being German by law and Dutch by birth.[48]

On May 26, 1908, the contractors began digging the foundation of a two-story brick building halfway up the hill between the convent and the rectory.[49] The building would be a combination school and church and was scheduled to be completed for classes in September. No one was happier over this news than the sisters, who were now squeezing eighty-four children into the original schoolhouse.

From the very beginning of their work in Mississippi, the missionaries had hoped to expand their activities to other cities in the South, especially within the state, and now, with Father Hoenderope firmly established in Vicksburg, Father Heick was free to move on. Jackson, the capital of the state, seemed the most likely place for the second mission; but there was no Catholic congregation as at Vicksburg, and no one could predict the outcome. Merigold had failed; Vicksburg had prospered. How would the missionaries be received in Jackson? They didn't have long to wait for the answer.

Visit of Fr. Boden (left) to Fr. Heick (right center), 1909

Chapter II Footnotes: Sunshine in Vicksburg

1. 1900 U. S. Census.

2. Interview with Alex Peatross, Vicksburg, July 21, 1970.

3. *Mississippi W.P.A. Guide, 268 ff.*

4. DAH, Department of Archives and History (hereafter cited DAH); *Commercial and Historic Vicksburg, 1907,* Souvenir edition of *Vicksburg Herald.*

5. *Americana Encyclopedia, WPA Guide,* op. cit.

6. St. Paul's Centennial Book, *The River Sings a Song, 1849-1949;* Interview with Mother Hildegarde Schumann, July 16, 1970.

7. SVD, Heslin to Peil, December 9, 1904; SVD, Document, Agreement between Bishop Heslin and Society of the Divine Word, August 21, 1905.

8. SMR, sketch of property; handwritten note from Heick to Josephine Gerasci and Mary A. Walsh, May 5, 1906.

9. SSpSG, Sister Bertranda to M. Theresia, October 11, 1906; Vicksburg House Chronicle, 1906 (hereafter cited VHC).

10. SVD, Heick Report, op. cit., 7.

11. SMR, Chronicle, 3; Mother M. Bernard, *Story of Sisters of Mercy in Mississippi,* 1860-1931 (New York, 1931), 89; *Parish Book,* Vicksburg, 1906.

12. SMR, Chronicle; *1906 Directory of Streets* (Vicksburg); VHC, Early pages; Interviews with Sister Desiderata Ramb, November, 1971, and Leonard Rose, August 14, 1974.

13. Interview with Sister Josephis Broeckerhoff, November, 1971.

14. VHC, op. cit.; Bertranda, October 11, 1906, op. cit.; Interview with Camille Cheeks, August 11, 1974.

15. Ibid.

16. Desiderata, op. cit.

17. *Parish Book,* op. cit.

18. School files Vicksburg, *Information Concerning Establishment, Development and Present State of Elementary Education for the Negro Conducted by Religious Communities of Women in Diocese.*

19. NJ, Peil to Heslin, July 19, 1906; Peil to Heslin, August 18, 1906.

20. SSpSG, Bertranda, October 11, 1906, op. cit.

21. SSpSG, Bertranda to M. Theresia, October 28, 1906.

22. Ibid.

23. Interview with Sister Celine Ulrich (undated).

24. SSpSG, Bertranda, October 11, 1906, op. cit.; Vicksburg Street Directory, 1906; Interview with Jake Holmes, August 18, 1974.

25. Hildegarde, op. cit.; Interview with Jack Robbins, August 21, 1974.

26. Rev. Julius Steinhauer to unnamed friend, February 13, 1917.

27. SSpSG, Bertranda, October 11, 1906, op. cit.

28. Ibid.

29. SSpSG, Bertranda, October 28, 1906, op. cit.

30. VHC, October 18, 1906.

31. SSpSG, Bertranda, October 11, 1906, op. cit.

32. SSpSG, Bertranda to M. Theresia, April 12, 1907; VHC, December 25, 1906-January 4, 1907.

33. SSpSG, Bertranda, October 11, 1906, op. cit.

34. Hildegarde, op. cit.

35. Ibid.

36. Bertranda, April 12, 1907, op. cit.

37. Sister Consuela Marie Duffy, SBS, *Katharine Drexel, A Biography* (Philadelphia), 17, 72, 74-75.

38. Ibid.

39. VHC, April 17, 1907.

40. Ibid, April 20, 1907.

41. Ibid, May 12, 1907.

42. SMR Chronicle, April 29 and May 12, 1907.

43. Ibid, June 13, 1907.

44. VHC, May 12, 1907.

45. Bertranda to M. Theresia, October 28, 1906.

46. VHC, September, 1907-October, 1907

47. PP, Vital Statistics.

48. SVD, Paper marked "Fathers."

49. SMR, Chronicle, 10.

CHAPTER III
Storm Watch in Jackson

As early as 1907 Father Heick visited Jackson to look for a suitable place for a mission.[1] He found the city delirious with excitement, exulting in an unprecedented growth. In the year 1900, the city had a population of 7,816, less than a thousand people a decade since the first state legislature met there on December 23, 1822. But around 1900 vast timber resources were opened in the southern part of the state and large lumber companies set up their offices in the capital. Mills opened to process the raw timber into finished products, and these, in turn, gave birth to dozens of small service industries. As hundreds of thousands of freight cars rumbled into the city with raw lumber and rumbled out again with carloads of wood products, industries doubled and the population tripled. By 1910 Jackson had grown to 21,161, half of whom were black, only one of whom was Catholic.[2]

Educational opportunities for black children were almost nil. Smith Robinson, which was named for two prominent black educators, was the only public school for black children in the city. Most of the teachers had 80 to 85 pupils in their classes, and one teacher had as many as 92.[3] Several churches in the city had tried to ease the lack of educational opportunities for blacks by opening their buildings during the week for classes. Here the children studied on uncomfortable pews and sprawled on the floor to write.[4]

Since its founding in 1823, Jackson had spent around $66,000 on school buildings for white children while spending only $7500 or one-ninth of that amount for blacks.[5] The city's phenomenal growth was one reason for the difference. The minutes of the city council and school board meetings indicate the difficulty the city was experiencing in keeping up with schools for only the white school population. No sooner was one building up then they began planning another. Under these circumstances, black children, whose parents had little political power, were forced to wait until the others were accommodated.[6]

If anywhere in the state, a school for blacks was needed in Jackson.

In the spring of 1908 Father Heick returned to Jackson with the intention of buying suitable property for the second mission in Mississippi. While in the capital, he enjoyed the hospitality of Father Charles A. Oliver, the pastor of St. Peter's Catholic Church on N. West Street. A native Mississippian of rare personal charm, Father Oliver was a convert to the Catholic faith and conversant not only in German, but also in Spanish, Italian, French, Russian, Dutch and fluent in Latin and Greek.[7] He welcomed the idea of a mission church and school for the blacks of Jackson and was helpful in directing Father Heick to several plots of land that were for sale. When Father Heick expressed interest in six empty lots located a few blocks north of the city limits between Crestview and Lamar streets (then called Lee and Grayson), he approved the choice, seeing no reason for anyone's objecting to a mission on the site. It was near the black section of town and there were no white residents within a block of it on either side. In addition, it was near the streetcar lines and had water and electricity.[8]

Pleased with the favorable outlook in Jackson, the missionary returned to St. Mary's to be present for the first holy communion Mass of eight school children on June 25th. After the celebration he said good-bye to his beloved congregation in order to devote himself entirely to the new mission in Jackson, the pain of separation lying heavily on his heart.[9] For the third time in four years he was plunging alone into the unknown, feeling his way through strange territory, facing possible rejection by the blacks and hostility and persecution from the whites. He was leaving a zealous core of people who sacrificed time and energy and money for their church and school. In Jackson he would begin with only one Catholic—Annie Williams, a young woman who was thinking of becoming a nun.[10]

The next day Father Heick was in Jackson where he signed the deed for the six lots he had previously chosen at the cost of $4200.[11] Two days later he received a check from Mother Katharine and engaged a

41

contractor to draw up the plans for a two-story, red-brick building similar to the one in Vicksburg, which would serve in the beginning as school, convent, and church.[12]

Then suddenly and without warning, clouds began to gather over the property site. By the end of the week, the Jackson *Daily News* carried a grossly confused account of the proposed school.

It reported:

Jackson has secured another large educational institution without the asking. The deal has just been closed for a large tract of 20 acres of land in the northwestern part of the city . . .on which is to be erected a colored religious college. . . .The investment will be between $50,000 and $75,000.[13]

The next day, Saturday, July 4th, the newspaper report on the nature of the school was slightly more accurate. It informed its readers:

A Catholic school for Negroes is to be established near the corner of Fortification and Grayson streets. The promoters hope to open the school in September.

But then as if some great conspiracy had taken place, the report continued:

. . .negotiations were conducted so quietly that the purpose of it has just been made known.

More misrepresentations followed:

The whole affair is being gotten up by the Society of the Divine Word, the Catholic organization founded by Miss Drexler of Philadelphia, whose history was a few years ago a matter of public interest and who since a certain alleged disappointment in a love affair with a millionaire has devoted her life to benevolent work in the Catholic faith having first spent several years in a convent.

42

It concluded the account by stating that all the sisters who would compose the faculty would be white women from the Northern states and that there didn't seem to be anything objectionable about the new project.[14]

But five days later the paper adopted a different stance:

A site has been purchased for a Negro Catholic college to be established . . . within a block of the homes of some of the best white families in Jackson . . . . This won't do.

The promoters of this institution must be made to understand that they will not be allowed to locate a Negro college in a white residential section, and they may as well make up their minds to seek another location.

Jackson is not hostile to the Northern philanthropists who believe that they are accomplishing a good work by spending money on Negro education, but they must not endeavor to establish their school in white residential sections. Our people won't tolerate it and in matters of this sort there is a law higher than property right. . . .[15]

By July 9, Father Heick knew that the storm was ready to break. He wrote in his diary:

I was told tonight that something is in store. People are aroused against the colored school. Much excitement among a certain class of people, especially among our neighborhood out there. They say they will never allow a colored school to be built on this property. Thus it seems impossible to open a school this year.

Then, in a tone of sadness, he added:

I am now in the same fix as three years ago at Merigold, yet full of hope that this will turn into blessing.[16]

On the following day he asked the contractor to stop with his work. *How sad!* he wrote in his diary that night.[17]

Since the newspaper accounts were whipping up the storm, Father Heick dashed off a letter to the editor which was printed in full on July 15. He explained that the undertaking was not the work of Miss Drexel, but of the Society of the Divine Word and the Holy Spirit Missionary Sisters. He said that before buying the property, he had sought the opinion of prominent citizens who assured him that there would be no objections to the school. It was not a college, he explained, but a parochial school taught by Catholic sisters. He wrote:

Your misrepresentations did a great deal in increasing the excitement of the people. They have caused us a . . . considerable expense. . . . If after this explanation they object to a small school being built on Grayson Street, the sisters occupying the lot closer to the white section, I am only too willing to remove the whole undertaking to another site. In finding this site, I would earnestly ask their good will and cooperation.[18]

In the midst of these difficulties, Father Heick received a letter from the founder, Arnold Janssen, which was not only encouraging, but almost prophetic, since the founder could not have known of events taking place in Jackson when he wrote.

I . . .wish you the same success that you achieved in Vicksburg. No doubt you will meet with difficulties because there are no Catholic Negroes in Jackson. But if God is with you, these difficulties, as well as others due to ignorance and prejudice, will gradually be

44

*overcome . . . . Have a good word for every one you
meet. In this way you will conciliate your enemies and
make friends.* [19]

The encouragement came at the right time, for
Father Heick's letter to the editor of the *Daily News*
failed to win over his adversaries. In fact, the opposition grew more vigorous when it became known that
Catholic sisters—white teachers—were going to staff
the school. On July 21st a prominent man in the area
visited the priest and warned him that if he persisted
in his plans for a school, he would have to take the
consequences of this action. [20]

The next day Father Heick left for Vicksburg where
he received a letter from his gentleman caller. It was
signed by forty-five people who were opposed to the
school and said that they would not consent to a
Negro schoolhouse being built upon the proposed
property. [21]

On August 1st Father Heick returned to Jackson;
but finding that nothing had changed, he left to visit
Father Gmelch in Canton to nurse his wounds and
seek comfort and advice. [22] In the meantime his
lawyer wrote a letter of explanation to each of the
persons who had signed the letter of protest, and a
few agreed to withdraw their objections. For a few
days it looked as if the sun was going to shine again
over the mission property. [23] But on August 20th, the
Daily News carried another story.

*. . .the people . . .are still wrought up . . .and declare
unequivocably that the proposed school shall not be
located there!*

After mentioning the attempts of the attorney to
persuade the citizens to withdraw their protest by
intimating that the law would be invoked, if neces-

sary, it ended by declaring:

The citizens . . .have never wavered from their posi-
tion and . . .threats of civil authorities would avail
nothing.

Again dark clouds covered the sun.[24]

When Father Heick returned to Jackson in October
to look for another site for the mission, wary land-
owners boosted their prices so high that he was unable to buy.[25] Discouraged, he went back to Vicksburg, where the success of the school was like balm
to his troubled heart. Beyond the missionaries'
greatest expectations, over 150 children were attending classes in the beautiful new building and the
bond of love had grown deeper between them and
the people. It seemed as if this was not meant to be
the case in the capital city of the state.[26]

In November Father Heick took a train to Techny,
where he discussed the situation in Jackson with his
superiors.[27] Taking into consideration all the animosity the mission had generated, they were inclined to abandon the idea of a mission there for the
time being,[28] but when Mother Katharine learned of
their decision, she would not hear of it, saying:

I could not bear to think that the capital of a state
which is the home of almost a million blacks should
not have a Catholic mission for them.[29]

There had to be a plot of land somewhere in Jackson for this purpose, and, regardless of the price, she
would buy it. Father Heick returned to Jackson in the
early part of 1909 to try again. This time he found two
acres of pasture land lying between Bell and Ash
streets, only two blocks from his original site.[30] To
the northwest were cotton fields and more pasture
land with a scattering of houses under construction.

46

A path called Short Blair ran along the east side of the property and paralleled a wider street also called Blair. An unnamed path ran along the west side of the property.[31] The price asked for the two acres was $5,000.[32]

Mother Leonarda and Sister Willibalda, the superior of Vicksburg, were in Jackson on April 9th and approved the purchase. They were eager to begin the school in the capital of the State.[33]

On April 18th Father Heick took the night train to Philadelphia to discuss the transaction with Mother Drexel. Happy that the mission was about to open, she promised him $16,000: $5,000 for the property, $10,000 for the school and equipment, $1,000 for the rectory and $210 for the interest on the loan on the original property which had not yet been sold.[34]

On June 25, 1909, the Jackson *Daily News* carried the announcement of the groundbreaking, giving it a favorable report:

Ground was broken today for the erection of the new building to cost $15,000 to be used as a school for blacks in the northern portion of the city.[35]

This was twice as much as the city had appropriated for Negro education since its incorporation in 1823.

After reviewing the previous difficulties encountered by Father Heick, the newspaper continued:

In the meantime, the purpose of the Society has become better known and the objections to the establishment of such a school in the city have subsided . . . . Vicksburg has just such a school . . . . It has relieved the congested conditions of the public schools for Negroes, and those who are being taught at small expense are apparently benefited thereby with no ap-

parent evil effects.[36]

Both in Techny and in Vicksburg, the sisters who had sympathized with Father Heick in his struggle to open the mission in Jackson and had prayed fervently for a favorable outcome, rejoiced over the news of the groundbreaking.

Mother Leonarda was already experiencing a need for more teachers. There were now six in Vicksburg and four were to go to Jackson in September. She wrote to her superiors in Steyl on July 14th:

Probably in the course of the next year a third station will be opened and then we'll be short of personnel again. What shall we do? Next year Vicksburg will absolutely need one more sister, perhaps also Jackson.

It was true then as it has always been in the Church:

The harvest is great, but the workers are few.[37]

Sister Maria Heinemann was one of the first sisters assigned to Jackson as she had been among the first to go to Vicksburg. The other three sisters were from Steyl and had been in the United States only a short time. The superior was Sister Cyrilla Hullermann, a calm, soft-spoken woman who could take everything in stride without becoming the least ruffled. She had done her practice teaching at St. Mary's during the previous year after completing a Normal Course offered by the Interstate School of Correspondence in Chicago. Teaching the primary grades was Sister Otgera Roth, who was a newcomer to Mississippi. Like her superior, she was short, but more energetic and vivacious. Sister Severina Knapp, her full round face bearing the scars of smallpox, was homemaker for the faculty and priest.[38]

Despite the favorable nod the Jackson *Daily News* had given the school, Father Heick worried about the white people's attitude toward the sisters and suggested that they come to Jackson on the night train from Vicksburg in order to make their entrance into the capital less conspicuous.

The moon shone a bright welcome when the train bearing the four sisters pulled into the Jackson station on Mill Street on the night of September 29th. But Sister Severina scarcely noticed it as she faced the prospect of coming to a new house in the darkness of night.

"I wonder if Father Heick will have a light for us so we can see our way around," she wondered aloud.

Sister Maria laughed and pointed to the moon. "Look, Sister," she said. "We've nothing to worry about. Mr. Moon will give us enough light tonight."

There was hardly a chance to say anything more. Before the sisters had time to glance around the dimly-lit station, Father Heick whisked them to a curtained hack and hustled them inside. A ten-minute ride in the stillness of the night, broken only by the dull clop-clop of the horse's hooves and a few whispered words, brought them to the mission.[39]

As they alighted from the carriage, they could distinguish two buildings in the moonlight: the two-story, school-convent-church building of red brick and the one-story frame rectory standing on the corner of Ash and Short Blair. Father Heick led them over the dirt to the larger building. Downstairs there were four large classrooms completely furnished with double desks and blackboards. The sisters' "convent" was two rooms on the south side of the second floor, which to their surprise, were also completely furnished. Across the hall was the chapel containing only a small altar, but no pews. Father

Heick was hoping that the pews would arrive in time for the dedication on Sunday, October 3rd, the feast of the Holy Rosary.[40]

Arnold Janssen, the founder of the two orders of missionaries, had taken a great interest in the Jackson mission and had written to Father Heick that he would like to see it named in honor of the Holy Spirit. Since this mission was in the capital of the state, he hoped it would flourish and become a model for all other stations in Mississippi as well as in other places of the South.[41]

October 3rd dawned bright and beautiful. The pews had arrived the day before and had been placed in the chapel immediately.[42] Father Heick, Sister Maria and Sister Cyrilla were happy to see them being occupied by many of the Catholics from St. Mary's who had come for the dedication, among them Lucy Gilland and her son, Eddie; Eliza Collins and her husband, John, the first adult convert to St. Mary's; and Hester Winlock, another faithful parishioner.[43]

Bishop Heslin presided at the Solemn High Mass and preached the homily, taking the Sacrament of Penance for his theme. The sisters and a young priest, Rev. P. H. Striewe, sang the Latin Mass. Throughout the afternoon many visitors, both black and white, dropped by to see the building, and all seemed visibly impressed.[44]

Despite the flow of visitors, the missionaries remained uneasy. There had been no canvass made of the city as had been done before the opening of the school in Vicksburg; nor were there any black Catholic children in Jackson; the school was not free; it had been denounced by some of the ministers; and the public school had been in session for three weeks already. Realizing that all of these conditions worked against the success of the school, the missionaries could not even guess what the next day would bring when the school opened its doors for classes.

Not even Bishop Heslin could contain his curiosity and decided to remain overnight in Jackson to see for himself how the school fared on opening day.

Father Heick noted jubilantly in his diary:

His Lordship wanted to stay for the opening of the school. He wanted to see the children coming to our place. And he saw them coming. From all quarters they came. Soon the rooms and seats were occupied. I counted 111. Sister Otgera has been blessed exceedingly. She has 61 today; Sister Maria, 28; and Sister Cyrilla, 22.[45]

Apparently the opposition to the school had only served to make it better known throughout the city. By the end of the first week Sister Otgera's pupils in the first and second grades numbered in the 70's, and a distress signal was sent to Mother Leonarda in Techny. On October 12 the tall, robust but gentle Sister Marcellina Wefers arrived in Jackson to relieve Sister Otgera of her first graders. Now all four classrooms were in use and continued to fill.[46] Three weeks after the opening of Holy Ghost School, the enrollment had risen to 140.[47]

One of the first students, Fannie Coleman, recalls that she had become very nervous at Smith Robinson. Her sister, Eula, had already enrolled at Holy Ghost but her parents were hesitant about doing the same for her. The family was poor: her father was a millworker, her mother, a laundress, and they had just bought a new home and were making payments on it. But the reports of Holy Ghost School were so reassuring that the parents decided to make the additional sacrifices needed to send her there, too. She entered the fifth grade shortly after school opened, and the one characteristic of the school that she remembered years later about those early days was that all persons were treated alike whether they were rich or poor.[48]

The children loved their teachers and were easily drawn to the Catholic religion. By the end of the month, a third of them were attending Sunday afternoon religion classes taught by the sisters although they had attended services earlier in their own churches at the insistence of their ministers.[49]

At first the parents were disturbed when their children showed an interest in the Catholic faith. It was something that they had hoped wouldn't happen. All that they had really wanted was an education for their children, not a change in church affiliation. But the love and concern that the priest and sisters had for their children was not lost on them and when they saw how their children loved and respected the missionaries in return, many withdrew their objections.[50]

The little chapel was often crowded on Sundays with standing room only for latecomers. On Easter Sunday, 1910, Mary Roden, a child in the third grade, was baptized by Father Heick in the presence of many school children and adults. The ceremony deeply impressed all of those present, and many asked for baptism.[51] On May 15, Pentecost Sunday, fifteen children and two women were baptized. As before, many attended the ceremony and every seat in the second floor chapel was occupied.[52]

The missionaries believed that it was important to

give the black child an opportunity to perform on a stage before an audience since such opportunities were otherwise denied him. Because of Sister Bertranda's illness and the danger of typhoid fever in Vicksburg in 1907, the performance that year had been suspended; but from 1908 it became a tradition in all of the schools established by them in the South. Every child was given the opportunity to participate in a major production which was usually held at the end of the year. At St. Mary's the parents sat on chairs set up on the playground while the children performed on the back porch of the school. But this primitive setting did not diminish the excellence of the performance.

The first commencement exercises in Jackson were held in the American Theater on Pearl Street, located about a mile from Holy Ghost School. Despite the inconveniences they experienced in walking the children back and forth to the theater for practice, the sisters thought the benefits far outweighed the time and trouble. Sister Maria, who was in charge of the program, worked incessantly to develop all the latent talents of the pupils.

On June 7, the evening of the performance, the youngsters, costumed as lilies or roses or dressed in the national clothing of England, Ireland, Spain, China, Turkey, and the American Indian, assembled on the playground and when everyone was ready, they paraded down Bell and Mill Streets with their teachers, drawing many people to their porches to watch them as they passed by. That evening they had the unforgettable experience of performing before an audience of 300 people.[53]

The next day was the last day of school and report

cards were handed out to fifty-two boys and ninety-eight girls.[54]

In September, the enrollment at Holy Ghost School came to 180 the first day, and continued to grow until it reached two hundred. When Sister Auxilia Haag came from Techny on September 23 to take the overflow of first and second graders, there was no classroom for her. The sisters could not give up the two rooms they were using for living quarters, and the chapel where the Blessed Sacrament was reserved was too sacred. The missionaries finally made a temporary classroom by moving some desks into the dimly-lighted hall on the second floor between the sisters' rooms and the chapel.[55]

The success of the school in Jackson, as well as the one in Vicksburg, did not go unnoticed throughout the state. Pastors in north and central Mississippi took note of the rapid growth and vitality of the two missions. On March 19, 1910, Father Heick received a letter from Rev. Wenceslaus ten Brink, pastor of St. Patrick's Church in Meridian, inviting him to come and look over some lots that he thought would make a suitable site for the mission.[56]

Chapter III Footnotes: Storm Watch in Jackson

1. Jackson House/School Chronicles, 1909 (hereafter cited JHSC), 1.

2. 1910 U. S. Census, DAH, William D. McCain, *The Story of Jackson*, A History of the Capital of Mississippi, 1821-1951, Vol. 1 (Jackson, 1953), 9, 311.

3. Telephone conversation with William Dalehite, Jackson historian, September 30, 1974. *Jackson Daily News* (hereafter cited JDN), October 4, 1909.

4. McCain, op. cit., 252; Interview with Leola Gross Brown, June 18, 1971.

5. Ibid, 249 ff.

6. Dalehite, op. cit.

7. St. Peter's Parish archives, Jackson paper "Dr. Charles A. Oliver."

8. JDN, Rev. Aloysius Heick to JDN, July 15, 1908.

9. SMR, Chronicle; VHC, June 25, 1930.

10. Heick Report, July, 1923; Heick Chronicle, August 13, 1909; Interview with Mrs. Henry Denton, June, 1971.

11. Heick Chronicle; Dates conflict with Sisters' chronicle in Vicksburg unless Father Heick traveled back and forth between the two cities.

12. Ibid., July 7.

13. JDN, July 3, 1908, 8, Col. 5.

14. JDN, July 4, 1908, 5, Col. 5.

15. JDN, July 10, 1908, 4, Col. 2.

16. Heick Chronicle, op. cit., July 9, 1908.

17. Ibid., July 10, 1908.

18. JDN, Heick to Editor, July 15, 1908, 5, Col. 1.

19. Heick Report, op. cit.

20. Heick Chronicle, op. cit., July 21, 1908.

21. Ibid., July 22, 1908.

22. Ibid., August 4, 1908.

23. Ibid., August 14, 21, 1908.

24. Ibid., August 21, 1908, quoting JDN August 20.

25. Heick Report, July, 1923, op. cit.

26. Heick Chronicle, op. cit., October 19, 1908.

27. Heick Chronicle, op. cit., November 5, 1908.

28. Heick Report, July, 1923, op. cit.

29. Heick Report, July, 1923, op. cit.

30. Ibid.

31. Interview with Goldie Adams, June 15, 1971.

32. SMR, March 26, 1905, op. cit.

33. SSpSG, Sister Leonarda Lentrup to Rev. Mother Theresia, April 4, 1909.

34. Paper in Archives of the Blessed Sacrament Sisters at the Drexel Motherhouse, (hereafter cited BS).

35. JDN, June 25, 1909, 2, Col. 5.

36. Ibid.

37. SSpSG, Leonarda, op. cit.

38. VHC, September 10, 1908; Convent of the Holy Spirit Archives, Manila, Philippines, November 12, 1974, Letter of Sister Lucy Agnes to author.

39. JHSC, September 29, 1909.

40. Interview with John Grisham, June 20, 1971.

41. Heick Report, July, 1923, op. cit.

42. Heick Chronicle, October 3, 1909, 27.

43. Ibid.

44. Ibid.

45. Ibid.; JHSC, October 3, 1909; BS, Heick to Mother Katharine Drexel, October 15, 1909; Heick Chronicle, October 4, 1909, 28.

46. JHSC, October 12; Heick Chronicle, October 12, 1909, 28.

47. JHSC, October 25, 1909.

48. Interview with Fannie Coleman, June 16, 1971.

49. Heick Chronicle, November 14, 1909, ff.

50. Coleman, op. cit.; Interviews with Dock Gordon, June 22, 1971, and Jimmie Neil Stewart Banks, June, 1971.

51. JHSC, April 1, 1910.

52. Ibid., May 15, 1910.

53. Heick Chronicle, op. cit., 44, June 7, 1910; Coleman, op. cit.; Heick to Drexel, June 10, 1910.

54. Heick Chronicle, ibid.

55. JHSC, September 26, 1910.

56. Heick Chronicle, 40, March 10, 1910.

CHAPTER IV
Among the Pines in Meridian

Lying in the southernmost Appalachian foothills in a region of pine trees and buff-colored limestone, Meridian with a population of more than 23,000 had become the largest city of Mississippi by 1910.[1] Vicksburg had shrunk to third place with a population of about 21,000, and Jackson had moved into second.[2] Among the 12,000 blacks in Meridian, three were Catholics—Mattie Printens, of whom little is known; Lillian Oliver, who had come to Meridian from Vicksburg; and Thomas Foster, formerly of Mobile, Alabama. For some time Mr. Foster, who had been born into a devout Catholic family and baptized as an infant, was the only black Catholic in the city, a fact which made him a curiosity among his own race.[3] There was a saying in Mississippi that to be born a Catholic was bad; to be born a black was worse; but to be both black and Catholic was to really have the odds stacked against one.[4]

On March 22 Father Heick accepted Father Wenceslaus ten Brink's invitation to come to Meridian to look over a lot he had selected as a suitable place for a third mission and school. He was in Meridian again on April 14 and 15 and examined three other locations that all seemed favorable for their work. In the meantime, the pastor of St. Joseph's Church in Greenville, Rev. Paul J. Korstenbroek, visited the missionaries in Jackson, and after a tour of the buildings strongly urged them to come to Greenville. Father Heick, together with his friend, Father Gmelch, spent April 21 and 22 in Greenville, where he found a number of people, like Father Korstenbroek, interested in having the missionaries establish a church and school for the blacks in the city.[5] However, it seemed better to continue with the plans for Meridian since suitable land was available, and on April 29 he returned there and took option on two acres of land atop a clay hill capped with pines, fronting Eighteenth Avenue between Nineteenth and Twentieth streets in the northeast part of the city.[6] It was within the precincts of a rapidly growing black settlement on Meridian's east end and only two blocks from the East End Street car line. Its price of $2200 was reasonable, and Mother Katharine had generously promised the mission $10,000, if she lived.[7]

Unwilling to have another debacle like the one in Jackson, Father Heick sent a notice to the city newspaper, *The Meridian Star*, before making the final purchase of the property. He gave the exact location of the site, mentioned that the Holy Spirit Missionary Sisters would staff the school, signed his name and waited anxiously for three weeks.[8] On May 25, he joyfully wrote to Mother Drexel, *No word was spoken against our undertaking.*[9]

Was the opposition to the missionaries over in Mississippi? Had the missions proved themselves? This would only be revealed later. Perhaps that spring Meridian was too engrossed in its own activities to fret about a school for blacks, for the city had proudly hosted the annual convention for 2000 white Mississippi school teachers and rumors had it that it was planning to bid for the State Normal School in the fall.[10]

Meridian had a right to be proud of her schools. Under Superintendent John C. Fant, the Meridian public school system for both races had become a model for other city schools throughout the state. White students attended Meridian High, Highland, Whitfield, Stevenson, Witherspoon, Georgetown, Southside, and Chalk; while the black children studied at Wechsler, Valley Street, East End, and a newly-opened school also called Southside.[11]

Wechsler, built in 1888, was named for Rabbi Jacob Wechsler, an influential German-born Jew, who had supported black education and had taken this cause to the city fathers. It was the first brick public school for blacks in Mississippi. In 1910, it offered an eight-grade education and had eleven teachers and a principal on its staff. The other two schools—Valley Street and East End—went to sixth grade. Southside had a principal and one teacher. Besides the public schools there were also private elementary schools for both black and white.[12]

Mount St. Joseph, as the mission school was called, would have to offer quality education if it was to successfully compete with the other schools in the city.

As in Jackson and Vicksburg, a two-story brick building designed for school, chapel, and convent was planned; and Father Hoenderope, the builder priest, came from Vicksburg on June 23. The very next day, he was at city hall where he obtained a building permit for $16 and then went to the brick-yard to order 200,000 bricks.[13] The building would be ready for the opening of school in the fall.

He must have wondered about the future of Mount St. Joseph. He and the sisters at St. Mary's had just passed through a difficult year. Only 78 children had enrolled in September of 1909 as compared to 150 in September, 1908. Prompted by their ministers, Protestant parents, fearing their children would join the Catholic Church, had sent them to the public schools. But the children staunchly protested the transfer, declaring they wanted to be with the sisters, and by October 1 they were all back at St. Mary's. That wasn't the end of the matter, however, because another campaign was launched against the school during Christmas vacation and was followed by another exodus of children. Again the children protested, and by the first of March 130 had returned. Surprised to learn how much their children loved the sisters and knowing the quality of education they were receiving, the parents finally decided to allow their children to remain at St. Mary's. After these experiences in Vicksburg, Father Hoenderope could only wonder what lay ahead for Mount St. Joseph.[14]

On September 17 he met the sisters at Meridian's newly-built plush railroad station on Front Street in a mule-drawn buggy.[15] Sister Romana Lauscher was the superior of the new mission. Like Saul, the king of the Israelites, she stood head and shoulders above her companions, was even taller than Father Hoenderope. Born in Merzenich, Western Germany, she had been educated in an Ursuline boarding school for girls of aristocratic families and had studied English with the Sisters of Mercy in Chicago after coming to the United States. She was bursting with energy— the army officer of the community, some called her— and was gifted in music, a master in violin, organ, and piano. Sister Praesentata Kappel, 27, was the first grade teacher. She was Austrian and had been in the U.S.A. a year and a half. The third sister appointed to Mount St. Joseph was Sister Lamberta Kludt, a shy, reserved woman who had a gift for communicating with children and developing latent talents. The homemaker for the sisters was Sister Sebastiana from Vicksburg, now enjoying her fifth year in the South.[16]

Knowing that Bishop Heslin was coming the next day for the dedication, the sisters were dumbfounded to find the building far from presentable. Though it was already late, carpenters were still hustling about, hastily adding the finishing touches to the rooms. Shavings and sawdust lay everywhere. The chapel was completely empty, not even having an altar. How would they have Mass? Where would they keep the Blessed Sacrament?

Although the sisters had been on the train for the past twenty hours, they dropped their suitcases in their rooms on the second floor, took a hurried lunch, pinned back their wide blue sleeves and long habits and set to work sweeping up the shavings and sawdust and preparing the chapel for the next day's celebration.

While one sister prevailed upon a carpenter to nail some boards together for a simple table that could be used for the altar, another lined a brown-painted wooden cabinet with cloth for the tabernacle. The few available chairs were brought into the room and

61

the furnishings of the chapel were completed.

The night was well spent before the carpenters left and the sisters retired to their quarters for rest. But they were up again early in the morning to take care of a number of last-minute details.[17]

The day was beautiful and sunny, and the priests and sisters were pleased that almost 200 people were present for the dedication.[18] Bishop Heslin did not look well and appeared drawn and weak as he performed the blessing of the school and chapel. For some time the 63-year-old prelate had been suffering from serious bronchial and kidney disorders. Earlier in the year he had cancelled several confirmation appointments while he sought a cure at Armstrong Spring, Arksansas, *drinking the mineral water copiously*. Instead of finding the relief he sought, however, his feet and ankles became painfully swollen.[19] On his way back to Natchez, he was forced to stop in Memphis, where he was confined to bed in St. Joseph's rectory and given the last sacraments. By July 20 he had recovered enough to return to Mississippi and resume some of his work, although he never fully regained his health. The missionaries considered themselves fortunate to have him present on this occasion.[20]

In his address to the people crowded into the chapel in Meridian on September 18, 1910, Bishop Heslin acknowledged that the education of blacks had been seriously neglected and that it was time for the Catholic Church to become involved.[21] He welcomed the Divine Word Fathers and Holy Spirit Missionary Sisters to Meridian.

On the following day, September 19, Mount St. Joseph School opened with 45 pupils. Sister Romana took charge of the older children; Sister Lamberta, the middle grade pupils; and Sister Praesentata, the primary ones. The monthly tuition for the children from kindergarten to Grade 3 was 50¢, while those in grades 4 to 8 paid 75¢.[22]

Having received an excellent education in their former schools, the children expected to be placed in the grades indicated on their report cards. But Sister Romana set her own standards for each grade and when a pupil did not meet them, she placed the child in a lower grade, sometimes even two grades below the one indicated on the report card. These transfers aroused resentment and anger on the part of both children and parents and created a few disciplinary problems in the classrooms, but gradually the parents began to understand that the teachers had the children's true interest and happiness at heart.[23] More children applied for admission, and Sister Damascena van Ackeren, a light-complexioned, portly sister, arrived from Techny on November 13 to help with the teaching.[24]

The pastor at the mission was Father James Wendel, 29, who had spent four years in New Guinea.[25] Father Hoenderope, his work completed in Meridian, had returned to St. Mary's in Vicksburg. As tall as Father John, but not as robust, Father Wendel was an articulate, dynamic missionary with a drive that equalled Sister Romana's. He began in the chapel by replacing the makeshift table altar with one that he ordered from Techny.[26] At a time when a church was not complete without statues, he added these. He bought bells which rang out for the first time on Thanksgiving Day.[27]

As the missionaries had hoped, the people became

interested in the Catholic Church, and the first two children received the sacrament of baptism on Christmas eve.[28] On the feast of St. Joseph, March 19, fourteen people—ten children and four adults—joined the church. Thomas Foster and Mattie Printens stood as sponsors on April 2 when five more children received the sacament.[29]

In March 1912, a year and a half after Mount St. Joseph Mission opened, Father Wendel wrote to Mother Katharine Drexel that the mission had 50 Catholics and 150 children enrolled in school. But, as the missionaries feared, the success of the mission also stirred up bitter opposition.

Father Wendel wrote:

God has blessed us so far, but not without many a trial and anxiety. It seems sometimes as if the whole force of hell has been waging war against us.[30]

Meridian, proud of its many churches, was a stronghold of Protestantism. Understandably, the new mission was an affront to the people's religious convictions. Some citizens went so far as to solicit signatures to have the school closed as a nuisance to the community and presented the petition to the city council. When this effort failed, there followed threats of violence against the mission personnel and the building.[31]

In a letter to his superiors, Father Wendel wrote:

The animosity of the preachers, white and black, really explodes sometimes in very strange actions—actions not becoming Christian gentlemen, especially not ministers of the Gospel. They distribute calumnious literature among the blacks like "Thirty Years in Hell," and "The Devil in the Church."[32]

He believed that some wealthy person in the

North was paying for weekly copies of *The Menace*, an anti-Catholic paper published in Aurora, Missouri, which was distributed to the more prominent blacks by an agent. This person visited the black Protestant churches and preached against the Catholic Church.

One day Father Wendel confronted him in a Baptist church and a spirited argument ensued. As the congregation shouted, "Alleluia, put him out . . . . Glory be to God, put him out . . . ." the priest vigorously defended the Church and the mission.

He wrote to his superiors:

It's not the welfare of the black that prompts them, because I find none of them reaching a helping hand to the starving black despite the hard times that are prevailing in this section.[33]

One day the sisters learned that a minister had told his flock that Catholics go straight to hell. "If that's where you parents want to send your children, then send them to the Catholic school," he thundered. Hearing this, a devout father of five school-age youngsters threatened them with death if they ever dared set foot in Mount St. Joseph's.

May God have mercy on him, wrote the sister in the school chronicle. The Lord evidently heard her prayer, for the father later joined St. Joseph's Church and became one of its most faithful members.[34]

Besides the opposition from church leaders, the Ku Klux Klan, angered that white women were teaching black children in Meridian, was also spreading false information and reports about the church that wreaked havoc upon the mission.

It was a difficult time for the missionaries, but they placed their entire confidence in God and turned more than ever to prayer, inviting the people to join them in a weekly hour of adoration. About twenty-five parishioners responded and gathered with the priest and sisters in the little chapel on Wednesday evenings to implore God's blessing and protection on the mission.[35]

During the second school term the opposition united to deal a devastating blow to Mount St. Joseph's. Protestant groups formed a society whose goal was to collect funds to pay the tuition of the pupils who were attending the mission school if they would transfer to one of the three other private schools in the city, all conducted by Protestants. Within three weeks, the sisters watched their enrollment drop from 150 to 70. With the children also went their means of livelihood.

Father Wendel wrote to Mother Katharine Drexel:

We are powerless against them since the sisters depend upon the monthly tuition for their support. Our average income up to now was $60 to $70 a month. Somehow we managed by doing all the work ourselves.[36]

The few parents who remained faithful to the school did so because they believed Mount St. Joseph offered their children a quality education that they wouldn't find elsewhere. It took courage for them to declare their convictions to white people, often their employers, who wanted to know why they were sending their sons and daughters to a *Catholic* school taught by *white* sisters. In some instances, their decision placed their jobs in jeopardy.

One father declared, when asked why he sent his daughter "to those white nuns":

It's true I can hardly afford it, but I want to have the

best for my children. I consider the Catholic school to be the best school for them, educationally as well as for its religious atmosphere.[37]

The opposition did not prevail against the school for long, however, since the enrollment soon rose again.

In September of 1912 the sisters and priest at Mount St. Joseph began monthly school conferences to maintain their professional competency and study how to improve the quality work done by the students. The minutes of their conferences read as though taken from pages of modern educational manuals.[38]

At this first meeting, Sister Zitta Hilbich, the teacher for the fourth, fifth and sixth grades, delivered a paper on Arithmetic.

Arithmetic (she said) *must be made interesting . . . . The child will look at the numbers as at poles, too heavy for him to handle. But those poles turned into little sticks, he will handle with pleasure . . . . In solving problems, children must be trained to read the problem carefully and if they don't understand, to read it over twice or thrice . . . .*

In November Sister Bartholomaea Seelhorst spoke on manners:

Children should not laugh at the mistakes of others or at their way of speech, especially if they are new children . . . . Among the children you will find a few who always like to play tricks and want to have their own way. How can you make them better? Be kind to them, ask them to do you a favor . . . .

Sister Damascena spoke on the subject of character training in January, 1913.

As long as a teacher does not know the character of the

child, there is always danger of treating him wrong-
ly . . . . A good teacher, who knows the character of a
*child, is able to teach him according to his **individu-***
ality. This is a very important factor in teaching,
and the success of a teacher depends on it to a
***great extent.** How much can a teacher do with a look*
when she understands the child. On the contrary,
how wrongly can a child be treated, if the teacher does
not understand him. She may sometimes see a fault
and punish where there is only a weak point in his
character that would have been restored or made
strong by a good word or even by a kind look.

The sisters, in their efforts to improve their work in
the classroom, were true daughters of Mother Leonarda. As noted earlier, she wanted to have her
teachers prepared when they entered their classrooms: Only the best was good enough for their work
among the blacks. Soon after she came to the United
States from Steyl in 1901, she approached St. Ignatius Liberal Arts College in Chicago, now Loyola
University, and engaged a Professor, Francis
Tschan, to come to Shermerville to conduct classes
for her future teachers. In February 1906 he taught
weekly classes in language, literature, history, geography, civics, and Latin. In the summer he taught
politcal economy and college mathematics as well.

All of the sisters teaching in the South, even if they
had graduated from the Normal School in Steyl,
Holland, before coming to America, attended some
of Professor Tschan's classes.[39] By the summer of
1912, however, the number of sisters in the Southern
missions had increased to such an extent that Mother
Leonarda arranged to have the summer normal
school in Mississippi.

Choosing the site was not difficult. She invited the sisters from all the stations to meet in Vicksburg, where the sisters were living in the two-story antebellum Geiger house which Father Heick had purchased along with the surrounding property. The spacious convent and grounds would offer the visiting sisters comfortable places to study. Behind the convent was a hall which could be converted into a dormitory, and classes would be held in the school.[40]

Besides the three schools in Mississippi, the sisters were also staffing St. Bartholomew's School in Little Rock, Arkansas, which they had opened in 1910 along with Mount St. Joseph in Meridian. This mission had already been in existence for over a year and the school had been staffed by the Benedictine Sisters of Shoal Creek, Arkansas, when the Holy Spirit Missionary Sisters came. Bishop John Bartholomew Morris had named the mission after his patron saint, St. Bartholomew, because, he said, the saint was martyred by having his skin peeled off him alive so that the color of one's skin really didn't matter.[41]

Sister Bertranda was teaching there when the sisters assembled for the first six-week summer school in 1913. Sister Romana and Sister Damascena were among the sisters from Meridian. Sister Afra Horstmann was the new superior in Jackson. Sister Cyrilla and Sister Sebastiana had been transferred to the congregation's newly-opened missions in the Philippine Islands.[42]

The sisters were no longer wearing the beautiful, light-blue habit, but had changed to a more practical navy blue color while retaining the crucifix and medal of the Holy Spirit suspended from a red ribbon.

The priests from the missions were also present for the summer courses, opening them with a Solemn High Mass and offering spiritual conferences and lectures. Sister Dominica Ogrodowski, prefect of studies, assisted Mother Leonarda in teaching the courses. The sophisticated, patronizing deportment of the tall young sister was the direct opposite of her superior's humble, modest manner, but what she lacked in gentleness and tact was offset by her learning and zeal. Courses were offered in pedagogy, church and world history, speech and literature, mathematics, physics, and gymnastics.

An effort was made to unify the school program in all of the schools by choosing the same books and subject matter to be taught, deciding on the length of the school term and the kind of records that should be kept. Following the lead of the faculty at Mount St. Joseph, the teachers resolved to hold monthly faculty meetings in the stations and send copies of the minutes to Mother Leonarda and Father Heick.

Toward the close of the summer school, a day was set aside for a pleasure trip on the Mississippi River to Louisiana where the community enjoyed a picnic before returning to their boat. Then back to their respective missions the sisters went, eager to apply in their classrooms all that they had learned in the courses as well as from one another.[43]

The sisters at Mount St. Joseph continued to keep the minutes of their monthly faculty meetings. In October the topic was Individualism in Education. The chronicler wrote in perfect penmanship:

Individualism is necessary for justice and efficiency's sake. It is the only way to effective education. Every child must be studied according to his mental capac-

ity, his health, and peculiarity.

At another meeting a speaker prefaced her subject, "Teaching Mathematics", with the words:

The teacher is tempted to follow the textbook slavishly, page after page, operation after operation, all as set down in point. To have as aim the completion of a certain part of a textbook within a set time is villainous and shows a most pitiful ambition.

Then she launched into her subject:

The aim we ought to have in the teaching of mathematics is twofold—cultural and practical. The cultural aim is to have our pupils secure a grasp of principles. Students who after years of mathematical study have but slight conception of the principles whereon the science is based have not been taught by the teacher with a cultural aim in view.

On the topic of teaching geography, the chronicler noted:

*Geography is not only the description of the earth's surface as some books define it, but a description of the earth's surface as the **home of men**.*[44]

At this time these quiet efforts of the Holy Spirit Missionary Sisters to improve themselves professionally went unnoticed in educational circles of the State. Within a few years, however, the sisters would have the educators around the State talking about them. Even the Bishop in Pass Christian would take note of it.

Sr. Afra, Holy Ghost School, Jackson, MS, 1910

Chapter IV Footnotes: Among the Pines in Meridian

1. Earl L. Bailey, *Economic Analysis of Mississippi Community*, University of Mississippi, 1935; WPA Guide, 228.

2. U. S. Census 1910.

3. *Colored Messenger*, March 17 and February 1, year unknown, NJ, Report by Rev. Anthony Jacobs, 1937.

4. Interview with De Witt Webster, June 7, 1970.

5. Heick Chronicle, 40, ff., March 19, 1910-April 22, 1910; BS, Heick to Drexel, March 24, 1910.

6. NJ, Jacobs Report, 1933.

7. BS, paper, op. cit.

8. *Meridian Evening Star*, May 3, 1910, Vol. XXIV, No. 120.

9. BS, Heick to Drexel, May 25, 1910.

10. *Meridian Star*, April 17, 1910.

11. *Meridian City Directory*, 1910, R. L. Polk and Co.

12. Roger Tilmon Smedley, Jr., *The Gel of a Dream* (Institutional Research, 1968), 32 & 33; *Citizens of Color*, "Development of Schools."

13. Jacobs Report, op. cit.; Heick Chronicle, op. cit. 45, June 23, 1910.

14. VHC, September 10, 1909; January, 1910.

15. Jacobs Report, op. cit.

16. PP, Vital Statistics of sisters; *In Memoriam* of sisters; Interview with Sister Uriele Isermann.

17. Meridian House Chronicle (hereafter cited MHC) tr. from German, 1.

18. Ibid.

19. *Meridian Evening Star*, June 24, 1910; NJ, Heslin Diary, op. cit., 277.

20. Most Rev. Richard O. Gerow, compiled by *Catholicity in Mississippi* (Marrero, LA), 75.

21. MHC, op. cit.

22. MHC, op. cit.

23. MHC, op. cit.

24. MHC, op. cit.

25. *St. Augustine Messenger*, May, 1960; Jacobs, Report on History of Parish given at a 1935 Clergy Conference.

26. Meridian Rectory archives "Description of Church."

27. MHC, op. cit., October 27, 1910.

28. "Description of Church," op. cit.

29. MHC, op. cit., March 19, 1911; Interview with Rev. Arthur Winters on parish records.

30. Rev. James Wendel to Drexel, March 12, 1912.

31. Ibid.; James Wendel, "Foundation," *Colored Messenger*, March, 1917, and February 1; Jacobs Report, op. cit.

32. Jacobs Report, op. cit.

33. *Colored Messenger*, op. cit.; Meridian Rectory Archives, no date.

34. Jacobs Report, op. cit.

35. Wendel to Drexel, op. cit.

36. Ibid.

37. Interview with Mamie Sudbury, June 3, 1970.

38. This and following paragraphs are taken from a handwritten notebook *School Conferences*, now in the Archives of the Paraclete Province.

39. Telephone conversation with Loyola University, Chicago, Illinois, librarian, March 4, 1975; Interview with sisters in Paraclete Wing, after reading chapter 1, undated; *Paraclete Chronicle*, 1951, sisters' intercommunity communication.

40. SMR, Chronicle, February 7, 1909, ff.; VHC, 1912 and 1914 (summers).

41. Sister Aelicia Hess, *Master's Work*, November, 1960, sisters' house organ; Rev. Hubert Singleton, *The History of St. Bartholomew Parish*, 50th Anniversary Booklet.

42. Sisters who attended the conference are taken from respective house chronicles.

43. VHC, op. cit.

44. *School Conferences*, op. cit.

CHAPTER V
Past Septembers

Bishop Thomas Heslin died on February 22, 1911, and was buried on the last day of the month. According to a note in Father Heick's diary, black Catholics were prevented from attending the requiem Mass at the Cathedral because of *the unchristian spirit of the Knights of Columbus.*[1]

On June 29 John Edward Gunn, a Marist priest, was appointed Bishop Heslin's successor. Born in Ireland in 1863, the eldest of eleven children, he studied in England and France before going to Rome where he received a Doctorate in Theology and was ordained. After a few years of pastoral work in London, Father Gunn was assigned to Washington, D.C., to teach at the Marist House of Study; and in 1898 he was appointed the superior of the mission opened by the Marist Fathers in Atlanta, Georgia.

Under his administration a beautiful brick church dedicated to the Sacred Heart was built on Peachtree and Ivy streets and here on August 29, 1911, Father Gunn was consecrated the sixth bishop of the Diocese of Natchez. At 48, he was a man of large build with a receding hairline, a square ruddy face with a finely-chiseled nose and sensitive lips. He possessed a ready wit and had become an eloquent speaker.[2]

A few weeks after his consecration, accompanied by his brother, Edward, and officials of the diocese, Bishop Gunn came to Natchez on a chartered train to take possession of his See. A throng of people welcomed him at the station. He was amused to find a victoria, drawn by four white horses and surrounded by out-riders, bridle holders, and others *in medieval-looking attire*, waiting to drive him down Main Street to St. Mary's Cathedral. Only later did he learn that the attendants in their colorful regalia were in the procession for more than mere pageantry.

He wrote in his diary:

It seems that the horses were borrowed from the Fire Department. Had the fire siren rung during the procession, there would not have been a force powerful enough in Natchez to keep the horses from bringing the Bishop to the fire. This was the reason for the out-riders, the lackeys, the bridle-holders. How little does a man know how close he is to danger,

he ended with tongue in cheek.[3]

After the celebrations in Natchez, Bishop Gunn set out to make the rounds of his state-wide missionary diocese to assess its strengths and weaknesses and become acquainted with its people.[4] On September 30 he arrived in Vicksburg, where Father Mallin met him with an impressive delegation. The next day he dined with the Sisters of Mercy at St. Francis Xavier Convent, and on the following day he visited St. Mary's. Now in its fifth year, the mission numbered 99 Catholics. The enrollment in the school had again risen to 150 and appeared to have become stabilized.

Bishop Gunn took note of the brick school building in Vicksburg, as well as in Jackson and Meridian, and would later make a note of them in his diary. He visited Holy Ghost mission on October 8. In the third year of its existence, 40 people were coming for Mass on Sundays and 60 children were attending religious classes on Sunday afternoons. There were 207 students in school.[5]

On November 11 the Bishop administered confirmation in both parishes in Meridian.

Returning to Natchez after his tour, Bishop Gunn noted in his diary:

The towns and villages are well supplied with churches. There are six brick churches in the northern part of the diocese—one at Natchez, Vicksburg, Greenville, Canton, Meridian, and Jackson, and two along the Mississippi Coast—one at the Bay and the other at Biloxi. All of the other churches are frame work. With the exception of Greenville and Biloxi all the brick churches, even the Cathedral, looked dingy and in need of repairs and whitewash. The frame buildings were miserable makeshifts with perhaps a few exceptions such as Pass Christian, Long Beach, and Brookhaven.

The schools are numerous and well-attended, but the buildings are poor-looking and apparently cared for by nobody. The Brothers of the Sacred Heart have three brick schools—Natchez, Vicksburg, and Bay St. Louis. The Sisters of Mercy have one brick school at

Vicksburg; the Sisters of Charity, one at Natchez; and
*the **Sisters for the colored have brick schools at***
***Vicksburg, Jackson, and Meridian**. All the other*
schools of the Diocese are frame buildings and sorry
substitutes for schools of any kind.

It is interesting to note that the other religious have names—the Brothers of the Sacred Heart, the Sisters of Mercy, the Sisters of Charity. But the Holy Spirit Missionary Sisters are the *Sisters for the colored*.

At times Catholic Church leaders in Mississippi have stated that the Church has done more for blacks than for whites in Mississippi. In one sense, history bears this out. Until the second half of the 20th century, the Catholic Church in Mississippi constituted a minority without political power or prestige. Lacking adequate money and personnel to care for its own members, it had little means to evangelize either white or black Mississippians.[6]

Records of the first black Catholics in the state go back to the Spanish era between 1786 and 1798. In the intervening years until the diocese was established in 1837, baptismal records indicate that perhaps a dozen slaves were baptized by priests who came to Natchez off and on to tend to the needs of the Catholics living there.[7]

When Pope Gregory XVI established the See of Natchez in 1837, four years passed before a priest was found who would be willing to accept the responsibility and loneliness that would be demanded of him as Mississippi's first bishop. This was John Mary Joseph Chanche, a Sulpician priest and president of St. Mary's Seminary in Baltimore, Maryland.[8] When Bishop Chanche came to Natchez, he had no church and only two priests who were temporarily on leave from the Diocese of New Orleans: Rev. M. D. O'Reilly in Vicksburg and Rev. Joseph N. Brogard in Natchez.[9] Besides these two congregations, there were a few Catholics along the Coast in Pascagoula, Biloxi, Pass Christian, and Bay St. Louis and perhaps a hundred families scattered in the interior of the state. The bishop found two black Catholics in Natchez when he arrived in 1841. No doubt, there were others living on plantations owned and operated by Catholics. Some historians estimate their number to be as high as four or five hundred.[10]

Father Brogard wished to leave Natchez at once and return to New Orleans; but Bishop Chanche persuaded him to remain while he toured the North to beg for men and money.[11] During his absence, a Rev. Jean Claude Francois appeared in Natchez and offered his services to the diocese. Although he had left the Diocese of Vincennes to the north without the permission of his bishop, Bishop Chanche was so desperately short of priests that he sought the necessary authorization from Father Francois' ordinary to let him remain.

He wrote to Bishop Blanc in New Orleans:

I have a notion of trying to do something for the black people. Perhaps he might succeed in this mission. We will see.[12]

Before a month had passed, Bishop Chanche was congratulating himself for accepting Father Francois' services. He wrote to Bishop Blanc:

I thank God that Father Francois is here. I have had him open a mission among the blacks which promises to be successful.[13]

Before long Father Francois' congregation grew from two to sixty people, and fifteen adults asked for baptism. By June 1842 from 150 to 200 blacks were receiving instructions in preparation for baptism.

Father Francois also visited various Catholics, pockets in the counties north and south of Natchez—Rodney, Port Gibson, Grand Gulf, and Woodville. True to Bishop Chanche's wishes, the priest instructed and baptized the Negro slaves of the Catholic plantation owners wherever he went. Four years later Father Francois left the diocese to join the Congregation of the Missions.

The lack of priests—never more than two at a time—continued to plague Bishop Chanche. In 1850 Rev. John Fierbras became the first resident priest of Port Gibson. From 1852 to 1864 the baptismal register reveals the baptism of 138 black children and three adults. In Vicksburg about the same period, the records show the baptism of 112 children and 40 adults. At the same time, there were probably not more than 30 white Catholics around Port Gibson and about 700 in and near Vicksburg.[14]

Bishop James Oliver Van de Velde, SJ, Bishop Chanche's successor, governed the diocese for only two years, and in 1857 he was succeeded by Bishop William Henry Elder. There were now more than 309,000 slaves and 1000 free blacks in the diocese, and Bishop Elder was deeply concerned about their spiritual welfare.[15]

He wrote to the Propagation of the Faith that same year:

The masters do not like to let the Negroes go to a public church, because there is danger of their misbehaving when they are away from home and out of sight of the overseer; and because various inconveniences result from the servants of one plantation mingling with

80

those of another. Each master has something particular in his regulations and his method of management, and if the servants have free intercourse they are apt to make each other jealous and dissatisfied.[16]

The bishop lamented not having enough priests to send one around to the plantations as a traveling missionary.[17]

During the Civil War, Natchez and Vicksburg fell to the Union Army and became refugee centers for thousands of blacks fleeing from their plantation owners. Not knowing what else to do with the flow of freedmen who arrived with only the clothes on their backs and worshipping the Union Army as their liberators, the military authorities in Natchez blocked off an old cotton press grounds below the bluffs of the city along the river and herded them into it. Here the refugees camped, crowded together without adequate food and water, proper sewerage, and protection from the elements. Thousands were struck down by scarlet fever, small pox, measles, and dysentery.

Bishop Elder and his priests went to the area daily to minister to them, instructing and baptizing those who were in danger of death. As they passed the headquarters of the Northern military authorities on their way in and out of the camp, they could not refrain from taunting them for not bettering the living conditions of those they had so magnanimously "liberated."[18]

After the War, the Church made noble efforts to establish schools for the Catholic children of both races in the state. In Natchez Rev. Mathurin Grignon, the vicar general of the diocese and rector of the Cathedral parish, gathered the black Catholic children in the basement of the Cathedral and opened a school taught by lay teachers. In 1867 Rev. Charles Van Queckelberge on a plantation near Port Gibson wrote to Bishop Elder that he was trying to establish a school for about twenty black children.[19] In 1870 the Sisters of Mercy were conducting separate girls' schools for each of the races in Pass Christian.[20] About the same time, Rev. Henry LeDuc in Bay St. Louis opened a school for black children taught by lay teachers at first and later by the Sisters of St. Joseph, who were conducting a boarding school for girls.[21] In 1882 the Sisters of the Most Holy Sacrament from New Orleans came to Pascagoula and opened a boarding school for white children and a day school for the blacks.[22]

In 1880 Bishop Elder was appointed Bishop of Cincinnati, and Rev. Francis Janssens was named his successor.[23] The new bishop had come to the United States from the American College in Louvain, Belgium, in 1868, the year of the Second Plenary Council of Baltimore. The Civil War had just ended. Thousands of blacks were without homes, without work, without opportunity for religious services. The bishops, who represented both the North and South, wrestled with the emotionally-charged situation as best they could and decided that no general rule of action could be taken in such a vast area as the United States. It seemed best to leave these matters to the zeal and prudence of the respective bishops and their provincial councils.

After all aspects of the matter have been thoroughly considered and it seems good in the Lord to the bishops that the salvation of the blacks is benefited best by the erection of separate churches for them, then that priest

*who undertakes this work with proper permission is
duly to be praised. But if in another place it is decided
that it is better to invite the blacks to churches that
have already been built and to worship in them simul-
taneously with the whites, then let the ordinary take
care that this be done in such a manner that
the church later on be not subjected to any accusation
or become the pretext of such an accusation. This
whole matter weighs heavily on our consciences that
to everyone who wants to come to Christ the door is
open.*

Decree of the Council

The Decree also urged the erection of schools and
orphanages since the War had left many children
homeless and with no one to care for them.

In the Third Plenary Council in 1886, which Bishop
Janssens attended, the bishops again reviewed the
black apostolate. The Decree noted that some
churches and schools for blacks had been built while
in other churches places had been reserved for them
to attend Mass and receive religious instructions according to the recommendations of the Second Plenary Council. Then there followed two important
sections.

*Experience shows the spiritual welfare and Christian
education of the blacks cannot be provided for effec-
tively except through missions, instructions, and
other spiritual exercises proper to their temperament
and culture. We decree, therefore, that the bishops
make serious efforts to build churches, schools, orphanages and homes for the poor wherever this is
possible. For other localities we wish that they not
only provide a fit and proper place in a church where
blacks are given the sacraments gladly without dis-*

83

crimination, but we further decree that bishops take
for this important task priests, whether diocesan or
religious, whose sole duty will be to preach the Word
of God to the faithful, to teach the children the truths
of our faith and to perform other ecclesiastical services
for them. The pastors of the churches should not only
be helpful to these missionaries, but we forbid them to
become obstacles to all who have been appointed to this
sacred trust by the bishop.

Title VIII, Chapter 2, Section 242 of the Decree

In the following section it exhorts the bishops to
search for workers who are aflame with zeal for
souls, who will go to those who are still not in the fold
of the Church and invite them to come in.[24]

According to Bishop Richard Oliver Gerow in his
book *Catholicity in Mississippi*, Bishop Janssens

tried to comply with the Decree for separate churches
proposed at that renowned gathering by seeking an
opportunity as well as the means to establish a sepa-
rate congregation for the colored people of Natchez,
but . . . his subsequent appointment to the Archdio-
cese of New Orleans prevented him from fulfilling his
zealous design.

It was Bishop Heslin who carried out the policy of
separate churches for the races in Mississippi.[25]

On October 18, 1889, Rev. A. N. Peters, a diocesan
priest, wrote to Bishop Heslin asking to leave the
diocese, adding, however, that he would be interested
in coming to Natchez to minister to the blacks.[26]
Bishop Heslin accepted his offer and had a frame
building put up on Beaumont Street for their use as
school and church. In July 1894 Father Peters succeeded in collecting enough money in the North to
build a beautiful brick church on the corner of St.

Catherine Street and Orange Avenue. A few days after its dediction the zealous priest died, worn out from his labors, and in 1899 the parish was turned over to the Josephite Fathers.[27]

St. Joseph's Society of the Sacred Heart (SSJ), popularly known as the Josephite Fathers, was founded in 1866 at Mill Hill, London, England, by Bishop Herbert Vaughan. In 1871 four priests had come to America to work among the blacks at the express invitation of the American hierarchy. Although Bishop Elder had written to Bishop Vaughan in 1875 asking him for missionaries for Greenville, where the 12,000 blacks outnumbered the whites six to one, it was Bishop Heslin who succeeded in obtaining the services of the Society. In 1889 they were given charge of Holy Family parish in Natchez. That same year Rev. E. E. Reilly came to give missions and lectures and open schools and churches in Mississippi.[28]

The Josephites were working along the Coast when David Bremner approached Bishop Heslin with his proposition at Merigold. Before granting permission to the Society of the Divine Word and the Holy Spirit Missionary Sisters to begin work in the diocese, the bishop consulted the wishes of the Josephites.

In a letter dated November 23, 1904, the Josephite superior, Rev. Thomas Donovan, reassured him:

Your letter was received, and it delights me to know that such an excellent offer is made you in behalf of the colored work in your diocese . . . . We don't object, but heartily concur in and hope always to extend our good will toward the progress and development of this contemplated enterprise . . . .[29]

By 1912 there were nine Catholic churches in Mississippi exclusively for blacks; six in care of the Josephite Fathers and three in care of the Divine Word Fathers. Black Catholics numbered 2,800.

There were ten Catholic schools for black Mississippians: the three schools in Vicksburg, Jackson, and Meridian staffed by the Holy Spirit Missionary Sisters with an enrollment of 643 students; Holy Family School in Natchez, now taught by the Franciscan Sisters of Glenn Riddle, Pennsylvania, with 125 students; schools in Harrison, Laurel Hill, and Springfield staffed by lay teachers with 128 students; schools in Pass Christian and Bay St. Louis conducted by the Sisters of Mercy with 140 students; and the day school in Pascagoula, staffed by the Sisters of Perpetual Adoration with a total of 75 pupils.

The ten schools had a total of 1121 pupils, of whom 643, or more than half, were in the three northern schools staffed by the Holy Spirit Missionary Sisters. At the same time there were 20 Catholic schools for white children in the diocese.[30]

Bishop Gunn jotted in his diary under the heading EDUCATION:

I found the diocese far in advance of its numbers and finances in the matter of education. In fact, I have found that with the Archdiocese of Philadelphia as the only exception, Natchez has provided more educational facilities for its Catholic children than any other diocese in the country.[31]

He credited this to the 100 Sisters of Mercy in the diocese who were staffing 10 of the 20 schools for white children. Besides the Sisters of St. Joseph in Bay St. Louis, the Sisters of Perpetual Adoration in Pascagoula and the schools of the Brothers of the

Sacred Heart in Vicksburg, Bay St. Louis, Natchez, and Meridian, the bishop noted that the Sisters of Notre Dame

> have a boarding school at Chatawa and a parochial school at Brookhaven; the Sisters of St. Vincent de Paul, a school and orphanage in Natchez; and the Sisters of Nazareth, a school in Yazoo City.
>
> The Catholic teachers are simply splendid, full of zeal, interest and Catholic ambition. But their school buildings are primitive and defy classification. For the most part they are falling to pieces.[32]

Despite Bishop Gunn's lamentations over the conditions of the schools, the diocesan schools were no worse than the public schools in Mississippi.

In pre-War rural Mississippi, public schools were really not needed. Tutoring and studies abroad or in eastern cities took care of the educational needs of the plantation owners' children.

After the Civil War the Constitutions drafted for Mississippi established a uniform school system for both races.[33] Northern enthusiasts pushed school buildings and equipment, and when there were not enough Southern whites to staff the schools for the blacks, they recruited teachers from the North, offering them salaries high enough to attract them to the state even though the school term was only four months long.[34]

The cost of buildings, equipment, and teachers' salaries fell heavily upon the impoverished Southerners trying to recover from the havoc created by the War. There arose a violent opposition to the free school system, and school houses of both races were burned to the ground and the Northern teachers driven from the state.[35] In 1886 eighteen superintendents reported that churches were being used for schools in their districts, especially by blacks.[36] During the next two decades, efforts were made to change this situation and by 1910 about 4500 school buildings were put up, mostly for the whites.[37]

During this period, efforts were also being made in educational circles to improve the quality of education in the state.

In his biennial address to the legislature in 1903, State Superintendent of Schools, H. L. Whitfield, pointed out that the public school curriculum in Mississippi was one of the lowest in the United States. He said that the twelve subjects taught could be completed before the children were old enough to be sent to school. He also claimed that 90% of the teachers were not professionally trained and that 75% had never attended any school other than a rural school. Professional training of the white teachers came from summer normals, county institutes, and the departments of pedagogy in state institutions. For the blacks there was Holly Springs State Normal School, which offered two to three hundred students three years of preparatory work and a two-year normal course; but the curriculum hardly went beyond secondary subjects. The school ceased to exist in 1904 when the legislature refused to vote appropriation for its support. A state normal school for white teachers came into existence in 1911.[38]

That year the average expenditure of each child in Mississippi enrolled in schools exclusive of separate districts was $7.82 for whites and $1.95 for blacks. In the separate districts it was $14.83 for whites and $4.04 for blacks.[39]

This was the educational scene in Mississippi

when the mission schools were opened in Vicksburg, Jackson and Meridian. It also explains why parents chose to send their children to the Catholic schools even when they feared they would join the Church. Parents interested in their children's welfare sacrificed their hardearned pennies to pay the tuition, while the pupils—some only ten or eleven years old—picked cotton, swept sidewalks and porches, and carried in coal in order to buy their books and school supplies. They were serious about their education.

Chapter V Footnotes: Past Septembers

1. Heick Chronicle, op. cit., 49; February 23, 1911.

2. Gerow, op. cit., 77-78.

3. NJ, Most Rev. John E. Gunn Diary, 1 and 2.

4. This and the following paragraphs are from Gunn's Diary, 3-7.

5. JHSC, October 8, 1911.

6. Interview with Most Rev. Joseph Brunini, May 31, 1971.

7. NJ, File: *Negro History*, "Catholicity Amongst the Negroes in the Diocese of Natchez," 6-page typewritten paper (hereafter cited CAN).

8. James J. Pillar, *The Catholic Church in Mississippi, 1837-65* (New Orleans, La., 1964), 3.

9. Pillar, op. cit., 7.

10. Pillar, op. cit., 37.

11. Pillar, op. cit., 7; Letters of Most Rev. John Joseph Chanche, May 27, 1841 (U. of Notre Dame).

12. Pillar, op. cit., 8.

13. Ibid.

14. Ibid.

15. Chanche letters, December 3, 1841; January 2, 1842; January 31, 1842.

16. NJ, CAN, op. cit.

17. Ibid.

18. Pillar, op. cit., 268 ff.

19. NJ, CAN, op. cit.

20. NJ, History File P Pass Christian.

21. Bay Rectory files, paper.

22. NJ, Janssen's file S, February 2, 1882.

23. Gerow, op. cit., 113.

24. II Plenary Council of Baltimore. Title X—*Concerning the Salvation of Souls*, Chapter 4, Section 485 (Baltimore, 1868); III Plenary Council 1886, Title VIII, Chapter 2, Section 242 and following.

25. Gerow, op. cit., 113, "Early Religion," *Journal of Mississippi History*, Vol. 9, August, 1947.

26. NJ, P file, Letters of Rev. A. N. Peters, October 18, 1889.

27. Gerow, op. cit.

28. NJ, Elder Letter book no. 15, 477, July 19, 1875; *Diary of Janssens, Meerschaerts, Heslin,*, op. cit. 200-202.

29. NJ, Heslin file D, Letter in envelope marked "Donovan, Thomas SSJ," November 23, 1904.

30. NJ, File *Negroes*, January, 1913, "Application for Aid to the Commission for the Colored and Missions."

31. Gunn Diary, op. cit., 7.

32. Ibid., 8.

33. Billy N. Bishop, Thesis: *Public Education in Mississippi, 1910-1954*, August, 1961.

34. Stuart Grayson Noble, *Forty Years of the Public Schools in Mississippi* (New York, 1918), 35.

35. Ibid., 37.

36. Ibid., 65.

37. Ibid., 67.

38. Ibid., 86 ff.; *Biennial Report of Superintendent of Education, 1905-06 and 1906-07.*

39. *Biennial Report of State Superintendent of Education, 1910-1911.*

1st Holy Ghost Convent and Church, Jackson, MS

CHAPTER VI
A Return to the Delta

For several years there had been talk about opening a mission in Greenville, 60 miles south of Merigold. Both the pastor of St. Joseph Church in that city, Rev. Paul J. Korstenbroek, and Mother Katharine Drexel were interested in the project,[1] but because of the mission schools opening in Meridian and Little Rock, the work could not begin until 1913.

Greenville, the seat of Washington County, was the center of the greatest cotton-producing region of the world and was famous for its Bender Cotton, acclaimed for its long fibers and extra strength. Experts in grading and classifying cotton and buyers for spinners around the world had their offices in the downtown business section where cotton was the only language understood or spoken.[2] The field work was done by the blacks, and this explained their predominance in the city. Of the 12,000 people living in Greenville, 9,000 were black.[3]

The races shambled along in outward harmony and peace, adhering strictly to the social structures of the South: the white children reared to consider themselves superior to the blacks, and the black children raised to accept that inferiority.[4]

But the black population in the city observed its own social structure. Property owners, well-to-do farmers, skilled laborers and professional people—the doctors, dentists and teachers who ministered to their own race—maintained a self-important aloofness from the common day laborers who eked out the mere necessities of life in the cotton fields around the city.[5]

There was integration in Greenville as in the other areas of the Delta, but only according to the white man's rules. The variety of skin colors—copper, olive, and cream as well as the various brown and black hues of every shade attested to this phenomenon. Whether the white family knew or not, it was common knowledge in the black community that many white men had two families, one on each side of town.[6] Though forbidden by Mississippi law to marry his black concubine,[7] he more than likely loved her, offered her financial support, provided her with the home in which she lived, opened doors for their children, paid for their education, and helped them or their spouses to find good-paying jobs. Such a man would welcome a private school for blacks as a means of bettering his children's education.[8]

There were two public schools for black children in Greenville: No. 4 on the south end of the city and No. 2 on Nelson Street. These were frame buildings that bulged with pupils who sat three to a desk on the double seats cast off by the schools for the white children. There was also a Seventh Day Adventist School on Union Street.[9]

Father Korstenbroek had two black Catholic families in his parish, the Millers and the Casa Calvos.[10] Dr. James Miller and his wife, Irene Davis Miller, had moved to Greenville from Natchez, where Mrs. Miller and her sister, Laura Lee, had attended grade school in the basement of the Cathedral.[11] The couple had three daughters, Emilie, Daisy and Edna. When the family moved to Greenville, Dr. Miller was not yet a Catholic, but Mrs. Miller and their three daughters faithfully attended the services at St. Joseph's Church. Since the children could not attend the segregated parochial school, they received weekly religious instructions from the Sisters of Mercy.[12]

Deploring the crowded conditions in the public school, the Millers at first sent their two youngest daughters, Daisy and Edna, to the Seventh Day Adventist School. However, not satisfied with the discipline or the quality of education (and perhaps for religious reasons), they transferred the girls to Public School No. 2 when Daisy entered the third grade.[13]

Ernest and Nannie Casa Calvo, originally from Baton Rouge, Louisiana, were devout Catholics of Spanish and Negro descent. They had five children: Nita, Ernest, Iva, Maymee and Tony. In order to provide a suitable recreational place for their children and for those of other middle class parents, the couple operated and rented out a dance hall to the elite on the corner of Nelson and Redbud streets. This caused hard feelings among the young people who were not considered patrician enough to be admitted. One summer evening, as the fashionably-dressed dancers glided gracefully around the brilliantly-lighted upstairs hall, they took their revenge by tossing rotten eggs through the open window.

Needless to say, the dancing ended abruptly that evening.[14]

Confident that a mission would eventually be started in Greenville, Father Korstenbroek and a partner, Elizabeth J. Meade, through the Greenville Land and Trust Company bought 63 acres of rich lowland in the heart of a new black settlement east of the city in 1911, paying $200 an acre for it.[15] When Father Heick was ready to buy land in Greenville, they offered him as many acres as he wanted at cost.[16]

In a letter to Mother Drexel, the missionary suggested that ten acres appeared reasonable, stating that the property could be used at first as a means of support and later as a site for a hostel or boarding house.[17]

Mother Katharine accepted his proposal and promised him $10,000 for the Greenville mission—if she lived.[18] With this assurance Father Heick purchased ten acres near the Columbus and Greenville Railroad along Gloster Street on April 24, 1913, immediately renting out six acres to a farmer who put it into cotton.

The news of the school aroused a great deal of interest in the black community, even among the children who heard their elders talking about it. One Sunday afternoon nine-year-old Daisy Miller, her cousin, Ed Hill, and three of their friends strolled over to Gloster Street to satisfy their curiosity. The children walked down Nelson Street, a dusty, narrow road lined with stores and cottages, crossed the Columbus and Greenville Railroad and turned left on Railroad Avenue. There were only a few houses here. On their right were small fields of sturdy young cotton plants preparing to transform the area into a fairyland of cream white, soft red, and pink blossoms.[19] The land was rich and good for cotton and had been so since it was settled. It would not surrender itself to structures of brick and concrete without a struggle, as the missionaries would soon discover.

The youngsters reached the site of the new school where they stood in amazement, unable to believe their eyes. In the yard was an enormous pile of bricks.

"Wow!" Daisy finally exclaimed. "Bricks! We're gonna have a brick school—just like the whites!"[20]

This was Father Hoenderope's fourth building in the South, and he certainly didn't anticipate any major problems. Once the building was under way, however, the workers ran into one difficulty after another. The soft, fertile soil, fine for growing cotton, would not support the foundation of the two-story building. But the priest-builder proved its master. Under his able direction, pillars of brick and concrete were sunk into the ground so deep that workmen razing the building in 1969 abandoned their plan to remove them from their 56-year-old bed.[21]

Once the foundations were secured, the building rose in the dirt, sound and stable on its sunken pillars. But the missionaries soon discovered that the rich humus soil became a sea of mud after a rain, making the building inaccessible a great part of the year. Worse still, the land was so low that there was little drainage. To solve this problem, truckloads of cinders and gravel were brought to the area until the property in front of the school was high enough to lay a concrete sidewalk the length of the building even though Gloster Street itself was still unpaved.[22]

The new mission was dedicated to the Sacred Heart. Its pastor, Rev. Joseph Stein, was a young, timorous priest who had been in the United States only ten months. He was apprehensive about his new responsibilities and insecure with the language and the customs of the country. Father Hoenderope tried to cheer him by reminding him that experienced sisters would be there to help him.

During the summer of 1913 the two priests lived in the attic of the unfinished school, climbing to their airy loft by means of a ladder. The pastor prepared their simple breakfast and supper, but at noon they walked downtown to a boarding house near the railroad station on Main Street where the proprietress served them dinner without charge. In a letter to Father Julius Steinhauer, who was taking Father Hoenderope's place in Vicksburg, Father Stein confided his joy that the sisters were coming soon. "The sisters will be here Friday this week. I am glad when they come because the way of life is not very pleasant so."[23]

Sister Auxilia Haag was appointed the superior at Sacred Heart. Of stocky build, she was not more than 4 feet, 6 inches tall and had a broad face with dimpled cheeks and thin lips that often parted into a roguish smile. She took great pains to speak proper English and asked for corrections as well as offering them to others.[24] She had completed the Normal School Course in Steyl and had studied English with a teacher from England, Isabelle Sandiford, who had joined the congregation, taking the name of Winifrede.[25] After coming to the United States in May 1909, Sister Auxilia taught at Holy Ghost School in Jackson for three years and was impressed by the deep religious beliefs of the people and their hunger for more religion. "There are no pagans in my class," she would say.[26] Appointed for the Philippines in 1913, she left Jackson to return to the mother house in Techny, where it was discovered that she had malaria. Her appointment was cancelled, and she was assigned to Greenville.[27]

Sister Seraphim Bukase, a vivacious and out-going nun, tall when standing next to her superior, was the teacher for the four lower grades.[28] She would need all of her vitality to handle her classroom of lively youngsters. Sister Marianna Mockenhaup was the capable homemaker. Not expected to teach, but to acquaint herself with the culture of the South and practice her English, play the organ for church services and be the jack-of-all-trades, helping wherever she was needed, Sister Susannah Rivinius, tall and robust, was also assigned to Greenville.[29]

The four sisters arrived in Greenville by train on September 20. Although there had been no indication of trouble over the school, Father Stein was cautious and met them at the station with a closed, one-horse buggy.[30]

In the other missions two rooms had been set aside in the school for the sisters' living quarters until they were needed for classrooms and a convent could be built. But this arrangement had proved impractical because the classrooms were needed before there was money available to build the convent. In Greenville, therefore, this plan was changed, and Father Stein took up living quarters on the second floor of the school while the sisters settled in the unfinished, one-story brick building originally intended for a rectory.[31] It had four rooms and a kitchen, a wide hall, and a spacious veranda along the back. The night the sisters arrived they found only a sack of onions, a favorite food of Father Hoenderope's, and a barrel of flour in the house, and before they could prepare their evening meal, it was necessary for two of them to walk to the nearest grocery store for staples.[32]

While they were gone, Sister Marianna set about heating water for coffee. The only container available for the water was a good-sized tub in which she later boiled the laundry. There was no stove in the unfinished kitchen, but she found one in another room. No sooner had she started the fire than the smoke poured out from every joint and crack and out the end of the stovepipe, which didn't quite connect with the chimney. She called for the priests and Father Hoenderope rushed over from school and pulled and pushed the stove from one room to another in a frantic effort to find a connection that would fit, but without success. The little community took their evening meal in a house clouded with smoke that lingered for the rest of the night.[33]

As had been done in the other stations, two classrooms facing the street on the lower floor of the school building were set aside as the church. The table in the attic which the priests had been using for Mass and meals was carried downstairs to the chapel, and the sisters covered it with sheets, hanging one across the front as an antependium. Father Stein fashioned a crude wooden tabernacle, and Sister Auxilia lined the inside with a remnant of silk she had brought from Techny and embroidered a white lace curtain to drape over the outside. There was no other furniture in the room. When the sisters met for

100

Mass during the week, they first swept away the *hobelspane* (shavings) left by the carpenters from the day before and knelt on the floor.[34]

On Septembr 28 about thirty people attended the first Sunday Mass offered in the church. The table altar was adorned with wild asters and goldenrod gathered along the railroad tracks. During the Mass Father Hoenderope announced the opening of school and stressed the religious benefits it offered the children. He encouraged the parents to enroll their children and pass the word on to their friends and acquaintances.[35]

Classes could not begin until October 2 because the problems encountered earlier with the laying of the foundation had set the building schedule behind by a month.[36] About eighty children had registered; but Sister Auxilia was confident that many would not come the first day or even the first month and that she and Sister Seraphim could manage until January when a third teacher was to come.

She was right. Only fifty children appeared the first day.[37] The others were in the cotton fields, transported there by pickup trucks which arrived in the city before sunrise, one of them parking under a massive oak tree near the Millers' home on Broadway and Nelson streets. Under the watchful eyes of an overseer (There were no guns as in Merigold), the pickers, ranging in ages from eight to seventy, filled their long canvas sacks that hung around their shoulders and dragged along the ground behind them. The fastest among them could earn a dollar a day. Most of them earned 50¢.

If cotton-picking looked romantic, exciting, and fun to children of middle-class families, they had to try it only once to be cured of their romanticism. The sun was hot; bugs and mosquitoes tormented the pickers; the bushes scratched their arms and legs; their ankles blistered; and overseers prevented any dawdling along the way.

When evening came, the pickers climbed into the waiting trucks and were returned to their starting point. If a carrier with its precious cargo did not pull into its regular corner at its accustomed time, worried parents lined the porches of their homes, peering anxiously down the street until it came into view.

The picking continued until the fields were stripped bare sometime in early December and the plants stood in rigid rows like tattered soldiers at attention, untidy cotton scraps clinging to their leafless branches. New pupils appeared at school proudly wearing their brightly-colored dresses or store-fresh shirts and pants and carrying paper and pencils and books—all purchased with the money they had earned themselves in the cotton fields.[38]

Understandably, the children were more or less a year behind in their studies; but Sister Auxilia allowed them to remain in their respective grades while she and Sister Seraphim worked with them as well as they could. In addition to teaching grades five through eight, Sister Auxilia had several pupils who had graduated from the eighth grade of Public School No. 2 and were working. They were sent to the mission school by their employers, who wanted them to have more education and who saw in Sacred Heart School an excellent opportunity for this. Teaching four grades already, she could hardly offer these pupils a full high school course; but she did manage classes in algebra and world history. She was a strict disciplinarian and did not spare the rod even on the older boys who stood strong and sturdy and as tall as light poles. Before the year was over, she had whipped every boy in the class.[39]

In a classroom on the northwest corner of the building facing the Columbus and Greenville Railroad, Sister Seraphim had grades one through four, plus a number of pre-schoolers. To her surprise, every time the train rumbled by, the smaller tots would fly to the windows to see it. It took all of her ingenuity to keep the class in order, but somehow she managed.[40]

On December 3 Bishop Gunn was in Greenville to dedicate Sacred Heart Church and school and confirm seven children: Daisy and Emilie Miller, Nita, Ernest and Maymee Casa Calvo, John Mays and James Marshall. The last-named boys were boarding in the school attic.[41]

Basic to any missionary work is the establishment of a native clergy and sisterhood, and the South, despite its racial bias, was to be no exception to this standard procedure of evangelism. Greenville, with its dense black population, seemed to be a good place to start, and Father Stein received approval from his superiors to set up a dormitory in the school attic and take in boys. The first boarders, ranging in ages from six to twelve, were four Catholic boys from Jackson, three of whom were brothers, and an unbaptized youth from the Greenville area. It was hoped that by living as boarders they would earn a reputable position among their people and perhaps one would even be called to the priesthood. Father Stein was in charge of their spiritual and moral training. Sister Marianna cooked for them. Sister Seraphim checked to see that they kept their quarters clean and a woman in town laundered their clothes.[42] Although the project did not result in any vocations, it showed that the missionaries were serious about establishing a black clergy in Mississippi nine years before a seminary for black priests was actually opened.

By December, so many pre-school children were coming to Sister Seraphim that Sister Euphrosine Buelter came from Holy Ghost School in Jackson on December 8 to begin a kindergarten.[43] Despite this siphoning off of these younger children, Sister Seraphim still had 72 children after Christmas vacation. They were sitting on boxes, on the podium near her desk, on the floor—everywhere—writing their lessons on their laps for want of desks, and Sister Susannah was asked to take the first and second grades for a few weeks until help could come from one of the other stations.[44]

By Easter the school was running smoothly. Ten children were baptized on Easter Sunday and four more a few weeks later. Several adults were also baptized, bringing the number up to twenty.[45]

Along with the annual programs at the end of the year, the students in the mission schools began to exhibit their handiwork at the Negro State Fair in Jackson in 1914. The German-born sisters were skilled in needlework, and it was natural for them to pass these skills on to their pupils. In their weekly classes the students learned how to hook rugs with figures of birds and animals; crochet and embroider tablecloths, doilies, bedspreads, curtains and quilts; monogram sheets and pillow cases; and sew dresses and boys' shirts. Even the younger children learned how to crochet napkin rings and washcloths. The thread could become soiled from constant unraveling and reusing, the pupils could make jokes about ever being able to wash it clean, but eventually each object they struggled over became a thing of beauty.[46]

In 1915 Sacred Heart School walked off with almost twenty blue ribbons at the Negro State Fair,[47] the same year St. Joseph won five.[48] In 1916 Holy Ghost School won a blue ribbon for a kindergarten exhibit, another for the best exhibit among denominational schools, and a first place in an oratorical contest won by a seventh grade pupil.[49]

There are no records to show that the students of St. Mary's participated in the State Fair. But the two papers in Vicksburg, the *Morning Democrat* and the *Evening Post*, praised the work of the students exhibited in the school. The article stated:

> *These devoted people have established an institution in our midst that can favorably compare with any educational institution in our city. On June 2 they exhibited a creditable display of handiwork, from bric-a-brac work of kindergarten children, raffia and wicker work of juniors, to fancy and domestic needlework and embroidery of the more advanced classes. There were also freehand drawings and paintings. During the evening program there were vocal and instrumental pieces. In a word, all that is **useful** and **ornamental**.*[50]

In every way the sisters strove to encourage excellence in their students.

St. Rose de Lima School, Bay St. Louis, MS, 1910

Chapter VI Footnotes: A Return to the Delta

1. BS, Heick to Drexel, May 25, 1910; note in archives dated April 19, 1909.
2. 39th Anniversary Edition, *Greenville Times*; Second ed. (reprinted 1970).
3. U. S. Census 1910; Rev. Matthew Christman, "Foundation," *Our Colored Messenger*, September 17, February 13 (year unknown).
4. Interview with Mamie Sudbury, June 3, 1970; NJ, Gunn to Msgr. John Burke, January 25, 1917; David Cohn, *Where I Was Born and Raised* (Notre Dame Press, 1967), VIII.
5. Cohn, op. cit., 21.
6. Cohn, op. cit., 57, 22; Interview with Charles W. and Josephine M. Wiley, December 27, 1970.
7. Mississippi State Law Library, Mississippi Code 1906 of the Public Statute Laws.
8. Interviews with Joseph Williams, July, 1970; Gladys Clark, December 8, 1970; Sadie Crowther, June 7, 1970; Daisy Miller Greene, December 5, 1974.
9. Daisy Miller Greene, December 19, 1974.
10. SVD, Rev. Joseph Stein, Paper, *History of the Sacred Heart Mission among the Colored of Greenville, Mississippi*.
11. Greene, December 5, op. cit.; *Negro History and Directory*, 8; Sister Immolata Reida, "Mother Miller," *Christian Family*, January, 1957, 7.
12. Greene, op. cit.; SSpSG, Auxilia Haag to Mother General, November 26, 1913.
13. Ibid.
14. Ibid. Interview with Vernandah Cook, December, 1974; Greene, December 5, op. cit.
15. Rev. Hubert D. Singleton, *1912-1962 Golden Jubilee of Sacred Heart Parish*, Sacred Heart Rectory (hereafter cited SHR); Washington County Courthouse, *Greenville Book of Deeds 135*, 134.
16. Ibid., 462.
17. BS, Heick to Drexel, September 29, 1911.
18. BS, Note on Letter of Heick, January 11, 1913, "If I live, we should give $10,000 in G."
19. Greene, op. cit.
20. Ibid.
21. Singleton, op. cit.
22. *Colored Messenger*, op. cit.
23. Stein Report, op. cit.
24. Interview with Sister Auxilia Haag, September 22 and October 27, 1969.

25. PP, Sister Assumpta Volpert, *The Life of Mother Maria Stollenwerk and Mother Josepha Stenmanns*, tr. German (Techny, 1931).
26. Auxilia, op. cit.
27. SSpSG, Auxilia to Assistant General received October 13, 1913.
28. Interview with Sisters Auxilia Haag and Liobina Schikora, December, 1973.
29. SSpSG, Auxilia to Assistant General, op. cit.; Greenville House Chronicle (hereafter cited GHC), 1.
30. Auxilia interview, op. cit.
31. Singleton, op. cit.; SSpSG, Auxilia letter, November 26, 1913.
32. SSpSG, Auxilia letter, op. cit.; Auxilia interview, op. cit.
33. SSpSG, Auxilia letter, op. cit.
34. Interview with Auxilia, November 11, 1970; with Auxilia and Liobina, op. cit.
35. Auxilia, November 11, 1970.
36. Stein Report, op. cit.
37. Interview with Sister Auxilia, December 19, 1973; SSpSG, Auxilia letter, op. cit.
38. Interview with Luella Mallet, June 21, 1970; Clark, op. cit.; Greene, op. cit.; Interview with Greene, Cook, and Jessie McBride, December 20, 1974; David Cohn, op. cit., 34.
39. Auxilia interview, op. cit.; GHC, undated.
40. SSpSG, Auxilia letter, October 13, 1913.
41. GHC, no date.
42. SSpSG, Auxilia letter, op. cit., November 26, 1913.
43. SSpSG, Letter of Auxilia to Assistant General, December 8, 1913.
44. GHC, undated.
45. Ibid.
46. Greene, op. cit.; Interview with Mary Ida High Jackson, June 9, 1970; Interviews with Sister Desiderata Ramb, January 22, 1970; Gladys Clark, December 8, 1970; Mrs. Henry J. Floyd.
47. GHC, undated.
48. SVD, James Wendel to J. A. Burgmer, November 25, 1915.
49. BS, Heick to Drexel, March 15, 1917.
50. SVD, St. Mary's Chronicle, op. cit.

CHAPTER VII
Poverty a Constant Companion

Poverty was a constant companion of the Holy Spirit Missionary Sisters and the Divine Word priests in the missions of Mississippi and Arkansas. Out of their monthly stipends of $20 per teacher (The homemaker was not paid.) the sisters managed their food, clothing, doctor, medical and traveling expenses, and sent money to Mother Leonarda in Techny to help pay for a newly-erected provincial house and the education of the young sisters.[1]

Accepting the radical poverty demanded by their work was not easy for the missionaries, who were for the most part from middle-class families and who didn't know what hunger and cold meant before coming to Mississippi. Sister Desiderata Ramb, a young kindergarten teacher in Vicksburg in 1915, could recall many nights when she cried softly into her pillow, unable to sleep because of gnawing hunger pains. Physically small, short, and frail-looking, she possessed a strong will and would have preferred to die of starvation rather than complain.[2]

The sisters bought as little of their food as possible, depending for vegetables from their own gardens and for milk, eggs and meat from their cow, chickens, and pigs. On weekdays, breakfast consisted of home-baked bread with butter and oatmeal. On Sundays and holydays, the fare was cold cereal or crackers and eggs when the chickens were laying well. Weekday dinners were often 20¢ worth of stew meat cooked with potatoes or vegetables to make them go farther. On Christmas and Easter they feasted on German coffee cake, together with apples and oranges given by the Knights of Columbus. Sometimes there was homemade raisin bread. The story is told that one day one of the priests found *one* raisin in his slice of raisin bread.

"What wonderful raisin bread, one raisin to a slice," he teased the cook.

Noticing that he had the crust—instead of a slice from the middle of the loaf—the sister exclaimed in embarrassment, "Oh, that's a mistake!"

"Oh?" the priest replied. "It's a mistake that *one* raisin got into the raisin bread?"[3]

When the sisters butchered, the community enjoyed a rare feast. One day, when the sisters at Holy Ghost were making sausage, the cook treated the community to apples baked in the sausage sauce. The day happened to be a Thursday and one of them jokingly remarked, "It's too bad tomorrow is Friday and we can't eat what's left of these delicious apples."

"How about getting up 20 minutes to 12 to finish them?" someone suggested, carrying the joke one step farther.

The sister who was in charge of ringing the convent bell that awakened the community and called them to religious exercises and meals took the remarks seriously and at 20 minutes to 12 she dutifully rang the bell and awakened the entire house. Needless to say, when the aroused sleepers learned what happened, they rolled over on their sides, blessing the bell ringer under their breath.[4]

People were good to the sisters, often sharing the little they had, and on special occasions the bishop sent them a donation he had received.

One day the community at Sacred Heart was shaken by a loud cry near the chapel. Rushing to the scene, they found Sister Maria, the superior, kneeling in the hall outside the chapel with arms outstretched, holding a check of $50 in one hand and exclaiming over and over again: "God, I thank Thee!" It was the week before Christmas, and the community was completely out of money for food and had already overextended its credit. The check, which had come from the Bishop, was reason enough to cry out with joy to the Lord.[5]

Despite their poverty, none of the sisters complained or asked to be taken from Mississippi. They were working for the coming of the Kingdom preached by the God-man who had no place to lay his head on, whose disciples had broken off the ears of grain on the Sabbath to still their hunger pains.

It was equally hard to witness the poverty of the people and experience the helplessness of not being able to change a system that kept them shackled. But the little they could do meant so much to the recipients. In Vicksburg Sister Desiderata noticed a boy in church barefoot on his first communion day and hurriedly rummaged through the poor box hoping to find him some shoes. Not successful, she noticed that her own—size 4—fitted him perfectly and after a brief consultation with her superior, offered them to the boy. His eyes opened wide as he exclaimed in unbelief: "S'tah, are they for me?" She nodded, amply rewarded by his beaming face. He never forgot this kindness, thanking her again whenever he met her.[6]

In 1916 there were 293 Catholics at St. Mary's and 241 children enrolled in school; 122 Catholics at Holy Ghost and 321 children in school; 120 Catholics at Mount St. Joseph and 185 pupils; 120 Catholics at St. Bartholomew's and 148 pupils; and 65 parishioners at Sacred Heart and a school enrollment of 150.[7]

Ironically, the missions were facing a financial crisis brought about by the success of the work: increases in enrollment demanded more teachers, which meant additional salaries and larger convents to house them.

By 1916 all of the sisters, except the nine at St. Bartholomew's in Little Rock, had moved out of the original classrooms in the school buildings; but the convents that had been provided for them had grown far too small to accommodate the number of teachers.

Only in Meridian, where the community lived in a two-story brick convent/boarding school, were the accommodations adequate. The basement was used for study hall, dining room and domestic science classes for boarders who attended classes at the day school. The sisters enjoyed ample space in the two upper floors, although some rooms remained devoid of furniture for many years.[8]

No one was more interested in the education of the blacks in Mississippi than Mother Leonarda. Yet, she noted the increasing housing problems in the missions with growing alarm. Father Heick, who was responsible for living accommodations, was asking for more and more teachers, but had no place to put them.[9]

St. Mary's in Vicksburg was the hardest hit. The seven teachers and the homemaker were living in what was once "the spacious Geiger home." They had tried to sleep on eight cots squeezed into the two upstairs bedrooms, but it was almost impossible and two sisters had moved their cots to the attic.[10]

But room was a minor problem compared to the hazardous condition of the antebellum home. The foundations were crumbling and punctured with gaping holes, and the roof wept for want of major repairs.[11] Despite the sisters' efforts to catch the water coming through the roof during one heavy October rain, some of it seeped through the floor of the bedrooms and cracks in the dining room ceiling, barely missing the sisters' plates as the community gathered for dinner in the gloom of the cloud-darkened sky.[12] When the storm passed, Father Steinhauer walked through the convent with a heavy pole, knocking down the loose plaster hanging from the ceiling lest it fall on some unsuspecting head.[13]

But crumbling foundations and leaking roofs were not the worst of the problems at St. Mary's. The house was a fire trap. On October 17, as Sister Basilissa Holzapfel, the homemaker, was returning to the convent after taking Father Steinhauer's breakfast of oatmeal and bread to the small house where he dined, she saw wisps of smoke on the roof around the base of the kitchen chimney. Her cries of alarm brought the others outside, and Father Steinhauer, who had a telephone in the rectory, called the fire department.

"You're lucky you saw it when you did," the firemen told the missionaries after drenching the area. "In another fifteen minutes, you wouldn't have had a house."[14]

The problem of space was even more acute at Sacred Heart Convent, although the building, only three years old, was in good condition. Ten sisters were living in the five-room, one-story building that was intended to house one priest, all of them eating, studying, and recreating in one small room. They were squeezed so tightly into the chapel that it was impossible to add a heater. Sister Auxilia and a companion had taken their sleeping cots to the open porch along the back of the house, which exposed them not only to the elements, but to the danger of prowlers, as well.[15]

There was a space problem at Holy Ghost Convent also, the fastest growing of the five missions. Nine sisters were crowded into a convent too small to accommodate them, and three sisters were sleeping in the school corridors, setting up their cots at night and removing them in the morning before the children arrived for classes.[16]

In Greenville three of the sisters had become seriously ill; a fourth was hospitalized in Memphis, Tennessee, and ordered by her doctor not to return. In Jackson, six were on the ill list.[17]

Mother Leonarda's patience began to run out. As the sisters' superior, she had no right to demand an obedience that placed their lives and health in jeopardy. Accordingly, on April 24, 1916, she wrote to Father Heick that the situation had to improve.

Otherwise, she would be obliged to withdraw the sisters from Mississippi—at least from Vicksburg.[18]

This was a hard blow for the priest.

"Without the sisters, we may as well pack up and go home," he wrote to Bishop Gunn.

To add to the priest's woes, a tornado struck the area of the Jackson mission on June 6, 1916, killing 14 people, wounding 68 others, and destroying 200 homes. Like a herd of frightened animals, people, wearing only their night clothes, flocked to the mission, where the sisters dressed wounds and comforted the injured and dying throughout the night in the hall that was turned into a temporary hospital.

In the morning Father Heick assessed the damage to the mission property: slate ripped off roofs, walls battered by flying timber, windows broken and fences uprooted around the property. Fortunately, the buildings escaped the worst of the storm, which tore a devastating path only a half block from the mission; but even these minor damages laid a claim on his already limp purse.[19] As if this wasn't enough, a few weeks later a tropical storm swept through Meridian blowing down fences, uprooting trees, damaging roofs, and destroying the vegetable garden at St. Joseph's.[20]

He did not fail to report his financial embarrassment to Mother Katharine Drexel, but for once she could not help him. She wrote:

I read your letter with deep interest and it pains me to think that you must be disappointed by my reply for I must say that we are unable to assist you in your present needs. The demands made by the work in which we are engaged among the Indian and black races are so many and so great that we can never hope to supply them adequately, and it is a cause of great regret that we must refuse . . . . I pray from my heart that God may send you benefactors.[21]

Mother Katharine was keenly aware that her wealth would never take care of all of the world's problems. It was her custom to assume initial costs of worthwhile projects, expecting others to carry on the work once it was started.

From where would help come? Unlike parochial schools, the mission schools could not depend upon the church members for new buildings or major repairs because most of the students were not Catholics and those who were often had non-Catholic parents. The parishioners in the various missions held their fish fries, picnics and raffles (often a quilt made cooperatively by the women), maybe taking in as much as $7 an event, which they proudly handed over to the parish.[22] Sunday collections, which amounted to less than $500 a year, were truly an example of the widow's mite, for many made great sacrifices for their church and school.[23] One woman in Vicksburg put newspapers in her shoes when her soles wore through, to have the monthly 50¢ tuition for her nephew and two sons.[24]

Father Steinhauer wrote to a friend:

We hear sometimes remarks that we missionaries don't make new Catholics take care of their church and school. Yet, these people contributed $471.21 in the offertory collection basket last year.[25]

Wages for blacks were extremely low. Best paid were the teachers, who earned from $25 to $75 a month, though this was far behind their white counterparts.[26] Women worked as housemaids and cooks from early morning until late afternoon, six days a week, for one or two dollars. Many were washerwomen, going to the home of their patrons to collect the wash, carrying it home, sometimes five and six bundles at a time, two under each arm and one on their heads, boiling it on a "cha coal" fire, pressing it with an iron heated on a coal stove and carrying it back, all for 50¢ to $2 a bundle, depending upon the size.[27]

Men were the ones who suffered the most when it came to wages. The few businesses that flourished were small: grocery stores, barber and beauty shops, funeral parlors, and insurance companies. The best jobs for men were in the sawmills where they could earn as much as $9.50 a week. But doors and opportunities were open only through the sufferance of the white ruling race who determined who should receive the better-paying jobs.[28]

Both races understood the reason behind job discrimination for the black man. By keeping the black man financially hobbled, there was no possibility of his ever marrying a white woman. As one parishioner at St. Mary's put it:

Although many white men had their black concubines, black men couldn't afford white women. They would be too expensive. They'd need as much grease for their faces as for their bread, and they couldn't afford it.[29]

Through the efforts of the parishioners, the weekly offertory collections, and tuition from the school children, the missions were able to meet their day-to-day expenses; but money for new buildings, repairs and improvements had to come from other sources.

There were three organizations in the Church which contributed to the missions, all in a limited way. A Commission for the Indian and Negro Missions had been established in 1884 by the Third Plenary Council of Baltimore for dispensing an annual collection taken up on the first Sunday of Lent in all the Catholic Churches in the United States.[30] The Natchez diocese with its large black and Indian populations was receiving about $2,000 a year from this collection.[31]

There were leaders in the Church who realized that more had to be done to educate and encourage Catholics to support the work of the missionaries in the black apostolate. At a meeting of the Archbishops on May 3, 1905, Archbishop Ryan, prodded by Mother Katharine Drexel, recommended that a bureau for the black apostolate be established similar to the one for the Indian missions. The proposal was discussed and accepted. In April 1907 a Catholic Board for Mission Work Among the Colored People was incorporated with James Cardinal Gibbons as chairperson and Archbishop Ryan, Archbishop John Farley of New York City, Bishop Thomas Byrne of Nashville, Tennessee, and Bishop E. P. Allen of Mobile, Alabama, as members. Father John E. Burke, pastor of St. Benedict the Moor's Church, New York City, was named Director.[32]

As early as 1913, the Board was sending each of the missions of the Divine Word Fathers and Holy Spirit Missionary Sisters $350 a year to help defray the monthly stipends of the sisters.[33]

The third source of support was the Catholic Extension Society, which was started on October 18, 1905, by Rev. Francis C. Kelley, a young priest of the Detroit Diocese who later became Bishop of Oklahoma City and Tulsa. Its primary purpose was to finance buildings and support the clergy, religious, and lay persons who were laboring full time in the home missions. From time to time it contributed substantial sums to the missions of the Divine Word Fathers and Holy Spirit Missionary Sisters; but the demands on its tenuous funds limited the amount it could give to any one mission.[34]

To supplement the contributions from the Commission for Indians and Negroes, the Catholic Board for Mission Work Among the Colored, and the Catholic Extension Society, the missionaries approached people directly by both the spoken and written word. It was not a task that any of them enjoyed, but one that had to be done.

Bishop Gunn refused to allow them to approach the bishops of the South for assistance. When Father Wendel suggested it, he replied that it would be like "taking candy from a baby."[35] So the missionaries confined their "begging" to the North. Two or three months each year, the priests traveled through the cities and towns of the North, preaching in churches wherever they were welcomed, and were gratified by the generous response they received.[36]

In the meantime, the sisters devoted their weekends and late night hours, especially before Christmas, writing letters in longhand to prospective benefactors across the country. Each sister was responsible for 20 to 30 letters and the thank-you notes to those who responded. In the letters they mentioned how God had blessed their respective benefactors with temporal goods, and they were asking them to share these with the poor people of their mission. One benefactor in California was so touched to receive a thank-you note for his small gift that he left a thousand dollars to the mission in his will.[37]

Father Heick hoped for more time in order to seek funds that were needed to make the repairs and extensions on the four crowded convents, and he wrote to Bishop Gunn to enlist his support. The bishop was no longer living in Natchez. Since coming to Mississippi, the prelate had made it a practice to take the place of parish priests who were ill or on vacation, and in January 1915 he had moved to Pass Christian to replace a pastor whose doctor had advised him to return to Europe for his health. The Bishop suffered considerably from rheumatism and he soon discovered that the warm climate of the coast offered him a pleasant relief from pain. When news of the pastor's death reached him by cable on March 7, he promptly appointed himself pastor of the Pass, returning to Natchez only on official business.[38]

Bishop Gunn was going North in a few months and Father Heick asked him to stop in at Techny and plead his cause with Mother Leonarda. The bishop agreed to the request. He had accidentally walked in on the first school conference in Vicksburg in 1912 and had been surprised to find her and the other sisters there, and had talked with them for a long time, leaving the conference deeply impressed with Mother Leonarda's dedication to the teaching apostolate in the South.[39]

On a trip to the North in the summer of 1916 he kept his promise to Father Heick and stopped to talk to the quiet-spoken nun, but his eloquence fell on deaf ears. The superior remained adamant. Kindly, but firmly, she told the prelate that she could not in conscience ask the sisters to live in their present subhuman, unhealthful conditions another year.

Disappointed over the failure of his mission, Bishop Gunn went on to Burlington, Wisconsin, where he had dinner with the David Bremners. He found the aging gentleman still interested in the work in Mississippi and very fond of the blacks. Upon returning to Pass Christian, the Bishop immediately informed Father Heick of this and suggested that he write to Mr. Bremner, enclosing a sample letter.[40]

Mr. Bremner, Sr.
St. Mary's Island
Burlington, Wisconsin

Our Bishop called at Techny, Illinois, and tried to induce the superiors there to leave our sisters in Mississippi. You will remember that you were the occasion of bringing us to the Diocese and in our emergency we think it right to appeal to you in our difficulty. The enclosed letter which our Bishop sent to Msgr. Burke will explain better than I can express it the difficulty which confronts us. Our sisters are living in conditions that are certainly not sanitary and our mother house objects to any prolongation of the agony. The condition is acute as far as Vicksburg is concerned. Seven or eight sisters are living in a one-story building that was intended for a family of two or three. Decency calls for more than the sisters have got and the superior of the community threatens to withdraw the sisters unless I can give them better accommodations. Financially, I cannot. The schools are barely self-supporting. In fact, without the assistance of New York, we could not live here in Mississippi at all. If the mother house at Techny withdraws our community from Vicksburg, we might as well bundle up and leave the diocese and give up all we have attempted and done in Mississippi since you brought *us to Merigold. In this emergency I appeal to you and ask you if you could share with us some of the charity which I know you distribute elsewhere. I promised to put another story on the bungalow which the sisters live in in Vicksburg. I appealed to the Bishop for help but he cannot help me. Owing to the war, the community cannot help me and the Negroes of Mississippi are so poor that they cannot help me and in this emergency I appeal to you to tide over a situation which means our removal from Mississippi or our staying in it. It will require about $3000.00 to give a sanitary house to the sisters in Mississippi and if you can help us in this emergency you will be not only our creator in Mississippi but something that is still more wonderful—our preserver.*

The Bishop tells me he went to our mother house in Techny to plead for an extension and he reports that the community is more interested in the lives of the sisters than in the conversion of the Negroes.

On August 14, 1916, Father Heick copied the bishop's letter word for word and signed it.[41] There are no records showing how Mr. Bremner responded to this appeal, but it's most likely that he did help.

On January 1, 1917, Bishop Gunn was at St. Mary's to receive the religious vows of several sisters and during the Mass he congratulated the superiors for the spirit present in the Congregation. He told the sisters that they could be happy that they belonged to a congregation like theirs.[42]

Later in his diary he reflected on the day:

I commenced the New Year in Vicksburg, where I had the privilege of professing several Holy Spirit Missionary Sisters and receiving the renewal of the vows of several others. It was a quiet little ceremony in the

*private chapel of the sisters and gave me to realize
what a wonderful force there was in organization and
religious zeal. These Holy Spirit Missionary Sisters
are highly educated ladies and their education makes
them better religious . . . . They teach exclusively the
blacks and they have the best school buildings in the
diocese. Their work speaks for itself and even bigots
patronize their schools.*[43]

Though the bishop could well note that the school
buildings were the best in the diocese, the accommodations of its teachers continued to be the poorest.

On March 3, 1917, Father Heick again appealed to
Mother Drexel. After repeating the conditions in the
convents of St. Mary's, Sacred Heart and Holy
Ghost, he continued:

*We can't leave the sisters under these conditions . . . .
The Fathers won't be disposed to carry on the work if
we have to reduce the number of teachers and consequently the number of children in the classes I
make another appeal. My suggestions: Add a second
story to the convent in Vicksburg; an addition to the
convent in Jackson. For the convent in Greenville and
Little Rock I will approach Msgr. Burke, following the
advice of Bishop Gunn.*[44]

On March 24 Mother Katharine responded to his
second plea, promising $2000 for Jackson and $2000
for Vicksburg, if he could match the amounts.[45]

Thus with the concerted efforts of the missionaries, parishioners, Northern friends, Mother Drexel, and the various organizations of the Church, the
crises passed.

On July 2, 1917, Father Heick wrote to Bishop
Gunn that they had started with the convent at
Vicksburg.[46] A month later he wrote that they had

made a start at Greenville, where the plans called for a second floor. Jackson would have to wait for another year.[47]

On November 29 Bishop Gunn paid a surprise visit to the sisters at St. Mary's. After his unsuccessful attempt to persuade Mother Leonarda to allow the community to remain in their crowded, subhuman accommodations, he wanted to see the renovations with his own eyes. He was pleased to see that the crisis was over, at least, for the present.[48]

Chapter VII Footnotes: Poverty,
A Constant Companion

1. Interview with Sister Desiderata Ramb, November, 1971; PP, "Academy," *Paraclete Chronicle*, 1951 (sisters' house organ).
2. Ibid.
3. Desiderata, op. cit.; Interview with Sister Uriele Isermann July 31, 1974; Sister Basilissa Holzapfel to author, October 13, 1974.
4. Interview with Sister Liobina Schikora, undated.
5. Interview with Sister Leonardine Huettemann, May 17, 1974.
6. Desiderata, op. cit.
7. SVD, Statistics for year 1916.
8. Rev. James Wendel booklet, *St. Joseph's Institute*, Vol. VIII, 1918; MHC, June 8, 1914.
9. BS, Heick to M. Drexel, July 24, 1916.
10. BS, Heick to Drexel, March 15, 1917.
11. VHC, October 1, 1916.
12. VHC, October 11, 1916.
13. BS, Steinhauer to Drexel, March 23, 1917.
14. VHC, October 17, 1916; Basilissa, op. cit.; BS, Steinhauer to Drexel, August 19, 1916.
15. BS, Heick to Drexel, op. cit.; *Colored Messenger*, December, 1917.
16. SVD, Letter to Bishop (possibly from Heick) May 8, 1916; Aloysius Heick, "Education," *Colored Messenger*, September, 1916, and January 3.
17. SVD, Letter to Bishop, op. cit.; SVD, *Colored Messenger*, December, 1917; SVD, Letter (handwritten) Christman to Provincial, January 20, 1917; BS, Heick to Drexel, op. cit.
18. SVD, Letter to Bishop, op. cit.
19. Interview with Goldie Adams, June 15, 1971; Heick, "1916 Destruction," *Colored Messenger*, September, 1916.
20. Wendel, *Colored Messenger*, op. cit.
21. SVD, Letter (handwritten) from Drexel to Heick, July 29, 1916.
22. Interview with Mrs. Camille Cheeks, August 11, 1974; *Vicksburg Parish Announcement Book*, March 21, 1915 entry; also May 16, 1915 entry; Interview with Joseph Williams, op. cit.
23. SVD, Steinhauer to Msgr. John E. Burke, February 13, 1917.
24. Interview with Jake Holmes, August 18, 1974.
25. SVD, Steinhauer, op. cit.

26. Meridian Financial Report, July 1, 1915-October 1, 1915.
27. Interview with Mrs. Ina Glass, May 18, 1970.
28. Cohn, op. cit., 203.
29. Williams, op. cit.; Interview with Connie Moore, June 6, 1970.
30. DAH, John T. Gilliard, *The Catholic Church and the American Negro* (Baltimore, 1929).
31. NJ, Heslin N file, Envelope handwritten from R. E. Dyer, November 8, 1898.
32. DAH, Gilliard, op. cit.; Duffy, op. cit., 243; Roy J. Deferrari, ed., *Essays of Catholic Education in U.S.* (Catholic University, 1942); Essay by M. Mary Agatha, President of Xavier University.
33. SVD, Steinhauer to Gunn, November 13, 1916.
34. *Catholic Directory*, 992; *Catholic Action of the South*, official organ of the Diocese of Natchez, Vol. 17, October 13, 1949, Silver Jubilee of Bishop Gerow Supplement.
35. Wendel, an unpublished report in Meridian Rectory Archives; Jacobs Report on History of Sacred Heart presented at 1935 Clergy Conference.
36. MHC, December 8, 1911.
37. JHSC, op. cit., January 30, 1910; Interviews with Sisters Amidea Sonneville, 1974, Anacleta Kaiser, 1974, Joan Liebhauser, undated, and Sister Cherubina, 1974.
38. NJ, Gunn Diary, op. cit., 93.
39. SVD, Heick to Bremner, August 14, 1916.
40. Ibid.
41. Ibid.
42. VHC, January 1, 1917.
43. Gunn Diary, op. cit., 123 (January 1, 1917).
44. BS, Heick to Drexel, March 15, 1917.
45. BS, Pencil Notation on letter above.
46. NJ, Heick to Gunn, July 2, 1917.
47. NJ, Heick to Gunn, August 16, 1917.
48. VHC, November 29, 1917.

CHAPTER VIII
After Elementary School —Then What?

Once the students of the five mission schools graduated from eighth grade, where were they to go to continue their education?

In 1916 there was neither a Catholic nor a public four-year high school for blacks in the entire state of Mississippi and only one three-year public high school in Yazoo City, north of Jackson. Students who wanted a four-year high school education had either to attend one of the five denominational high schools in the state or go elsewhere.[1]

The out-of-state schools were often called "Universities," but a report made by W. F. B. Williams in 1913 on twenty-two black universities in the South revealed that their work covered every phase of education from primary and elementary grades up to college work and professional schools. Only ten of the twenty-two universities in the study had twenty or more college students. Out of the 7605 students enrolled in the undergraduate departments of these ten universities, only twelve percent were in college departments, 33⅓ percent were in high school, and fifty percent were in the grades.[2]

Very few of the students graduating from the mission schools could afford to leave Mississippi to attend these out-of-state universities. Morever, for the Catholic students to attend denominational or even the public schools in the state was to risk nullifying the purpose for which the mission schools were established. Many of the Catholic children were neophytes and needed nurturing in their newly-accepted faith if they were to become mature members of the Church.[3]

The lack of a Catholic high school in the state had prompted the missionaries from the beginning to offer some high school classes to talented students who had completed the eighth grade.[4]This arrangement was not unusual for that time because secondary education was not an independent unit in the educational system. In most schools, elementary and secondary classes were often carried on in the same buildings and by the same teachers.[5]

In September 1914 Sister Bertranda taught the seventh and eighth grades at Holy Ghost School and managed courses in algebra, world history, and Latin for a few older students.[6] St. Bartholomew's in Little Rock, Arkansas, also offered a high school class.[7]

In Vicksburg Sister Michaeline Willsch offered older students a two-year commercial course with bookkeeping, office practice, Gregg shorthand, and Latin. In May 1915 four students completed the course and received a two-year office course diploma.[8]

However, Sacred Heart School in Greenville was to be the first of the mission schools to graduate a senior high school student.

In September 1915 Mamie Upshaw, a lovely, tall, slim, fourth-year high school student at Fisk University, Nashville, Tennessee, asked to be admitted to Sacred Heart School. Intelligent and serious about her studies, she wanted to complete her high school, but reverses in her family made it financially impossible for her parents to send her back to Fisk.[9] Although the Upshaws were not Catholics,[10] they were aware of the excellent reputation enjoyed by Sacred Heart School and knew that it was offering some high school classes.

The year that Mamie was accepted as a senior, four students enrolled as freshmen to be joined by seven more in October, all from prominent black families in Greenville.[11] Their courses included mathematics, Latin, literature, chemistry, physics, typing and shorthand. A science laboratory contained all the equipment needed for basic experiments.[12]

About 700 people were present for the commencement exercises on June 2, 1916, when Mamie, the first black student to graduate from a four-year Catholic high school in Mississippi, received her diploma from Sacred Heart School. Since the mission did not have a hall, the exercises and entertainment were held on the back porch of the school. The weather had been threatening on the morning of the graduation day, but it had cleared in the afternoon, and the evening arrived with ideal weather, neither too hot nor too cold. As the evening progressed, however, a strange wind blew and clouds gathered in the sky, soon covering the moon. Suddenly, there were flashes of lightning, crashes of thunder, a sprinkle and then a downpour. People ran for shelter—some to their homes, some to the classrooms, some to the exhibition rooms—until the rain stopped and all could go home. The second night, the attendance was even greater—possibly a thousand people gathered to the delight of the entertainers.[13]

Mamie successfully passed the state examination for a public school teacher's license, but returned to college for her degree before accepting a teaching position. She later became Dean of Women at Howard University.[14]

Black educators watched Sacred Heart High School with great interest. One was Fannie Williams Coleman, the principal of No. 2 Public School. Stout and unshapely, her unruly hair looking uncombed even at 8:30 a.m., she was not an attractive woman, but people forgot her looks when they began talking to her. Well-mannered, gracious, she mingled easily and was conversant on almost any topic although she had never received a college degree. Her knowledge came from books: she read every worthwhile book she could find, often reading far into the night. She was excellent in algebra and geometry, and from a casual conversation with her one would never suspect the fire burning within her, a fire that yearned to ignite her students and make them want to learn. Because many boys missed school in the spring and fall to work in the cotton fields, they were often 17 and 18 when they reached her eighth grade room. But she was a strict disciplinarian. Tall, muscular boys whose broad shoulders diminished her portly frame flinched under the sharpness of her tongue as she goaded them on to make something of themselves.[15]

"You can *be* anything you want to be," she hammered away insistently. "*All* you have to do is learn."[16]

Father Stein, who worried about having to teach religion at Sacred Heart School, sat in the classroom of this public school veteran a few times to pick up ideas on discipline and pedagogy.[17]

She saw Sacred Heart High School as an answer to her highest dreams for her students and conferred with Father Stein's successor, Father Christman, about directing her eighth grade graduates to it.[18]

Not everyone was that happy about the high school, however. Some ministers in Greenville personally visited the parents whose children were planning to enter in the fall and tried to persuade them not to send their children to the school. When Father Christman learned of this, he offered the eighth grade graduates of Public School No. 2 a free, three-month summer course to acquaint them with the curriculum they would have at Sacred Heart during the year. Thirteen students accepted his invitation and after attending classes three times a week, both they and their parents were convinced that the students would receive quality education at Sacred Heart. When the public school board quite unexpectedly announced in September that they were offering high school courses that year, none of the summer students left. Instead, eight others applied for admission. In 1916 the high school opened with twenty students who were accommodated in one classroom in the school and the rectory dining room.[19]

Mount St. Joseph in Meridian also began some high school classes in 1916.[20] In 1917 a science lab was added.[21] That year St. Joseph had thirteen high school students and twenty-four boarders. It advertised a "splendid auditorium equipped with moving pictures and stereopticon apparatus."[22] It had a band and an orchestra that traveled around the state[23] and a separate circular, pine-log, one-room building where the muscians practiced so as not to disturb classes.[24]

When the school had programs, it would place a piano and some songsters from the school on the back of a dray or a truck and drive it up and down the streets of Meridian advertising the event.[25]

In Septembr 1918 Mount St. Joseph began high school with two seniors, Alma E. Rose from Yazoo City and Bessie Anderson from Greenville. Alma became a boarder and Bessie lived with her aunt not far from school.[26]

Sister Willibalda was the high school teacher and taught chemistry, typing, Latin, Spanish, and shorthand.[27]

The first high school graduation was held on the evening of May 16, 1919, before an overpacked hall which flowed on to the playground. Music was furnished by the orchestra. Alma spoke on "Reputed and Real Ability," and Bessie on "Nature and Influence of Literature." A Japanese operetta in which the two seniors starred was a big success.[28]

Bishop Gunn watched the growth of the high schools with great interest. In 1919 he received $3,000 from Rev. Thomas McCarty of St. Edward's parish in Philadelphia, Pennsylvania, where the bishop had preached his first general mission. The congregation never forgot him and periodically sent him money, especially for the black apostolate of his diocese. In a letter to Father Heick, the bishop suggested that the money be used for the Greenville school.

He wrote:

I spent a few days in Greenville and I found your school there very flourishing, but very crowded . . . . You've reason to be proud of Greenville. There are 250 in school and I hear that 100 were turned away this year for want of room. Your school in Greenville has the best record and reputation in the entire Delta.[29]

In August, when the bishop sent in his annual report on the black apostolate to Father Dyer, Director of the Indian and Negro Commission, he added:

The priests and sisters are doing far more than they get credit for in this world, and that we are in existence at all and on the job is a miracle of divine assistance . . . . You will be glad to hear that a priest of Philadelphia gave me $3,000 to use for the black apostolate. I put that into a school at Greenville . . . . The Holy Spirit Missionary Sisters are doing magnificent work everywhere and only we are so dreadfully handicapped for the want of means so that we could produce an effect on the black people.[30]

A multi-purpose brick building seemed to be the best way to use the money offered by Bishop Gunn. The sisters wanted a hall for plays and exhibits, one that could also accommodate about 200 additional children if the school continued to grow, and two classrooms for the high school, which was still meeting in the priests' rectory.[31] The mission would contribute about $5,000 to the amount to construct a substantial building that would serve the mission for years to come.[32]

In 1918 Sister Maria Heinemann was one of the

two high school teachers and the superior in Greenville. She taught classes in English composition, American and English literary classics, and history.[33]

Also assigned to the high school was Sister Leonardine Huttemann, 28, a talented sister, German by birth, who had come to the United States in 1912. An excellent mathematics and science teacher, she had completed special courses in these subjects at DePaul University in Chicago.[34]

An announcement in the *Delta Democrat Times* noted that the high school department had a physics laboratory which was one of the best in the state and that a chemical lab would be added the next session.

"No high school can anymore claim to be complete without elementary courses in physics and chemistry," the announcement said.[35]

Sister Leonardine had taught high school at St. Bartholomew's in Little Rock for two years before coming to Sacred Heart. Her bluish-gray eyes danced with a quiet joy and she smiled easily. She carried herself with quiet dignity that commanded respect and admiration from pupils and parents alike.

Father Christman taught Latin and French, shorthand and typing, although the latter subject required great patience since the school owned only one typewriter.[36]

Perhaps the most striking feature of Sacred Heart School was the military training given the boys. From 1910 to 1925, Greenville had a Military Academy on Washington Avenue, operated by Col. F. J. Reilly. It annually attracted over a hundred boys from all over the Delta, many of them sons of planters. The Academy consisted of a school, a gym, an athletic field and two barracks that were used as dormitories. Father Christman prevailed upon Colonel Reilly to come to Sacred Heart and lead his boys through the marching drills. Once a week they paraded up and down the playground, learning turns and drills and various formations, and loved it. Twenty years later Winchester Davis, a music teacher at his alma mater, would conduct the award-winning Sacred Heart marching band and attribute its success in part to the drills he had mastered under the commands of Colonel Reilly.[37]

Father Christman also saw to it that the boys had equipment and outfits for sports. They had a good baseball team and wore professional breast protectors, all of which gave them a pride in their school.[38]

Girls were also encouraged to take part in sports, especially in the new game of tennis, an unheard of sport for blacks in the Delta at that time.[39]

Needlework, art, and music also had high priorities. Students who showed promise in voice were sent to a private teacher at the expense of the school. A lay teacher also taught the high school students such favorites as *Barcarolle* from Tales of Hoffmann, *Welcome, Sweet Springtime*, and *Indian Love Call*. Daisy Miller singing alto and her classmate, Carrie Roberts, as soprano were great favorites at any school performance.[40]

Even though the high school was not separated from the elementary school, Sister Maria had a way of making it special. Often it was just the way she said "the high school girls" (The first boy graduated from Sacred Heart High in 1924) that made the girls feel to be in high school was the greatest of honors. Midi-blouses were in style and because there was a war going on, the girls dressed in patriotic white midi-blouses with blue-starred collars and red trim rick-rack, fashionable ankle-length skirts, and high-topped shoes.[41]

On June 1, 1920, five high school students who had started as freshmen at Sacred Heart High School graduated before an audience of 600 people in the newly-erected multi-purpose building.[42]

School records of one graduate, Hattie Bell Dent, show that she had taken the following subjects: Freshman year—English, algebra, ancient history, boteny (sic), ethics; Sophomore year—English, geometry, modern history, zoology, ethics; Junior year—English, algebra II, physics, Latin I, ethics; Senior year—English, chemistry, Latin II, American history, and ethics.[43]

These courses may not seem much by today's standards, but a comparison of the recommendations of a commission appointed by the legislature in 1926, six years later, to study the public education system in the state and suggest improvements illustrates what a progressive program this was for blacks. The report recommended that foreign language, English grammar, and algebra be eliminated completely from courses of study in black schools. A special period for oral and written language was not to extend beyond the fifth grade. It was recommended that the study of history be confined to American history, especially that of Mississippi, and that it teach the blacks their status and make them familiar with American institutions, ideals and objectives. The reading lessons were not to be too idealistic and go beyond the sphere of the lives of blacks, but should rather concern themselves with nature and economics and social relations that would help the race adjust harmoniously and happily to their fellow blacks and the white race by whose side they must live in good will and mutual helpfulness.[44]

Clearly, Sacred Heart School had more in mind than educating its students to accept the status quo.

St. Bartholomew's in Little Rock graduated its first high school student on May 29, 1918.[45] It also had its first religious vocation that year when a former student made her first profession on August 15 in the Order of the Oblates of Mary.[46]

The sisters at St. Mary's in Vicksburg were having second thoughts about offering their students the two-year commercial course because there appeared to be no openings for office work for them after graduation.[47] Observing the success of Sacred Heart High School, they made plans to expand their curriculum into a regular high school program. Their first high school students, 6 girls, graduated in 1924.[48]

Although Holy Ghost School had no four-year high school until 1920, from the earliest days promising girls had been given courses to prepare them for teaching, one of the few better-paying jobs that the blacks could obtain, although the salaries here were still far below those of white teachers. Father Heick was especially interested in having the high school students pass the state examination for teachers which would make them eligible for higher salaries. He laid great stress on courses in pedagogy—psychology, educational psychology, methodology, and the history of education. The students were given opportunities to do their practice teaching in the elementary school under the supervision of the sisters. In 1917 three girls passed the teachers' first grade license examinations for the country which permitted the holder to teach any grade from one to twelve and any subject in the public school.[49] The license depended upon the score made on the tests. Teachers holding a second and third grade license were less qualified and received lower salaries. It was also possible to receive a license to teach without an examination, but this license ranked lower than a third grade one. To help the students earn a first grade license, Father Heick paid their tuition for a six weeks' normal course at Jackson College which ended with an examination for a license.[50] The examination included written tests in spelling, reading, practical and mental arithmetic, the elements of agriculture, civil government, physiology and hygiene with special reference to the effects of alcohol and narcotics.[51]

In 1921 Holy Ghost High School had its first graduation when two young women, Lillian Green and Ethel Moman, received their diplomas.[52] From 1921 until 1924 it was the only four-year high school for blacks in the capital.[53]

For some time the sisters had discussed the feasibility of applying for a teacher's license themselves. Father Heick suggested that they begin by taking county examinations to teach in rural schools, but Sister Leonardine thought this was beneath their professional competency. She urged the sisters to try for the State Professional license.

"We can lift ourselves up and lift up the blacks at the same time," she said.[54]

The battery of 22 tests for a professional license consisted of written examinations in algebra, geometry, rhetoric, English literature, the science of teaching, civil government, Caesar and Virgil and any other information that the examiners might want to ask. They were administered only in Jackson.[55]

During the summer of 1921 eleven sisters prepared themselves for the examination. The idea of religious sisters applying for the professional examination was unheard of in the state, and no one knew what to expect. None of them wanted to fail.

On August 23 the sisters from out of town received hospitality at Holy Ghost Convent in Jackson: Sister Louise and Sister Liobina came from Vicksburg; Sisters Maria, Michaeline, and Leonardine came from Greenville; Sisters Auxilia and Josepha came from Meridian; Sisters Otgera, Bertranda, Fredericka and Pauline were at Holy Ghost.

They slept little that night and were up early the next morning to attend a Mass in honor of the Holy Spirit offered for their intentions by Father Heick. Since the examinations lasted from early morning until 6 p.m., the sisters armed themselves with sack lunches. Apparently some became so excited during the tests that they forgot to eat, because the examiner, noting their abstinence from food, offered them refreshments.

Sisters Leonardine and Liobina completed the entire battery on the first day; the others returned on August 26. Three days later, when the results of the examinations were announced, all eleven sisters had passed. On September 15 Sister Marysia Michel passed the music examinations with highest honors and was qualified to teach music for three years.

The event in Jackson caused quite a stir in educational circles around the state. Bishop Gunn noted in his diary on September 2:

139

> *I went to Vicksburg and heard something very agreeable about the sisters who are teaching in the colored school. They created quite a surprise in Jackson when they asked for the professional examination, and they created a greater surprise when thirteen (sic) of these sisters teaching in the colored school took the examination and obtained certificates. This created quite a sensation in educational circles in Jackson.*[56]

Not all people shared the bishop's enthusiasm. Some thought the sisters were putting on airs. A white Catholic, prominent in education, remarked to Sister Leonardine when she met her: "I don't see why you have to go through all *that* for the niggahs."

"Because only the *best* is *good* enough," Sister Leonardine replied.[57]

After the sisters earned their certificates, the students in Jackson were able to receive First Grade licenses from the State Board of Examiners without taking the examination, on the condition that the school continued its normal courses as required by the State.[58]

In 1923 the high school department of Holy Ghost School was using two classrooms and another room for a lab and sewing lessons. Father Heick wondered if the expense of maintaining a high school for so few children was justified. And even it if were, he wondered how long the mission would be able to bear it.[59]

Chapter VIII Footnotes: After Elementary School —Then What?

1. SVD, Heick Report, July, 1923, 4; Bishop, op. cit.
2. W. F. B. Williams, Field Agent of the John F. Slater Fund, *Occasional Paper No. 13* (Trustees of the John F. Slater Fund, 1913), 4-13.
3. BS, Wendel to Drexel, May 12, 1916.
4. JHSC, op. cit.
5. Williams, op. cit.; Bishop, op. cit.
6. JHSC, op. cit., September, 1914.
7. St. Bartholomew's School Chronicle.
8. VSC, September 15, 1914; May, 1916; St. Mary's Rectory Chronicle, 19; Copy of newspaper ad in *The Light.*
9. Greene, op. cit.; VHC, September 1, 1915.
10. Interviews with Greene, December 5, 1970, and December 19, 1974.
11. GHC, September 6, October 4 and 12, 1915.
12. *Mississippi Register*, 1966. Article written by a Holy Spirit Missionary Sister.
13. GHC, June 2, 1916.
14. SVD, Christman Report, no date.
15. Greene, op. cit.
16. *Negro History and Directory*, 1929, 6; Greene, op. cit.; Greene, Cook and McBride, op. cit.; pamphlet for Coleman High School.
17. SVD, Report of Rev. Joseph Stein to Rev. Carl Wolf, July 26, 1934.
18. Greene, op. cit.
19. Christman Report, op. cit.
20. Rev. P. J. Wendel, *St. Joseph's Institute*, Fifth Annual Catalog.
21. Meridian School files, paper undated.
22. Wendel, op. cit.
23. Wendel, op. cit.; Interview with Mary Ida High Jackson, op. cit.; History, written by Rev. Anthony Jacobs, 1937.
24. Interview with James Luster, November 5, 1974.
25. Jackson, op. cit.
26. Interview with Helen Rose, November 22, 1974.
27. Ibid.
28. Flier attached to MHC.
29. NJ, Gunn to Heick, April 17, 1919.
30. NJ, Gunn to Rev. Dver, August 6, 1919.
31. SVD, Christman to Heick, May 8, 1919.
32. NJ, Gunn to Heick, op. cit.

33. SVD, Christman to Heick, September 3, 1918.
34. PP, vital statistics.
35. *Delta Democrat Times*, September 12, 1918, last page.
36. SVD, Christman to Heick, op. cit.
37. Interview with Winchester Davis, December, 1970.
38. Ibid.
39. Reminiscences of Daisy Miller Greene written for author.
40. Greene Interviews, op. cit.; SVD, Christman to Heick, April 26, 1920.
41. Greene, op. cit.
42. GHC, June 1, 1920.
43. Greenville School Files, 1920.
44. Professor M. V. O'Shea, Director, with the cooperation of State Superintendent, W. F. Bond, et al., *Public Education in Mississippi* (Jackson, 1926).
45. St. Bartholomew House Chronicle.
46. Ibid.
47. SMR, 1917, 63; BS, Steinhauer to Drexel, December 22, 1916.
48. St. Mary's School files.
49. JHSC, November 20, year not recorded; BS, Heick to Drexel, July 29, 1918.
50. Interview with Doris Tharp Hall, June 20, 1971.
51. JHSC, August, 1921.
52. Jackson School files, JHC, May 23-25, 1921.
53. McCain, op. cit., 247-253.
54. Interview with Sister Leonardine Huettemann, 1974.
55. Material on the Sisters' Examination and Certification are taken from the House/School Chronicles of Holy Ghost, Sacred Heart, St. Joseph, St. Mary's Convents; Interview with Sister Leonardine, 1974; also Code of Mississippi Law 1906; Law nos. 4536, 4538 (Laws 1902), 4543, 4544, 4547, 4553.
56. NJ, Gunn Diary, 217.
57. Leonardine, op. cit.
58. JHSC, August, 1921.
59. Greenville Rectory files, Heick to Jacobs, August 10, 1923.

CHAPTER IX
Barren Septembers

Except for a few brief periods the five mission schools experienced great success. Black parents wanted their children educated by the Holy Spirit Missionary Sisters and were willing to pay the monthly tuition even when it meant great sacrifices.

But the missionaries became aware of other needs that were not being met, and a variety of apostolates, such as an agricultural/industrial college, a hospital in Greenville, the building and staffing of rural schools, were discussed, explored, sometimes started, then reviewed and altered or dropped.

The mission high schools were preparing students for college, and yet there wasn't one Catholic college in the South that would accept them. As early as 1915, Father Heick received permission from his superiors to purchase the land opposite the mission property in Jackson for a Catholic College patterned after Tuskegee Normal and Industrial Institute in Alabama, which emphasized industrial and vocational training and which seemed to be enjoying prominence and acceptance by both races.[1] In fact, educators in Mississippi were urging agricultural schools for *white* children.[2]

A law authorizing each county school board to levy taxes for the establishment and support of one agricultural high school in its respective county was passed in 1908 only to be challenged by a black Jasper County taxpayer on its constitutionality because it didn't include agricultural schools for blacks.[3] Understandably, the one school per county would be for white children. In 1910 the bill was amended, allowing for more than one agricultural high school per county.[4] Theoretically this meant each county could have one school for whites and one for blacks, but in reality it was simply a paper chase. By 1917 the State had 48 county agricultural high schools for whites and one (in Bolivar County) for blacks, thus fulfilling the bare minimum of the law.[5] Each school was required to have a school building and dormitory for 40 boys, at least 20 acres of land donated by the county for dairy cows, chickens, an orchard, and a model garden large enough to provide the fruit and vegetables consumed by the boarders.[6] In 1917 the state superintendent of schools urged the legislators to discontinue preparatory departments in the other high schools of the state and allow the money to be used to maintain agricultural high schools instead. This was bringing the high school to the people, he said, rather than the people to the high school.[7]

Gardening was also encouraged in the elementary schools. In his Biennial Report of 1909-1910 and 1911-1912, the superintendent wrote:

Every school in Mississippi should have a garden sufficiently large for each pupil to have an individual

144

plot for the cultivation of flowers, vegetables, and farm crops under the direction of the teacher. It would give the pupils a first-hand knowledge of natural life, stimulate individual and community efficiency, transform character. In teaching the pupil to plant, to cultivate, and to reap the harvest, and as a social community to be responsible for the proper care of a school garden, we are training them in some of the most valuable lessons in life and are fixing in their minds lofty ideals of home and community life.

He really became eloquent as he continued:

Honesty is not merely preached here, but actually put into practice and the value of industry is exemplified. The great lesson of civic righteousness and personal honor stand out in bold relief as soon as the school engages in the cooperative work connected with the real activities of the community. Here the pupils learn through experience as well as by precept how to work out their physical, mental, and spiritual salvation and to grow in grace, power, and knowledge.[8]

There was another reason for teaching the children how to grow vegetables: pellagra, a deficiency syndrome marked by loss of appetite and weight, inflammation of mouth and tongue, diarrhea, and skin rash ending in death when left untreated, was breaking out in the South.[9] One case had been discovered in Jackson.[10] Sister Auxilia had come across the dreadful disease in a young girl of 10, whose case was probably never reported to authorities. The sisters had visited her once and talked to the mother, who had another daughter untouched by the disease. When the sisters returned, the mother had fled with her healthy child for fear she would contract the disease and die, leaving the sick child to be attended

145

by neighbors until death came for her.[11]

At a two-day conference on pellagra held in Columbia, South Carolina, in November 1909, the U.S. Assistant Surgeon General called pellagra a national health problem.[12] The disease was attributed to a dietary deficiency of vitamin B and could be remedied by eating liver, lean meat, dairy products, and green vegetables.[13] This was another reason for the school authorities to encourage gardening as part of the school's curriculum.

In the mission schools at Holy Ghost and Sacred Heart, an hour a day was set aside for garden work.[14]

Sometime in February the boys spaded the ground while the girls planted the seeds. When the plants appeared, the boys hoed and the girls watered. When the crops were ripe, each child received some to take home for eating. Others were sold to buy new seed for the next year.[15]

Not all parents or children liked the idea of the garden work cutting into the school's curriculum, but most were in favor of it.

In the educational climate of the state that favored agricultural schools, opening a Catholic central agricultural and industrial college similar to the one at Tuskegee seemed like a good idea to the missionaries.

Bishop Gunn was more than favorable to the proposal.[16] He had already secured five or six thousand acres of land on the Yazoo and Mississippi Valley Railroad for an agricultural school for whites and an industrial demonstration farm for the Choctaw Indians. Nothing would please him better just then than to establish a "kind of Negro Tuskegee in Mississippi."[17]

He wrote to Father Heick:

I think a scheme, something like Tuskegee, would appeal to Northern sympathizers. As I think of it I am in favor of putting the entire affair into the hands of the Divine Word Fathers and of the good Holy Spirit Sisters. [18]

He had several places in mind. Near Hattiesburg, the seat of Forrest County and a trade center for a rich agricultural region, the United States government was selling part of Camp Shelby. Nearby was a large black settlement. On February 12, 1919, in a letter to B. E. Eaton, legal advisor of Gulf and Ship Island Railroad Company, he wrote that he was thinking of one to two thousand acres of land on a railroad and close to a little town with freight and railroad facilities and he had taken note of the great tracts of undeveloped lands on both sides of the G & SI between Gulfport and Jackson. [19]

Bishop Gunn received a favorable reply from Mr. Eaton. The Company was happy to develop their cutover pine land along its line and create tonnage through an agricultural school, the attorney wrote, but the government had taken over the railroads for the duration of the War. The Company would have to wait until they were returned before they could proceed with plans. [20]

Bishop Gunn was also interested in two German settlements in the Diocese—one at Gluckstadt about 15 miles northeast of Jackson, the other at Seneca, near Lumberton, south of Hattiesburg. Since priests were scarce in Mississippi, in addition to directing the school the missionaries would be near enough to minister to the spiritual needs of the German people in the area. [21]

The missionaries were familiar with Gluckstadt, a small settlement of German farmers who had been induced by a real estate agent to come to Mississippi and settle near Jackson. By hard work and thrift they had managed to save enough money to buy the land they had settled. But when the last payment was made, an attorney informed them that the agent had no authority to sell the property, and they had no choice but to leave or buy the land a second time from the proper owners. They chose to do the latter.[22]

Since 1910 Father Heick had been going to Gluckstadt weekly to attend to the spiritual needs of the German Catholics, and the sisters taught religion school in the summer. They were paid for their services in farm produce—vegetables and fruit, a cow or a pig.[23] A typical gesture of the people's generosity happened one day shortly after the sisters' cow helped herself to the contents of an open paint can and died. The sisters were in Gluckstadt for a Corpus Christi celebration and while they were seated at the table with a family, the topic of their cow came into the conversation.

"Elizabeth," the man said to his daughter, "go to the stable. The best cow we have there—the sisters get today." Not only the cow, but a load of hay accompanied them back to Jackson.[24]

The missionaries would have been happy to put up an agricultural and industrial school near Gluckstadt, but the price of property was prohibitive—$30 to $40 an acre.[25]

The bishop had still another suggestion—a fertile tract of land owned by F. J. Schwierjohn near Lumberton. When Fathers Heick and Wendel visited the location, they found that it was near a railroad and the price was right! They could buy as much as they wanted for $15 an acre. But there was one problem: during the 26-mile ride around the property, they had not seen one black person. It hardly seemed advisable to open a Catholic educational institution for blacks in the heart of a white Protestant settlement.[26]

When they made their doubts known to the Bishop, he didn't think their reasons should deter them from buying the property, and he returned to the subject of the Schwierjohn land again and again.[27] But the priests bided their time. Even if they succeeded in overcoming the prejudice of the scattered settlers in the area, they couldn't see how they would be able to attract black students to a school in a white settlement.

When the bishop realized that their decision was final, he had yet another suggestion for Father Heick:

I think you ought to keep busy in selecting a location. When you decide on what you need, I'll try to make it materialize. What about Mound Bayou?

There were *only* blacks living in this small town founded by Jefferson Davis' servant.[28]

In the events that followed, it seemed that God's providence was guiding the decisions or rather the indecisions made about the agricultural and industrial college because a year later a college with a far different purpose would evolve.

A second project that received considerable time and effort was a hospital in Mississippi. From the earliest days of the sisters' foundation in Steyl, Holland, Arnold Janssen, the founder, promoted an interest in nursing among the sisters, allowing them to become midwives, an unheard of ministry for nuns in those days.[29] Sisters with a talent for healing and ministering to the sick were sent away for training courses. In 1914 Mother Leonarda had accepted a nursing home in Watertown, Wisconsin, and had turned it into a well-equipped hospital and nursing school.[30] But she was also interested in a Catholic hospital in Mississippi for blacks, who were often relegated to the basements of the city hospitals.[31]

Father Wendel hoped to have a hospital in Meridian and in a letter to Mother Katharine he proposed a site only two blocks from the streetcar line on a slope shaded by a grove of trees. It was selling for $3000.[32]

Father Christman was hopeful that a hospital could be built in Greenville, where the doctors were interested in replacing the present overcrowded and poorly-equipped hospital being used for blacks. At a meeting on July 19, they met with members of the Chamber of Commerce at the Elysian Club on the corner of Main and Shelby, where the present Percy Library stands, to discuss the means of raising funds for the hospital. Two leading Catholic men, Malcolm Robertshaw, who chaired the meeting, and Judge Emmet Hardy, backed the proposal. Mr. Robertshaw said that the physicians had discussed the matter with the Holy Spirit Missionary Sisters, who had manifested a willingness to administer the hospital and had agreed to provide $15,000 of the $30,000 needed if the citizens would raise the other $15,000. On April 28 a letter had been addressed to the public inviting subscriptions to bonds in sums of $100 and $500 and about $6500 had been subscribed. Mayor E. G. Ham, as well as several prominent doctors, spoke eloquently on the need for the hospital, and a resolution was passed by the group to provide the funds needed.[33]

Bishop Gunn gave his approval to the project. Writing to Father McCarty in May, he said that he was deeply impressed with the school in Greenville, which was now six or seven years old:

At the beginning the school had to fight its way for existence; but I learned this year that all of its competitors have practically disappeared.

The building is kept constantly filled, and since last September the sisters were obliged to turn away over a hundred children. The school has become the most thorough and most fashionable of all colored enterprises in Mississippi, and not only is it doing good, but is a wonderful advertising agency. The doctors have been so impressed with the work of the sisters that they have clubbed together and raised something like $15,000 to start a hospital for the blacks under the charge of the same sisters. This shows progress, especially in a community where priests and sisters were far from being an asset some four or five years ago.

Mother Leonarda would have smiled if she had seen his next sentence:

Sisters are numerous enough, or plenty of Sisters could be supplied to run an institution of almost double the size.[34]

Sisters were never plentiful, for the fields have always been ripe for the harvest and the laborers few. The truth of the matter was that when the Sisters accepted the hospital in Watertown, the community had not one registered nurse. Although the number of young women entering the community in Techny was at an unexpected high, it took years of study to produce a nurse or teacher.

Besides a lack of nursing personnel, Mother Leonarda noted a vigorous opposition to the proposal which caused her to fear that the hospital would only cause friction and tension and perhaps in the end destroy all that was already being accomplished in the school.

When Father Christman relayed her fears to the civil authorities, they sent him a letter signed by the mayor, the congressman, doctors, and members of the Chamber of Commerce, reassuring her that it was a worthwhile undertaking. The letter was loaded with paternalism.

> In a recent conversation with you in regard to the proposed black hospital to be built here, it was intimated that the ones in authority in the sisterhood which is to conduct the enterprise doubted the wisdom of the undertaking because of the possibility of racial prejudice.
>
> We wish to assure you that this community realizes it as both an economic and moral necessity to provide a suitable place where members of the black race can have proper treatment when sick. We have lived all of our lives in the midst of blacks and can freely say that we entertain no such fear as was intimated. Their walk in life and ours are different and each recognizes his bounds. We have the deepest interest of the blacks at heart and feel that we are morally obligated to provide for him any means that will tend to uplift him in a social, moral, or economic standpoint in his sphere.
>
> We believe that a hospital such as is contemplated would be a means of untold, unthought of, and ever increasing value toward attaining such an end.[35]

In the end, it was the lack of nursing personnel that determined the fate of the hospital in Greenville.

Mother Leonarda wrote to Father Anthony Jacobs, Father Christman's successor in Greenville:

While taking the hospital seems to be an excellent opportunity, we are unable to consider it on account of a shortage of sisters. Even three we couldn't spare.[36]

Lack of teaching sisters was also the reason for Mother Leonarda's not accepting rural schools in Mississippi although the need was great. In Meridian the problem was solved by the boarding school. In Vicksburg this was not feasible, and Father Steinhauer pressed Mother Leonarda for teachers for a country school outside of Vicksburg. She suggested that some of the Catholic graduates from St. Mary's take the teacher's examination and staff these schools instead.[37]

In 1915 Father Steinhauer opened a country school in Waltersville, about two miles north of Vicksburg, in a dilapidated hut with two small rooms and two lay teachers.[38] On January 25, 1916, Father Heick wrote to Mother Katharine that he had found some beautiful property on a hill overlooking Mint Springs Bayou and would be willing to pay for part of it, if she would assist. She agreed and a school/chapel was built the following year.[39] On Easter Sunday, 1917, when Father Steinhauer blessed the new chapel, six children were preparing for their first Holy Communion and four more were taking instructions.[40]

Although the school at Waltersville prospered, the church was never sucessful. At any one time there were only one or two Catholic families and eventually even these moved away. But some of the pupils who attended the country school accepted the faith and became some of St. Mary's staunchest and most fervent members.[41]

"Why did God make me a Negro?" was a query placed in a question box during a mission in Jackson given by Rev. John Dorsey, SSJ, one of the five black priests in the United States.[42] Unlike foreigners who could eventually lift themselves up and merge with the rest of society, the black person's skin always sets him apart as "different." In the South, he was imprisoned in his own blackness and had to

keep his place, not get sassy, not seek equality with the white race, and often take the rap for the white man's frustrations.

"Our sons are never safe," moaned one black mother in Mississippi. "We never know if they'll come home in the evening or not."[43]

Death could come swiftly, with no recourse to law and often for minor offenses, such as using offensive or boastful language, slapping a white child, or suing or testifying against a white person. The punishment was often accompanied by torture. Many of these deaths were never recorded, the perpetrators merely saying that the man was sassy and had to be killed.[44]

Although more often associated with hanging, the term *lynching* was used to describe any physical violence done without authority of law by three or more persons to prevent the law from taking its course. Records at Tuskegee Institute described the typical lynching mob as made up of younger men from relatively poorer and uneducated families, but there were also a few educated men of high economic social standing involved.[45] In 1900, there were 115 lynchings recorded in the United States. The number rose to 130 in the following year, then dropped to a low of 38. In 1919 the number of lynchings in the United States, 83, was the highest since 1901.

Georgia led with 21; Mississippi came in second with 12.[46] One of Mississippi's lynchings, a barbarous demonstration of insensitive cruelty, occurred just a few blocks from St. Mary's School.

The sisters of St. Mary's heard the news the next morning from the children as they gathered on the playground visibly shaken and in a state of shock. Some of them were neighbors of the young man, whose home was on East Avenue. One was a cousin.[47]

The victim was Lloyd Clay, whose widowed mother was a respected cook and laundress in the community. Hattie Clay had three sons who were home with her that night at 1907 Monroe Street, which was a few blocks from the A & V station. Mancy, 20, whose real name was Archie, was the oldest. He played piano and organ, often entertained close friends, and owned a barber shop on Washington Street which catered to white customers. Lloyd. 18, was a feminine, immature youth and thought by some to be a homosexual. When he was younger, he played with dolls instead of joining his brothers and the other boys in their games. As a young man he worked as a day laborer for C. J. O'Neil, who lived at 807 Belmont Street, just a few blocks from the Canal. Harry, 16, was the youngest of the boys and also owned a barber shop.

Around 8 a.m., Lloyd and Harry left the house together and walked the few blocks to the O'Neil's residence, where they parted. This was the last time any one in the family saw Lloyd alive.[48]

Tension had been mounting in Vicksburg and several incidents had already occurred in the city. A prominent black doctor had been given a quota of war bonds to buy, but he declared that since he was only a half-citizen, he would buy half the bonds. At the same time a white man living with a black woman in a large, colonial-style house on the southeast corner of Cherry and Main streets was trying to secure a job for his mulatto son, which his neighbors deemed too high for a black. Both men, the doctor for being too "uppity," and the white man for "going too far," had been tarred and feathered on the steps of the city hall.

The tar was cold, but the feathering was thorough. According to a bystander's report, the pair looked like two huge birds by the time the fire chief intervened and rescued them from the mob. The doctor was given seconds to leave town. The white man was released. His tormentors hoped that he had learned his lesson.[49]

A victim was needed to release the emotional buildup of Vicksburg's citizens. The victim was 18-year-old Lloyd Clay.

A young woman renting a room in the home of the Kelly Broussard family on Second North, three houses south of Clay Street and one block north of the Schumann's residence, had found the black man in her bed that morning, according to the Vicksburg *Evening Post*. Screaming and fighting, she kept him back and roused Mr. Broussard, who rushed to her assistance. One account said he found the door locked and ran around the house and fired as the man crawled through the window.[50] Another report said that her door was unlocked and her rescuer saw the back of the black as he struggled with his victim. In either case the would-be rapist escaped through a window.[51]

156

According to the paper, Lloyd was arrested at the A & V station on the opposite end of town as a result of a second hunt with bloodhounds. (The first time the hound had scented out a white man.) Lloyd was taken from his front porch to Warren County jail, where the lady was brought in and asked to identify her assailant from a number of blacks who were lined up for her inspection. Lloyd was among them. Her response was that none of the men present had entered her room. Lloyd was held pending investigation.[52]

In the meantime, hearing of the arrest, a crowd of two or three hundred people, many of them armed, had gathered outside the jail. By 8 p.m. the crowd had swelled to almost a thousand and included women and children. They broke into the prison, tore the youth from his second floor cell, and hustled him to the top of the stairs. Someone struck him a blow with a heavy weapon and he lost his balance and tumbled all the way down the steps to the concrete pavement below. The ruffians dragged him from the jail and pushed him east up Clay Street toward Second North.[53] At the corner of Farmer and Clay, the procession halted, and the young lady was again brought face to face with the accused and asked to identify Clay as her attacker. By this time people were pouring into the area, cars blocked the streets, and the cacophany of blowing horns, shouts and howls of the blood-thirsty mob were deafening.

"Is this the man?" she was asked.

"Say the word," someone shouted.

Clay looked at her with terror in his eyes. "I'm not the one, lady," he cried.

"Yes," she said. "He's the one." Although she

hadn't been able to identify him that afternoon, she said later that she had recognized him from his clothes and the side of his face.

Shouts thundered from the rabble when they heard the verdict. They fell upon the defenseless youth, stripping him of his clothes, kicking and beating him with their fists.

At the corner of Farmer and Clay stood a tall elm tree with a protruding branch extending over the sidewalk. Three men climbed the tree and one produced a stout rope that excited the mob into savage, unbridled barbarity.[54]

For the first time, news of her son's plight reached Lloyd's mother. She had not even known he had been arrested. Her grief was uncontrollable. As she screamed and sobbed, helpless and uncomforted, her neighbors rushed to their porches, trembling. "That's poo' Miss' Hattie," women said, glancing gratefully toward their husbands and childen, knowing that it could just as well have been one of them.[55]

The hanging was an unmerciful, bungled job. Lloyd's body was raised with no attempt to break his neck as is done in legal hangings. His hands were untied and in a futile effort to escape, he began to climb the rope. He was lowered, his hands were fastened and coal oil was poured on his head. Then he was lifted again, his bound hands raised in prayer.

Bystanders jerked his legs. Others smeared kerosene over his body. Another cadre prepared a gasoline-whipped bonfire and touched a match to it. The crowds gloated as the boy's flesh began to blister and his face became distorted with pain. The legs burned to the knees, exposing the bones. Shots rang out. Even women were wielding revolvers and a fusillade of shots kept up for several minutes. Stray bullets struck two of the onlookers, seriously wounding an elderly man, but this did not distract the crowd from the central figure in the orgy.[56]

Young people out for an evening's stroll either joined the mob or turned and walked the other way, tryng to close their minds to what was happening.[57] The Sisters of Mercy received a telephone call from friends warning them to stay off the streets.[58]

Around 10 p.m., their passions satisfied, the crowd began to disperse. Then it was time for the blacks, especially the young people unable to believe what they'd heard, to creep over to the scene to see for themselves. They left quickly, sickened.[59]

Around 11 p.m. the body was cut down and taken to Fisher's undertaking establishment. The distraught mother was counselled not to claim the body, which was given a pauper's burial the next day. Only the undertaker's assistant accompanied it to the grave.[60]

Although school went on as usual at St. Mary's, the children were tense and inattentive in the classrooms. Young men left the city in droves, their clothes tied up in a sack or sheet. Fathers departed overnight, sending for their families later. Those who had no money to go either borrowed it or worked and saved until they had the money for their tickets. Every day, there was a long line in the A & V station waiting at the ticket window.

One man handed the agent a hundred dollar bill.

"Where do you want to go?" he was asked.

"As far as that hundred dollars will take me," was the reply. Flight was their only hope.[61]

A record book of an insurance agent who had

many black clients was found at the scene of the hanging. Needless to say, he lost his clientele because the people refused to pay him when he came to collect the premiums.[62]

There were those who spoke against the reckless contempt for human life and the laws of the land. Msgr. John Prendergast, the pastor of St. Paul's Church, denounced the crime in the pulpit on the following Sunday and told his congregation that any one who participated or even witnessed the deed was guilty of murder.[63] The NAACP sent a letter to the governor, Theodore G. Bilbo, asking that the lynchers be brought to trial, saying,

Such crimes . . .are the crimes of degenerates. What can be said of a thousand people who stand and watch a human being burned to death?

There was no response.[64]

The Vicksburg paper may have expressed it more honestly in an editorial on May 16, two days after the lynching:

It is well for it to be known at home and abroad that this evil condition is aggravated if not provoked by such movements as the "black country-wide campaign for equal rights," published in the New York press dispatches yesterday. Together they make a mockery of policies and declarations of a better race relationship. One more kindly and just all may strive for. But never in the way of race equality in political and civil rights as this New York race propaganda calls for. That mischievous publication has acted like oil on fire . . . .[65]

Chapter IX Footnotes: Barren Septembers

1. Heick Chronicle, op. cit., May, 1915.

2. Bishop, op. cit.

3. JDN, November 2, 1909.

4. Ibid.

5. DAH, *Biennial Report of Superintendent of Schools, 1913-14 and 1914-15.*

6. Bishop, op. cit.

7. DAH, *Biennial Report, 1907-08 and 1909-10.*

8. Ibid., 44.

9. *Americana Encyclopedia*, Vol. 21, 485.

10. JDN, September 2, 1909.

11. Sister Auxilia Haag, September 5, 1969.

12. JDN, November 3, 1909.

13. *Americana*, op. cit.

14. Interviews with Sisters Auxilia and Liobina, September 5, 1969.

15. Ibid.

16. NJ, Gunn to B. E. Eaton, Esq., February 12, 1919.

17. Ibid.

18. NJ, Gunn to Heick, February 12, 1919.

19. NJ, Gunn to Eaton, op. cit.; Gunn to J. B. Semmes, May 30, 1920; J. B. Semmes to Gunn, May 27, 1920.

20. NJ, Eaton to Gunn, February 15, 1919.

21. NJ, Gunn to Heick, February 12, 1919, op. cit.

22. NJ, Gunn Diary, November 11, 1917.

23. NJ, Heick Diary, March 27, 1910.

24. Desiderata, November, 1971.

25. NJ, Heick to Gunn, May 30, 1919.

26. NJ, Heick to Gunn, April 29, 1919.

27. NJ, Gunn to Heick, January 7, 1920.

28. NJ, Gunn to Heick, March 3, 1919.

29. Verbum-Supplementum 21, Ad Usum Privatum Nostrorum Tantum, *P. Arnold Janssen* by Melchior da Pobladura, OFM Cap., Head of the Historical Section of the Sacred Roman Congregation for Canonization, Romae 1972. (Apud Collegium Verbi Divini, 15).

30. PP, Sister Leonore Scholter, unpublished manuscript.

31. SSpSG, Sister Ignaza von Acken to Rev. Mother, September 29, 1911.

32. BS, Wendel to Drexel, May 26, 1915.

33. *Delta Democrat Times*, Vol. 23, July 21, 1919, front page. Interview with Hubert B. Crosby, only living member of original members, December 12, 1974.

34. SVD, Greenville folder, Gunn to McCarty, May 14, 1919.

35. SVD, Chamber of Commerce members to Christman, August 10, 1919.

36. Greenville Rectory file, Leonarda to Jacobs, April 22, 1930, year uncertain.

37. SVD, St. Mary's Chronicle 1913, 12.

38. BS, Heick to Drexel, January 25, 1916; Burgmer to Drexel, March 17, 1916; Heick to Drexel, March 19, 1916.

39. Vicksburg Rectory Chronicle, March, 1916.

40. NJ, Steinhauer to Gunn, April 17, 1917.

41. NJ, Hoenderope to Gunn, October 21, 1925.

42. Interview with Hattie Therese Jackson, May, 1970.

43. Interview with Mamie Sudbury, June 3, 1970.

44. Daniel T. Williams, "Introduction," *Lynching Records at Tuskegee Institute*, (taken from Eight Bibliographies), (New York, 1970).

45. Ibid.

46. Lynching Record from Tuskegee Archives.

47. Liobina, January 13, 1970.

48. Interviews with Jack Robbins, August 21, 1974; Harry Clay, Lloyd's brother, August 16, 1974.

49. Robbins, op. cit.; Interview with C. J. O'Neil, August 23, 1974.

50. *Vicksburg Evening Post*, May 14, 1919.

51. Ibid, May 15, 1919.

52. Ibid.

53. Ibid., May 16, 1919.

54. Ibid., May 15, 1919.

55. Interviews with Camille Cheeks, August 11, 1974, Irma Dease, August 16, 1974.

56. *Vicksburg Evening Post*, op. cit.

57. Interview with Sister M. Henrietta, R.S.M., August, 1974.

58. Interview with Sister M. Hildegarde Schumann, August, 1974.

59. Interview with Charles Stevens, August 10, 1974.

60. *Vicksburg Evening Post*, May 14, 1919.

61. Cheeks, op. cit.

62. Ibid.

63. Henrietta, op. cit.

64. NAACP, *Burning at the Stake in the United States* (New York, 1919), copy of letter.

65. *Vicksburg Herald*, May 16, 1919.

Sr. Bertranda, Holy Ghost School, Jackson, MS, 1913

CHAPTER X
Ten Septembers to Build a Seminary

The 1913 *Negro Year Book* listed five living black Roman Catholic priests in the United States: Charles Uncles, John Dorsey, SSJ, Joseph Plantvigne, Joseph Burgess and Stephen Theobold.[1]

Father Dorsey, the Josephite priest, was a tall, heavy-set man with a round, full face that radiated kindness, and, according to his contemporaries, an orator of unusual force.

In 1913 Father Wendel invited him to give a mission at St. Joseph's.[2] In 1915 Father Dorsey gave a three-day mission at Holy Ghost Church.[3] In 1917 he preached a one-week "revival" at St. Mary's, where he was frequently interrupted with applause and "Amen!" by a record-breaking congregation that filled every available place in the church, even sitting in the sanctuary around the altar. Crowded into the hall outside and on the steps leading to the second floor classrooms were people who had never been near a Catholic church before. Men who had spoken against the Church came out of curiosity to hear a priest of their own race.[4]

Father Wendel wrote in the *Colored Messenger* in March 1917:

> *He has a strong, vehement love of our holy faith. If we had a hundred black priests to labor among their own race, they would be hailed as a hundred kings by a people who hunger for their ministry. Why shouldn't we be able to have those hundred priests?*[5]

The establishment of a black priesthood had been a matter of great concern to the priests and sisters of the missions. Urged on by Father Wendel, who became an unflagging, persistent battering ram against all die-hard opposition to a black priesthood, the Divine Word Fathers in the South met on December 29, 1914, and unanimously agreed to begin steps to open a seminary in Jackson that autumn for black candidates to the priesthood. They did this, the resolution stated, because of the racial prejudice that prevented candidates from entering established seminaries. Little did they know the difficulties that lay ahead.[6]

In the spring of 1915, Rev. Adolph Burgmer, Provincial of the Society of the Divine Word, and Father Heick attended a meeting in Richmond, Virginia, for missionaries in the black apostolate. Father Heick enthusiastically placed the proposition of a black clergy before the group and was surprised to learn that the majority opposed the idea. They were told that black priests who had tried pastoral work had found themselves socially unaccepted and had left the priesthood in frustration, broken in heart and body.[7]

It became clear to the missionaries that an in-depth study of the problems of black priests was needed.

This study was undertaken by Father Wendel. He sounded out members of the Catholic hierarchy, who he found were almost unanimously opposed to it. The bishops did not question equality of the races nor did they deny that vocations to the priesthood were given to all races and nationalities. They said that they were simply facing the fact that under the prevailing social conditions in the South it was impossible for them to accept black candidates. To do so would be equivalent to trying to break down the race barriers and would make Catholicism impossible in the South. Even Catholics would oppose it. And if they did choose to defy the system, what would they do with the men once they were ordained? They would be rejected by the white people, perhaps even by their own, not because they were not qualified, but because of racial prejudice. What would this mean to the priests themselves?[8]

From 1915 until 1919 the discussion of a black clergy was a burning issue in the Catholic Church. Father Wendel used the *Colored Messenger* to expound his views and keep them before the public. His articles, growing longer over the years, aroused both enthusiasm and opposition. He explained that the white priest was only half a priest to his black parishioners. He could not mix with them as he should because of racial prejudices. If he stopped to talk with them in the street, not to mention shaking hands with them, he became an object of scorn from passing whites. He was not allowed to address them as a gentleman. These seeming trifles were bars which kept the white priest from the pulse of black life, he said.[9] Black priests were needed who by their birth and experience felt the pulse of their own race

167

and had an inborn understanding for its needs.[10]

Father John Albert, a Josephite, probably put down the reasons for a black clergy best in a letter to the Apostolic Delegate on September 1, 1913: A white priest is a persona non grata in the religious life of the blacks who are not Catholics and there was very little hope of converting them if it was to be done by him. He said there was no doubt in his mind that the blacks would not only accept their own priests, but would prefer them. He said that it was urgent to begin since it would take fifty years to obtain even a small number of black priests. He lamented that his own order in the past six months had turned away fourteen applications because they were black and he asked:

Can this be the will of God? . . . How long, O Lord, will Thy Church close the priesthood gate in the face of this race of people?[11]

He pleaded with the Apostolic Delegate to speak to the hierarchy in the United States and with Rome and bring about some favorable action, assuring him that if he were successful he would have done more toward the spread of the Faith in America than had ever been done by any other churchman since Columbus discovered it in 1492.[12]

Monsignor John Burke was another strong voice that spoke in favor of a black priesthood, and as early as 1909 he had addressed the issue at the First American Missionary Congress.[13]

The position of the hierarchy had not changed in 1919 when Father Peter T. Janser succeeded Father Burgmer as Provincial. An advocate of the black priesthood, he visited the Apostolic Delegate, Msgr. Giovanni Bonzano, John Cardinal Gibbons, Archbishop Mundelein and other members of the Church. Msgr. Bonzano told him that a committee of blacks had visited him earlier and requested that blacks be admitted to the priesthood and that he had sought out the opinions of the bishops, who assured him almost unanimously that it wasn't time, basing their reasons on the deep-seated prejudice and bias that such a move would arouse, especially in the South, and the innate fear of failure. All without exception said they would not accept black priests into their diocese.[14]

In a letter to Father Christman, Father Janser wrote:

The position taken by the bishops compels us to walk cautiously while working for the end. I have told Archbishop Mundelein that I could not agree with him, that the black man had not been given a fair chance . . . .

It became clear to the priests of the Society that if anything was to be done, the Society would have to do it by establishing a religious community either directed by them or affiliated with them.[15]

Archbishop Mundelein listened to this plan with more interest, although he preferred the establishment of a religious community of brothers trained along industrial lines. Father Dorsey did not approve the plan at all. He told Father Janser that the blacks were out for social equality and that nothing less would satisfy them, not a separate religious community for them, but an acceptance into already established seminaries was the answer.[16]

Bishop Gunn, while still opposed to a secular clergy, was more tolerant to the idea of a religious community of priests formed and trained by the Society of the Divine Word and gave his formal approval in a letter dated June 18, 1920. Although he had to dictate the letter because he had been nearly blinded from a cinder in his eye,[17] he seemed to be the *one* prelate in the United States who could *really* see.

The man who had vigorously led the long struggle for a black priesthood was not present to celebrate the victory. On February 14 Father Wendel had contracted the flu and ten days later, exhausted from his labors and unable to fight off the inroads of the disease, he had died at the age of 39.[18]

About this time the Procurator General of the Society of the Divine Word approached Cardinal Laurenti in Rome. As the former Secretary of the Propaganda, he understood the situation well since the United States had been under his jurisdiction until it was removed from a missionary status in 1908. He immediately arranged to have the Procurator General speak to the pope himself. Pope Benedict XV listened to the objections and difficulties raised against the seminary and dismissed them all with a wave of his hand:

*If the episcopacy cannot be won over for this work, it doesn't matter; **we** want it. If your provincial meets with any difficulties, let him turn directly to **the Holy Father**. But tell him to start.*[19]

The Vicar of Christ himself had spoken. The missionaries could now begin the work without fear.

Sacred Heart Mission, rather than Jackson, was chosen for the site of the seminary, and Father Christman, with fewer strands of hair combed across his balding head, was appointed its director. Father Janser voiced his doubts about the location in Green-

170

ville, noting that Father Christman was alone and could hardly manage the parish and seminary by himself. This would mean that the sisters would have to teach some subjects and he could hardly reconcile himself to the idea that women, though sisters, were to teach candidates to the priesthood.[20]

That July letters were sent to all pastors of black and mixed parishes, as well as to all sisters teaching black students. The response was minimal: Some pastors didn't even bother to make inquiries. One pastor in New Orleans tossed the letter into his wastebasket only to have it discovered by a tall, lanky lad of 14, Maurice Rousseve, who answered it unknown to anyone, not even his parents.[21]

In the summer of 1920, the attic of the elementary school building at Sacred Heart was turned into a dormitory for the boys and a small office for Father Christman. Several students came during the summer and work began on a two-story frame house that was to be designated as the College.[22]

At their annual meeting in September, the bishops of the United States chose to close their eyes to what was happening in Greenville. When the topic of the black clergy came up, Archbishop Mundelein described it

as a plan under consideration for the formation of black Brotherhoods and Sisterhoods under white superiors wherein teachers would be trained, especially teachers for technical schools in the South.

The chairperson then told the assembled bishops that all that they needed to do for the present was to give the project their blessing without committing themselves to anything or without touching the financial issue.[23]

On October 24 Father Anthony Jacobs, lonely and homesick for his beloved Germany, arrived in Greenville in a downpour to assume the parish work at Sacred Heart and relieve Father Christman for full-time service at the seminary. He had been an army chaplain in World War I and was still suffering the loss of loved ones in the war and the sting of defeat. Instead of applying himself to the study of English which he detested, he was soon on the scaffolds hammering and sawing with the carpenters working on the seminary building.[24]

On November 5 Father Christman arrived from New Orleans with three students, among them Maurice Rousseve, a "real city slicker" noted Father Jacobs, "whimsical, tears in his eyes, short pants and bashful."[25] The next morning when Father introduced the newcomers to Sister Maria, Maurice thought he had never seen a more beautiful sight and fell in love with her on the spot.[26]

Sister Maria taught the seminarians literature and English; Sister Leonardine, algebra and science; Father Christman, Latin and French. When it was discovered that many students didn't have sufficient elementary school background for high school work, special classes in grammar and spelling were added to the curriculum.[27]

A few weeks after the first students arrived, Father Christman called on Mrs. Miller.

"You have to help me," he told her. "They're homesick. Be a mother to them."

Irene Miller took Father Christman literally and opened her home to the boys. In the kitchen was a large cookie jar which belonged to them.

"If I'm not home, just go right in," she said, "and if

there's something in the jar, it's yours." The jar was only empty when the boys tripped out with the pockets of their dark suits bulging with the goodies. More often than not, Mrs. Miller was home and welcomed them with open arms, trying to take the place of their own mothers in some little way. Maurice was her "youngest boy;" Vincent Smith, a man who had wanted to be a priest for years, but could find no seminary that would accept him, "her oldest." Each seminarian's birthday was remembered with enough ice cream and cake for all the students, even when the number rose to around 40. Dr. Miller gave free health care.[28]

It was a difficult life for the homesick boys. The attic dormitory was cold in winter and suffocating in summer. The windows were without screens, exposing them to annoying mosquitoes and dreaded malaria. The boys and their prefect ate in the convent, and the food, though well-prepared by Sister Basiliana, was tart and sour—German cooking, they called it—though this didn't prevent them from downing it with gusto.[29]

Sister Maria encouraged them to "stick it out," to study hard, to bear the inconveniences imposed by their vocations, and tried to do whatever she could for them.[30] On Saturdays she rose around 4 a.m. to wash their clothes, on rainy days carrying it to the tenth grade classroom and hanging it on ropes across the room. The Japanese Laundry, Sister Leonardine dubbed it.[31] In the evening the sisters were a familiar sight to the seminarians as they sat on the back porch of their convent, darning the students' socks and shirts and patching their pants and jackets. Every piece of clothing was darned until it couldn't accept another stitch.

Toward the end of December the frame building was completed. It was an attractive dwelling, painted green with white windows and doors. It consisted of three rooms downstairs—kitchen, dining room and study room—and four rooms upstairs—three classrooms and an office for the Father Prefect—all varnished with golden oak.[32]

Now that the students had their own dining room, a woman was hired to cook and wash for them. Food was never plentiful and was most often soup, cornbread, and beans. Meat was rarely seen. Sister Maria seemed to sense their needs and at times invited them to the convent for a treat or sent over an entire meal to their dining room. A favorite was a Friday fare of toasted bread and cheese sandwiches. German cooking wasn't so bad after all.[33]

Toward the end of the academic year there were eleven students at the seminary and more were expected in September. The missionaries were having second thoughts about keeping the seminary in Greenville. The closeness of the seminary and the school made it impossible to separate the high school boys and girls from the seminarians. Sleeping in the attic during the hot season was impossible and some of the students who were sleeping in the hall had to camp out in an old shack about six miles away every time the school had an entertainment. Although the people in Greenville were tolerant of the seminary, it seemed better to build more substantially in a more Catholic atmosphere on the Coast, closer to New Orleans, where the Sisters of the Blessed Sacrament founded by Mother Katharine had opened Xavier University. It would be a rich source of vocations and a place where the seminarians could later earn their degrees.[34]

Another reason for moving was the activities of the Ku Klux Klan in the area. Parade after parade was held in Leland and Greenwood to the east of Greenville and Rolling Fork to the south, although the Klan never succeeded in organizing a parade in Greenville. In fact, they were practically driven from the city following a rally on March 2, 1922, at the Washington County Courthouse. After listening to the speaker castigate the Catholic, the Jew, and the black, Senator LeRoy Percy, a native of Greenville, urged on by the audience, ascended the platform and denounced the Klan as an outlaw organization going about their work behind masks and clown suits. He spoke of the harmony existing in Greenville among the Catholics, Jews and Gentiles and said that they were not going to let a foreign element come in and sow seeds of discontent. A resolution was drawn up on the spot and passed by all present condemning the KKK, declaring that it had no connection with the real KKK, which had served its purpose and had dissolved many years before.[35]

When ugly rumors of bombing the school and seminary or burning them persisted, the mission personnel brought them to the attention of the Senator, who only laughed them off. "Don't worry," he said, "the Klan won't touch you."[36]

The sisters were the target of the slanders.

"Those goddam sisters over there oughta be killed foolin' with those little black niggahs," a white man remarked menacingly to a black parent whose children attended Sacred Heart.[37]

The sisters supervising the playground during recess noticed members of the Klan walking up and down Gloster Street, watching to see if they would touch the children in an affectionate way. One of them even approached Sister Maria on the playground to warn her not to do so.[38]

One day, when Sister Leonardine was on duty, she caught a Klan member on the street watching the children as they enjoyed their games on the playground. Sauntering over to him, she looked him straight in the eyes and asked audaciously, "Are you trying to help me supervise the children?"

He looked at her with scorn and retorted, "I don't do dirty work like that."[39]

It was not the local Klan, however, that gave the seminary its worst trouble. In April the Klan in Houston, Texas, through its paper broke loose against the seminary, printing a tirade in its April 8 issue. Across the front page were splashed the headlines *Rome Calls for 1000 Negro Priests.* The editor charged that the Catholic Church was going to force integration in worship. He called on black pastors to protect their flocks from *the Catholic invasion.*[40]

Other KKK papers claimed that white women would soon be forced to confess their sins to a black priest. Another flyer carried the heading: *White Women Act as Scullery Maids for Young Negroes at Greenville, Mississippi.*[41]

Printed on yellow paper, some of the flyers came into Father Jacobs' hands and he shared them with the sisters. After reading the slanders and slurs against them, Sister Leonardine tore the paper into tiny scraps and disposed of them. Sometimes the community of sisters could laugh about the things they heard, but at other times they were fearful. With the exception of Sister Maria all of them were German aliens and there were still bitter feelings toward the Germans although the War was over.[42]

The civic leaders in Greenville were well aware that the flyers were meant to arouse bitter feelings and incite possible violence against the seminary, if not in Greenville then in adjoining counties where the Klan was very strong. Judge Emmet Hardy and other men went about armed, not knowing when they might be called upon to defend the personnel and property of the mission.[43]

The Knights of Columbus of San Antonio, Texas, where the original charges were made, sent a telegram to the Greenville mayor, J. Allen Hunt, asking him to investigate the seminary and report back to them.[44]

Father Jacobs was on the porch of the school building working on the chapel windows when a committee of four men came to the seminary for the investigation. They were Mayor Hunt, Rev. Philip G. Davidson, rector of St. James Episcopal Church, Judge Hardy and E. G. Ham, the former mayor, a Baptist and a high official of the masons. The priest answered their questions and showed them the facilities, and the men left favorably impressed. Fortunately, the cooking and washing were no longer being done by the sisters.[45]

The letter refuting the charges against the seminary was addressed to the Hon. William Clark in Dallas, Texas.

The committee wrote:

> . . . *We visited the school and are satisfied that there is no foundation for these charges and there is nothing in the conduct of the school that is contrary to the ideas*

and traditions of our Southern people touching the relationship of the races . . . . There is absolutely no social intercourse or menial service done by the sisters or any white person.[46]

So the move to the Coast was not because of any hostility in Greenville. The KKK would have attacked the seminary verbally regardless of its location. But it seemed important to move it into the more Catholic atmosphere that existed along the Coast.[47]

Father Gmelch was now the pastor at Our Lady of the Gulf Church in Bay St. Louis and was eager to have the seminary in his parish. When Bishop Gunn proposed not only the seminary but also a school and parish, he was agreeable to all three although he moaned the fact that he was going to lose a third of his parishioners.[48]

In 1924 Bay St. Louis had a population of 4,000 people. The business section consisted of a few shops and hotels clustered near the water's edge along roads paved with semicrushed oyster shells. A broad, concrete boulevard stretched along the beach for about eight miles, slipping in and out between magnolias and live oaks whose spreading branches dripped with long gray strands of Spanish moss, forming a picturesque archway along the route.

The town was a resort center for people from New Orleans, descendants of the city's Creole aristocracy. They owned the beautiful homes with deep cool verandas set back from the highway and surrounded by large shady lawns. Winter and summer they came in for weekend parties and enjoyed the cooling breezes of the Gulf while they swam, sailed, or fished, far removed from the heat and bustle of city life.

In the winter the town was filled with tourists from the North, who came to bask in the semitropical climate where comfort and conveniences were provided for in furnished homes, cottages, boarding houses and first class hotels.[49]

In the Bay twenty-seven acres graced with oaks, pines, dwarfed cedars, magnolias, graceful palms, and fruit trees were purchased at the cost of $6,000 for St. Augustine's Seminary, as it was to be called, and without delay work was begun on a three-story brick building for the students. The Mission Board donated $12,000. Mother Katharine, who had given $14,000 to the seminary in Greenville, gave the $6,000 for the property, and Father Dwyer of the Board for the Indian and Negro Missions gave $20,000. An old house on the premises was remodeled for the priests and another for the brothers' quarters; a third remained unused.[50]

A large crowd of people, many of whom came on a special sixteen-coach train from New Orleans and other coastal towns, was present for the dedication ceremonies and Mass, which were held in the open on September 16, 1923.[51]

Bishop Gunn, who had taken much criticism from his episcopal brothers for allowing the seminary in his diocese, was happy to see it well established before his death. He had grown old and weak and knew that he had but a short time to live. Perhaps it was because of his weakness that he let down his guard during his dedication address and encouraged the blacks to stay in the South, where there was "plenty of watermelons and chickens," words that were not well received by his listeners.[52]

The dedication of the seminary in Bay St. Louis did

not go unnoticed in Rome. His Holiness, Pope Pius XI, the successor of Pope Benedict XV, wrote the Superior General of the Society a letter in which he said in part:

> *In your new undertaking, you are following the very principle which . . .has always guided the Catholic Church. To this mother has arisen, especially in recent times, a numerous progeny among the black race—a host of children who have frequently displayed virtues so splendid that they sealed their faith with their blood as in the most glorious epochs of Christian history. . . . It is indispensable that priests of the same race shall make it their life's task to lead this people to the Christian faith and to a higher cultural level. . . . Experience has shown that the young black is not poorly gifted mentally so that he cannot assimilate higher education and the theological sciences—and the latter, not in a superficial and abbreviated form, but as our Predecessor commanded, in the full courses as prescribed. . . . The blacks of the United States greatly exceed ten million souls, for whom a capable mission and secular clergy of their own race must be created as soon as possible.*[53]

Father Janser did not hesitate to send a copy of the Pope's letter to every bishop in the United States.[54]

Chapter X Footnotes: Ten Septembers to Build a Seminary

1. *1913 Negro Year Book,* 183.

2. Meridian Rectory file, Wendel, "Father Dorsey," *Colored Messenger,* March, 1917.

3. Heick Chronicle, December 19-21, 1915; Heick, *Colored Messenger,* March, 1916.

4. Vicksburg Parish Announcement Book, February 18, 1917; Flier in Rectory files; St. Mary's Chronicle, 1917 clipping.

5. Wendel, op. cit.

6. SVD, Letters 1-15, Meeting in Jackson, December 29, 1914; Christman, "St. Augustine", *St. Augustine Messenger,* November, 1925.

7. Christman, op. cit.

8. Rev. Charles W. Malin, *Integration of the Catholic Clergy in the U. S.,* "The Colored Secular Priesthood," Chapter 3, 16-18. A Thesis submitted to the Faculty of the Graduate School, Marquette University (Milwaukee, June, 1964), Courtesy of author.

9. Rev. Joseph Eckert, "Seminary," *St. Augustine Messenger,* January, 1945.

10. Malin, op. cit., 8.

11. Ibid.

12. Ibid., 10.

13. Ibid., 43.

14. SVD, Rev. Peter Janser to Wendel, February 10, 1920.

15. SVD, Janser to Christman, February 16, 1920; Janser to Gunn, June 18, 1921.

16. SVD, Janser to Wendel, op. cit.

17. NJ, Gunn to Heick, June 28, 1920.

18. MHC, February, 1920; *Morning Star,* New Orleans, Louisiana, February 26, 1920.

19. SVD, Folder, Letters of Pius XI to Superior General Gier, April 5, 1921.

20. Janser to Christman, February 16, 1920; Christman to Gunn, February 21, 1922.

21. Interview with Rev. Maurice Rousseve, December 6, 1974.

22. Handwritten composition book by Rev. Anthony Jacobs (Springfield, Illinois, 1945); "Seminary," *St. Augustine Messenger*, January, 1932.

23. Archives of the Archdiocese of Chicago, *Minutes of the Second Annual Meeting of the American Hierarchy*, September, 1920, 8, 9.

24. Ibid.; Rousseve, op. cit.

25. Jacobs Report, op. cit.

26. Rousseve, op. cit.

27. Rousseve, op. cit.; Rev. Anthony Bourges, June 17, 1971.

28. Greene and Bourges, op. cit.; Reidy, op. cit.

29. Bourges and Rousseve, op. cit.

30. Jacobs Report, op. cit.

31. Leonardine, op. cit.

32. Jacobs Report, op. cit.; Rousseve, op. cit.

33. Bourges and Rousseve, op. cit.

34. Jacobs Report, op. cit.

35. *Delta Democrat Times*, March 1, 1922, and March 2, 1922.

36. Jacobs Report, op. cit.; Interview with Rev. Louis Benoit, November 11, 1970.

37. An interview with Sister Leonardine.

38. Ibid.

39. Ibid.

40. From Father Jacobs' Report.

41. Ibid.

42. Ibid.

43. Letters of Judge Hardy; correspondence with *Commonweal*.

44. Ibid.

45. Ibid.

46. Ibid.

47. Ibid.

48. Letter of Father Gmelch.

49. Ibid.

50. Ibid.

51. Ibid.
52. Ibid.
53. Letter of Pope Pius XI.
54. Letter of Father Gmelch.

1st Communion Class, Sacred Heart School, Rev. Fr. Stein, Greenville, MS, 1920

CHAPTER XI
A School on the Coast

On February 19, 1924[1], six months after the dedication of the seminary at Bay St. Louis, Bishop Gunn, a loyal and devoted friend of the missionaries, died. He had nothing to leave, his will read. He had relatives who had given him much but expected nothing from him in return beyond his thanks and prayers. In life he had given them his prayers and in this, his last will, he gave them his thanks. He left to the diocese all that he had used in his office as bishop: bonds, papers, furniture, jewelry, and the like.[2]

Almost three years before his death, he had urged the missionaries to hurry, not only with the seminary plans in Bay St. Louis, but also with plans to establish a separate parish and school for the 600 to 700 black Catholics who were members of the integrated Our Lady of the Gulf Church, the only Catholic Church in town. He had written to Father Christman on June 16, 1921:

> It would be well for those in authority to attend to this matter before there is a new bishop in Natchez. I am

home again, but very weak.[3]

Neither he nor his successor would be present for the dedication of the church/school building for the new parish in Bay St. Louis on September 20, 1924. Instead, the priest who had been pastor of Our Lady of the Gulf Church until 1918 and who had opposed the idea of forming a new parish for his black Catholics would be the one to dedicate its buildings.

Black Catholics had a long history in the pleasant resort town of some 4,000 people. At one time, four aristocratic black families, the Labats, Prudeaux, Barabinos and Piernas, had homesteaded land in the northern end of town fronting the beach between Leopold and Felicity streets and extending west beyond Dunbar Avenue, about a half mile back from the water. The families had their own landing wharf and a schooner, which brought in supplies from New Orleans, and in time they established a prosperous oyster factory on the beach.[4] With the coming of the railroad the beach area south of the settlement became populated by white settlers from New Orleans, and as a consequence, taxes on beach property began to rise. Except for the family of the French-speaking Joseph Labat, Sr., and his Choctaw Indian wife, Philo, the children of the first families, unable to pay the taxes, were forced to surrender their property and move inland.[5] Even after the death of the senior Labat, his four unmarried daughters continued to live on the family estate and every year their niece, Inez, a principal of one of the largest public schools in the South, paid the taxes on it. The ownership of this choice property had long been a thorn in the side of greedy officials, but there was little they could do about it, unless they resorted to trickery. This they did by promising a member of the family a good price for the property, persuading him to obtain the five signatures necessary to put the property up for sale. Joseph Labat, Jr., who had refused to sign, together with his daughter, Inez, who had been paying the taxes, and a son were present at the sale, intending to buy back the property. But the perpetrators of the crime brought in a woman from New Orleans who was to outbid any price made by the "niggers." Later, when she learned who the victims were, she regretted her participation in the deal, but the damage had been done. The original owners received $36 from the sale.[6]

Friends urged Joseph to take the matter to court, but he only shook his head sadly. He had just learned that the lawyer he had hired was part of the deal. The father of thirteen children, he was a contractor for many of the houses and churches built in both Bay St. Louis and surrounding towns and with the large influx of settlers work was plentiful. His four brothers, three of whom were carpenters and one a brick-layer, worked for him. One was the brother who had obtained the signatures.

"I've a houseful of children," he said with tears in his eyes. "These crooked lawyers would take everything away from me. I wouldn't get any more work in town."[7]

Instead of taking the matter to court, the younger Labat placed the city official who had pushed the sale and profited from it into the hands of the Lord. A short time later this man met with a fatal accident while working on the property.[8]

Aside from individual incidents like these, there was a warm, friendly, and a more relaxed relationship between the races in the Bay than in any other area of Mississippi. They dropped into each other's homes and chatted over cups of coffee and worshiped in the same churches.[9]

For Catholics this was Our Lady of the Gulf Church, built in 1847 by the first pastor of Bay St. Louis, Rev. Louis Stanislaus Mary Buteux. The black parishioners were proud of the church and took active part in its support, holding their fund-raising events separate from the whites. Returns from an entertainment by the black parishioners on May 3, 1908, was $115.90, according to an entry in the church announcement book. A note for the fifth Sunday after Easter gave them credit for $85.[10] In 1909 a baseball game on the college campus and an entertainment on the grounds of St. Rose School to help pay the debt on the church netted $114.44.[11]

St. Rose School, where the entertainment was held, had been established for black children in 1867 by the second pastor of Our Lady of the Gulf Church, Rev. Henry LeDuc. Carrying his shoes in his hands to save on leather, the zealous priest had walked the bayous to visit the families in the area, encouraging them to attend church and send their children to school.[12] This was a two-room school house attached to the east side of the church where grades one through six were taught in one room while the teacher lived in the other.[13] As the school prospered, the priest built a one-story, two-room building with a porch along the back for programs, near the end of the church property on what is now Second Street opposite the town hall.[14] In a letter to his bishop in 1879, Father LeDuc wrote that the school was doing well. "I have two teachers, many pupils, and no

188

money."[15]

In 1885 the Sisters of St. Joseph from New Orleans agreed to accept the supervision of St. Rose. They were conducting St. Joseph Academy in the Bay, a boarding school for young girls of wealthy New Orleans families.[16] At the time there were about 35 boys and 50 girls in attendance at St. Rose, and until the public school was opened in 1890 it was the only school for black children in Bay St. Louis.[17]

Despite their good will, the sisters were often absent from the classrooms because of their duties in the Academy. At one time teaching was assigned to two sisters who were in charge of the convent laundry and academy dining room. Often in the mornings the children at St. Rose were given written assignments—busy work—while the sisters were elsewhere. In the afternoons the pupils often helped in the laundry, waxed floors, and cleaned dormitories. In the spring they planted a garden and in the fall they raked leaves and picked pecans. Their pay was bread and zip (molasses).[18]

Although the children enjoyed their work and loved the pay, their parents were far from happy about this arrangement, and by 1918 the school population had dwindled away to almost nothing.[19] The gentle admonition of Father John Prendergast, the pastor, reminding them from the pulpit every September to send their children to a Catholic school, fell on deaf ears.[20] Instead, the parents chose the public school on Washington Street directed by a Mrs. E. F. Ross and her two daughters.[21] Algebra and other advanced courses were taught in the eighth grade, and both girls and boys who graduated were sent to the court house to take the examination which qualified them for a teacher's license.[22] The Joseph Labats sent their children to St. Rose until they made their first communion and then reluctantly transferred them to the public school.[23]

Not only did the school attendance drop, but about this time some black Catholics were beginning to feel as if they were being relegated to the back places in the church and treated like second-class members. This was especially galling to the descendants of the black aristocratic families whose fathers and mothers had helped build and support the church, and some refused to take a back seat while others stopped going to church altogether.[24]

For several years there was talk about separating the parish. Protestants in the Bay were building churches for each of the races, and some people were disturbed that the Catholic church was not doing the same; but Father Prendergast was opposed to separation.[25]

It was not a mere coincidence that the priest was transferred to St. Paul's in Vicksburg in 1918 and Father Andrew Gmelch was assigned as the pastor of Our Lady of the Gulf Church. The new pastor felt differently about the separation and believed that the situation of the black Catholics in the Bay could be improved by a separate church and school.

Indeed, in a letter to Father Gmelch dated June 19, 1921, Bishop Gunn mentioned the fact that they had already discussed the new parish and school in Bay St. Louis and that Father Gmelch had given his verbal approval, but now it was time for him to put it in writing for the records.[26] Believing that a separate parish was in the best interest of his black parishioners, Father Gmelch gave his consent in a letter to the

Bishop dated July 19.

It is with a heavy heart that I arrange to give up the charge over the black Catholics of my flock. There are among them many good and holy souls who are to me a source of joy and to the white Catholics a source of edification. But I realize that unless the blacks of this parish receive special attention, there will be a considerable leakage among them. The establishment of a parish for the black Catholics will check this—hence, my consent to the separation. That good relations exist at present in Bay St. Louis between the white and black communities is in a great measure due to the fact that many blacks are Catholics and good Catholics. A separate parish will tend to increase their number, and consequently will make the continuance of existing good relations all the more secure.[27]

In a report entitled *A Few Reminisences of St. Rose School*, the Sisters of St. Joseph also expressed regret at the separation and praised the blacks of the community:

In social life, they had well-organized societies for men, women, and children. They took good care of sick members and all expenses were paid by their respective societies. When someone died, the funeral was attended by all members. They were a peaceful people. When the United States entered World War I, a flag was raised on the school grounds and many present wept for joy. They were willing, even happy to see their boys entering the ranks of soldiers and some lost their lives. With regret, the report concluded, *the Sisters had to give up St. Rose in 1922.*[28]

The society that the sisters referred to was the Promote Benevolent Society, which was organized in 1878 by Louie Piernas, the first black person to

191

hold public office in Hancock County, a feat some considered all the more remarkable because he won the office over a former confederate soldier. Later Piernas became postmaster in the Bay and held this position for 17 years. His Society offered a kind of health and burial insurance for its members.[29]

It was agreed that the complete separation of the two parishes would not take place for five years, giving the people time to adjust to the changes they would be called upon to make. During this time the black parishioners would continue to attend Our Lady of the Gulf Church for baptisms, weddings, funerals, and other services. In the meantime, they would build their own school and chapel where Sunday Masses would be offered for them. The Divine Word Fathers would staff the parish and the Holy Spirit Missionary Sisters would staff the school.

Since the black parishioners of Our Lady of the Gulf Church had made substantial contributions to the parish over the years, it was only fair that some of the church property be turned over to the new parish. Accordingly, land between Necaise Avenue and Agnes Street and Esterbook and Union streets was assigned to St. Rose. Next to it was a narrow strip of land with a small house for the caretaker of St. Mary's cemetery, which lay directly across the oyster-paved Necaise Avenue. This property, owned by the Sisters of St. Joseph, was added for $240, and the caretaker was given permission to remain.[30]

In 1923 Rev. Francis Baltes, a professor at St. Augustine's Seminary, was appointed pastor of St. Rose. While he laid plans for a new school, classes were held as usual in the old school building on

Second Street.[31] Two lay teachers, Clotilde Caspelich and Portia Labat, were hired and later, when classes grew in numbers, a third teacher, Mary Bloom, was added. Classes included grades one through nine, with special classes for two juniors who came from the public school, Lillian Caspelich and Ethel Edwards.[32] Fr. Baltes taught all religion classes and one mathematics class.[33]

Mother Katharine Drexel pledged $4,000 toward the new building, which would serve as school and chapel, and Joseph Labat was hired as the contractor.[34]

A house with three rooms and a bath on the first floor and a garret was moved from the seminary grounds and placed about 50 feet from the caretaker's home, for the sisters' convent.[35] Father Baltes found excellent teaching positions at Tuscaloosa for Portia Labat and Clotilde Caspelich,[36] and on September 1, 1924, five Holy Spirit Missionary Sisters arrived in Bay St. Louis to take charge of the school.[37] Sister Leonardine, who had been teaching at Sacred Heart School, was among them.[38] The superior, Sister Matutina Holle, had studied with the Sisters of Christian Charity in Dortmund, Westphalia, Germany, and was a talented pianist and violinist, having studied at the Holtschneider Conservatory. She had already taught eight years at Holy Ghost School in Jackson.[39] Also acquainted with the South was Sister Charitosa Klug, who had been teaching for the past three years at St. Mary's School in Vicksburg.[40] The other teacher was Sister Ellen Marchner, a 21-year-old American sister from Rochester, New York. Sister Basilissa was homemaker.[41]

The inspection of their living quarters didn't take

the sisters long. As in the first convent at St. Mary's in Vicksburg, the sisters could look through the holes in the rough wooden floor and see the wild flowers under the house. Even when Father Baltes later added some straw mats to the floor, the sisters found it easy to clean by lifting a corner of the mat and literally sweeping the dust under the rug, letting it escape between the planks.[42]

The dining room next to the kitchen was just large enough for a table and five chairs. If a sister sitting away from the door wanted to leave, the others had to stand to let her pass.[43] The attic of the small building had been made into a dormitory with a section under the eaves partitioned off as an office for the superior. Even though Sister Matutina was of medium height, she could only stand in one part of the room, which was scarcely large enough for a bed, chair and desk.

"Big enough for a dog house," Father Jacobs had remarked when going through the house before the sisters came.[44]

Electrical wiring for the house was not completed, but in the dormitory this didn't matter, since the room was lit at night by a large incandescent light from the cemetery across the street turned upon the crucifixion scene. Local Italians were paying monthly dues to keep the light burning through the night.[45]

Four trunks they had brought with them from the Motherhouse in Techny contained all that the sisters had: clothes, kitchen utensils and dinnerware—two serving dishes, one platter, five cups and a few plates.

"Don't break anything," warned Sister Matutina half seriously, half jokingly, as they unpacked the dinnerware. "This is all we have, and we don't have money to replace them.[46]

The sisters had hoped to open school on the 15th of September, but the building was not complete nor were there desks for the pupils. Consequently, the opening day was postponed until after the dedication on September 20th.[47] Bishop Gunn's successor, Richard Oliver Gerow, a native Alabamian, had been appointed Bishop of Natchez on June 25, and his consecration date was set for October 15.[48] In the interim period the former pastor of Our Lady of the Gulf, Father Prendergast, served as vicar of the diocese and in this capacity he returned to Bay St. Louis to dedicate the chapel and school. Despite his earlier opposition to the separation of the parishes, he praised the people for their loyalty to the Church and told them that they had merited a free, independent school of their own.[49]

The carpenters were still sawing and hammering and singing and shouting on the second floor of the building when classes began on September 21. In some rooms there were no desks, no seats, and un-planed wooden planks served as tables and stumps of pine trees as seats.[50]

Sister Matutina taught the first and second grades and pre-school children in one of the first floor class-rooms. Next to her was Sister Ellen with the third, fourth, and fifth grades. On the second floor Sister Charitosa taught the sixth, seventh, and eighth grades in a room behind the chapel. Opposite the chapel Sister Leonardine instructed the two women who were now seniors and fifteen other students in ninth and tenth grades. Except for religion classes taught by Father Baltes, she carried the entire load:

chemistry, general science, algebra, geometry, world history, and English.[51]

Not every black Catholic in the Bay was happy about the separation of the parishes, but most of them not only wanted it, but supported it enthusiastically. The enrollment in school rose from 65 in the previous year to 155 pupils, and it soon became necessary to hire a lay teacher for the third grade.[52] Encouraged by the sisters and priest, those who had stopped going to church began attending Mass again, happy to see their sons serving at the altar and their daughters singing in the choir. Without complaining about the overcrowding or the heat in the summer, some 300 worshipers packed themselves into the chapel, the size of two classrooms, on Sundays for Mass.[53]

In the spring of 1925 the Apostolic Delegate of the United States, Archbishop Pietro Fumasoni-Biondi, came to the Natchez Diocese for a canonical visitation, spending five days in Bay St. Louis and offering Sunday Mass at the seminary. He told his listeners:

I'm greatly interested in the education of American young men, both black and white, for the priesthood. I think that the salvation of the black people of this country depends largely upon the piety and learning of black clergy.[54]

On his visit to St. Rose he noted that the church was obviously too small for the congregation and recommended that a church be built soon.[55]

While at dinner with the sisters that evening, he talked about his trip to Japan, where he had first become acquainted with the Holy Spirit Missionary Sisters, especially through Sister Pia, whom the German sisters in the Bay knew well from Steyl. He said that she was living like the Japanese sisters and was a model for all missionaries.

He told the small community several times:

Missionary sisters cannot be nationalistic because the Church is international. Catholic means universal. We can't have a national Catholic Church.[56]

After the Apostolic Delegate sent a report of his visit to the Natchez Diocese to the Sacred Congregation in Rome, Bishop Gerow received letters from the Sacred Congregation that glowed with praise about the progress that was being made among the blacks in the diocese.[57]

On the nineteenth of April, 47 children received their first Communion in St. Rose chapel,[58] and on May 27 the first graduation was held, the two young women from high school and six students from eighth grade.[59]

That spring, Bishop Gerow wrote to the Sacred Congregation of the Council in Rome, requesting the necessary permission to officially erect a parish for blacks in the Bay. Although the permission was promptly granted and on the bishop's desk in June, it was not made public until the new church was built and dedicated in November of the following year.[60]

Bishop Gerow showed great interest in the progress of the church, for which he gave $3,000. In a letter of May 5, 1925, he wrote to Father Baltes:

I have looked over the specifications: sand specified for concrete work is simply sand that is 'clean and coarse' —no mention made that it should be sharp sand. Sharp sand is much better than round sand. However, I notice the proportion in which the concrete is to be mixed is quite rich in cement, and I suppose the

richness makes up for the grade of sand used. Paint—
doesn't specify what kind. It is almost a waste of time
to put on the outside of a wooden building in this
climate anything but a lead and a linseed oil paint.
Any other paint lasts only a short while. It soon
washes or chips off. Be sure when the exterior of the
building is painted that you have a white lead mixed
with linseed oil, and if you want it tinted, this tint
may be added.[61]

The completed church was a beautiful building of Spanish stucco, 40 feet wide and 80 feet long, and big enough to accommodate 350 people. Its windows of stained glass shone in the morning sun.[62] Dedication day was set for November 14, 1926, with Bishop Gerow officiating, and on this occasion Father Baltes read the document that officially declared St. Rose a separate parish. That afternoon the bishop confirmed 40 children.[63]

As the parish and school grew, so did the number of sisters on the teaching staff, and the small convent was becoming very overcrowded. When Father Baltes asked for another sister, Sister Leonarda responded:

I should be glad to give you another sister, but I should
like to know where you are going to put her.[64]

Realizing the need for larger accommodations, the priest made plans to add rooms to the existing structure, and when Bishop Gerow learned of this, he pledged the missionaries $1,000, adding that he would try to find more.[65]

Chapter XI Footnotes: A School on the Coast

1. NJ, Gerow, *Catholicity in Mississippi*, op. cit.

2. *Seacoast Echo*, Bay St. Louis, March 1, 1924.

3. NJ, Gunn to Christman, June 16, 1921.

4. Interviews with Inez and Portia Labat, April 20, 1970, and November 4, 1974, respectively. *Seacoast Echo*, March 13, 1931.

5. Interview with Clement Hazeur, May 4, 1970; Inez Labat, April 14, 1970.

6. Portia Labat, op. cit.; Interview with Sister Matutina Holle, December 15, 1969.

7. Hazeur, op. cit.; Portia Labat, op. cit.

8. P. Labat, op. cit.

9. Ibid.

10. Our Lady of the Gulf Church Announcement Book, handwritten.

11. Ibid.

12. Matutina, op. cit.

13. Ibid.; Bay Rectory files.

14. P. Labat, op. cit.

15. Our Lady of the Gulf Rectory Archives.

16. Ibid.

17. Ibid.

18. Our Lady of the Gulf Rectory Archives, op. cit.; Inez and Celestine Labat, April, 1970.

19. I. Labat, op. cit.

20. Ibid.

21. Ibid.

22. Hazeur, op. cit.

23. Matutina, op. cit.; Bay Rectory file.

24. Matutina, op. cit.

25. P. Labat, op. cit.

26. NJ, Gunn to Rev. Andrew Gmelch, June 29, 1921.

27. NJ, Gmelch to Gunn, July 19, 1921.

28. St. Rose Rectory Archives, paper probably written by a Sister of St. Joseph, "A Few Reminiscences of St. Rose School," no date.

29. *Seacoast Echo*, May 8, 1911; Interview with Ridgley Curry, May 4, 1970.

30. NJ, Gmelch to Gunn, July 19, 1921.

31. Ibid.; Matutina, op cit.

32. Matutina, October 28, 1969.

33. NJ, Christman to Gunn, October 16, 1923; Matutina, op. cit.

34. St. Rose Rectory archives, Copy of Deed signed by Drexel and Janser.

35. Matutina, December 15, 1969.

36. P. Labat, November 4, 1974.

37. Matutina, op. cit.

38. Ibid.

39. PP, Matutina, op. cit.

40. PP, Biographical Notes.

41. Matutina, op. cit.

42. Ibid.; Sister Ellen Marchner, August 1, 1975.

43. Matutina, op. cit.

44. Matutina, op. cit.

45. *Seacoast Echo*, June 21, 1924.

46. Matutina, op. cit.

47. Bay Rectory Archives, "Early History."

48. NJ, Gerow Diary 1924-34, November 12, 1924, 12.

49. *Seacoast Echo*, September 27, 1924; Bay Rectory Archives, "Early Years of School."

50. Matutina, op. cit.

51. Interviews with Sisters Leonardine Huettemann, August 2, 1975, and Ellen Marchner, August 1, 1970.

52. Matutina, op. cit.; Lillian Caspelich Robateau La Bauve, undated.

53. Bay Rectory Archives, "History of the Church."

54. Ibid.; *St. Augustine Messenger*, Vol. II, Pentecost 1925.

55. Gerow Diary, March 18, 1925.

56. Matutina, op. cit.

57. NJ, Index, Vol. VIII N-O, 142.

58. Bay Rectory Archives, *Early Years of the School*, April 19, 1925.

59. Matutina, January 22, 1970; La Bauve, op. cit.

60. Gerow Diary, April 8, 1925; June, 1925, 44.

61. Bay Rectory Archives, Gerow to Baltes, May 5, 1926.

62. Ibid. "History of the Church."

63. Ibid., November 14, 1926.

64. Ibid., "History of the Church."

65. Matutina, op. cit.; Early History, op. cit.

Greenville, MS, 1987

CHAPTER XII
The River's Rampage

For a quarter of a century—in 1897, 1903, 1912, 1913 and 1922—the people of Mississippi had experienced devastating floods from the Mississippi River bordering its rich, fertile fields, and by 1927 they thought they had learned how to handle the river's unpredictable behavior. Following the 1922 flood, one of the worst in the state's history, the river levees had been built to a height of 56 feet, twice as high as the first levees constructed by slaves and Irish immigrants before the Civil War.[1] But what the people did not realize was that since the levee board commission had been formed in 1858 to join local levees along the river into one continuous system, gaps which had allowed the water to quietly settle into inland swamps were being closed one by one. With nowhere to go, the river could but fill up its channel and spill over the sides of its banks.[2]

Lulled into a sense of false security because of the superior height of the levees, the people of Mississippi paid little heed to the warning signals given in

September 1926 when the rivers in eastern Kansas, northwestern Iowa, and Illinois overflowed and again in December and January, when overflows occurred in Alabama, Kentucky, and the northern tip of the state.[3]

Throughout the winter months, unusually heavy rains fell steadily upon already saturated soil throughout the entire length of the Mississippi River system, causing heavy flooding along its tributaries —the Missouri, Ohio, Arkansas, White, and Red rivers. Slowly, the Father of Waters traveled southward, glutting itself with great volumes of water as it churned past each of its swollen tributaries.[4]

Greenville was still experiencing heavy rains in April, but no one seemed unusually concerned about them. On the first page of the Greenville paper, the *Daily Democrat Times*, dated April 9, the weather report read: "Fair tonight; Sunday increasing cloudiness with showers and thunderstorms." Relegated to page four was a photo and an account of a levee break in Laconia, Arkansas, that had driven thousands from their homes.[5]

In 1927 Sister Ambrosine Feldmann was the superior at Sacred Heart Convent. She had entered the congregation in Steyl, Holland, as a candidate in 1907, and had come to America as a postulant in 1912, teaching several years at the boarding school for girls established in Techny, Illinois, by the Holy Spirit Missionary Sisters, before being assigned to Greenville in 1925. A warm, gentle person, she was short with a head too large for her body. Her eyes, or rather, since one was glass, her *eye* was her most striking feature, the one, dark brown seeing eye, twinkling merrily enough for two. She was no stranger to discrimination and could empathize with her students because her own mother, a Jewess, orphaned at an early age, had been disowned and locked out of her brother's house when he learned that she was becoming a Catholic.

A childhood friend of Sister Ambrosine, Sister Gerasina Kneer, was also in Greenville. As children the two sisters had attended the same church in the town of Koerbecke, Germany. Sister Ambrosine's father owned a *Wirtschaft*, a combination beer parlor and village store, near the church, while Sister Gerasina and her parents lived in a distant village, about an hour's walk away. After Mass on Sundays the girls spent the time together while the elder Kneers enjoyed a mug of beer at the *Wirtschaft* before returning home. The girls never discussed their vocations, and Sister Ambrosine was the first to enter at Steyl and was already in the United States when her friend followed her into the congregation. Sister Gerasina remained in Steyl after taking vows, completing the Normal Course for teachers before coming to the United States. Now after more than a decade, the two childhood friends were reunited in Greenville.[6]

Also at Sacred Heart in 1927 were three sisters who had spent many years in the Southern missions: Sister Josepha Delort, Sister Seraphim Buskase, and Sister Basiliana Korte. The other members of the community were an American, Sister Ruth Wendelgass, from Rochester, New York; a Czech, Sister Yolandis Ritter, from Hungary; and a German, Sister Antonina Quandt, a teacher when she entered the convent.[7]

That April, Sacred Heart School continued as usual, and preparations were already in progress for the graduation exercises of four high school seniors in May. Because of the frequent spring rains, the mission grounds were more beautiful than they had ever been. As one sister described it, as far as the eye could see across the playground, the grass was like one vast, velvety green carpet. Red, white, and pink ramblers had endeared themselves to the evergreen trees and their fragrances mingled and were wafted over the playground by the playful breezes that rippled the branches of the young willow trees near the bell tower. Among the branches the birds twittered and chirped as they fashioned their nests. The hedges were neatly trimmed and their delicate, fragile leaves sparkled like bits of jade in the spring sun.

Beyond the school an orchard of young peach and plum trees laden with half-ripe fruit and sturdy pecan trees promised a bountiful harvest. Chickens scratched in the sand near the school building, while a little distance away Brownie, the cow, grazed on the luxuriant grass. Romping nearby were Father Jacobs' two dogs, Lady Flora von Blankenberg, a German police dog, and Tilly, a Scotch collie. The land was full of beauty and life and promised a bright future.[8]

On Wednesday, April 13, the *Daily Democrat Times* reported that there was no excitement along the river front around Greenville; that the levee was holding with no weak spots apparent; and that the water level was expected to be about 51 feet, less than the 1922 level.[9]

But elsewhere along the river, there was cause for alarm. By April 15 the levees farther north were slowly crumbling before the crushing force of the Mississippi swollen by its numerous tributaries. On Saturday, April 16, the water smashed the levees at Mounds, Illinois; Judsonia, Arkansas; Dorena, Missouri; and Alexander County, Illinois. Ten to fifteen feet of water whirled through the area at Dorena, washing away spring crops, killing livestock, and damaging homes and property. The crest of the river, traveling about 35 miles a day, was expected to reach St. Louis that Sunday.[10] The situation did not look good for Mississippi although the city of Greenville continued to be optimistic. Not even the fact that it had received 10.46 inches of rain that Friday and Saturday weakened its confidence in the strength of its levees.[11]

Nevertheless, precautions were being taken and camps had been established at strategic points under the supervision of experienced high water fighters. The governor requested General Curtis Greene to visit the levees at Greenville to see if the National Guard would be needed. Again the embankments were declared safe.[12] Realizing, however, that they were in for the greatest high water fight they'd ever made, the levee board had 200 convicts from Parchman Penitentiary brought to Greenville to lay down sandbags and reinforce the barriers still more.[13]

The atmosphere was quiet and peaceful at the mission on Sunday, April 17, and three high school students and a kindergarten child were baptized at Sacred Heart Church, which still occupied two classrooms on the first floor of the school building.[14] That afternoon the sisters walked to the levee about a half mile away to see how high the water had risen. Here they questioned the officials, who reassured them that the city was safe. Nevertheless, should the unexpected happen, they were told, the mayor had

207

decreed that the fire siren would not blow except to warn the people that the city was in danger, and schools and public buildings were designated as refugee centers. Even if flooding should occur, no one expected more than two or three feet of water at the most.[15]

On Monday, April 18, the high water reading at Greenville surpassed the 1922 record by .15 inches. The following day the paper reported that the water at Greenville had shown a rise of a half foot during the past 24 hours, but also noted that the crest seemed to be leveling off since the river level had been stationary at Cairo, Illinois, during the same period.[16]

It was not the levee in Greenville that was to give way, inundating most of the city under nine to ten feet of water, but one eighteen miles to the north. The weak spot was at Mounds Landing, near Scotts on a plantation owned by the Delta Pine and Land Company. According to one revetment worker, the money allowed for the district had been cut off, and officials had closed down the repair work in December, intending to begin again in spring when the new allotment came. When the rains swelled the river, engineers knew the levee couldn't hold, and in March there had been a scramble to mend the weak spots. On the night of April 20, some 1,500 men worked feverishly in a driving, cold rain, while the land shook beneath them under the mighty force of the water. They would throw the sand bags and two-by-four boards into the gaps, then stand by helplessly as the current kicked them out as if they were bean bags and matchsticks.[17]

On the morning of Thursday, April 21, the sisters

went to their classrooms as usual. Sister Ambrosine stopped to chat with the few children who had arrived early and had congregated on the playground. The missionary noted the tenseness and anxiety on the faces of the children and learned that many of their fathers had been working on the levee all through the night. Suddenly, their conversation was cut short as the piercing scream of the fire siren tore across the clear, cool morning air. Everyone froze.

"Go home! Go home!" the superior called out and someone began ringing the school bell. Within minutes, the grounds were empty.[18]

Father Jacobs hurried into town to find out what had happened and learned that the levee at Mounds Landing near Scotts, eighteen miles to the north of Greenville, had broken at 7:45 that morning.[19] The crevasse was over 3,000 feet wide and was discharging 468,204 cubic feet of water per second. It would be in Greenville in 24 hours.[20]

"How much can we expect?" asked the priest.

"Four feet—maybe ten," was the answer. "Who knows how deep it will be when all the water up river has passed through that gap?"[21]

Buying a supply of groceries for himself and the sisters, he hurried back to the mission, passing families who were feverishly constructing scaffolds for their furniture and other household goods. Some were fashioning boats and chinking them with tar, their children joining them in the race against time. Others prepared to leave the city by train or flee to the levee. It all seemed like a bad dream.[22]

When the sisters learned of the break, they hurried to bring up coal and firewood and canned goods from the basement and stored them in the attic.

Someone brought in the cow and staked her on the back porch with a good supply of hay. The chickens were put on the second floor porch. The one-story rectory, located on lower ground than the sisters' convent, was deemed unsafe for Father Jacobs, and he brought his belongings to the convent and placed the consecrated hosts from the church in the sisters' chapel.[23]

At three o'clock that afternoon, the fire siren blasted again. This time the dam at Willows Landing, three miles north of the city was on the verge of breaking. The sisters hurried to the chapel to pray that the Lord would divert the catastrophe about to fall on the city and its inhabitants.[24]

Sacred Heart School was a designated refugee center for the blacks in the area, and that afternoon four or five families arrived at the mission with their food and blankets. One family even brought their icebox.[25] The father was a carpenter, and he and Father Jacobs hastily put together a small boat.[26]

After supper Father Jacobs and the sisters spread out through the neighborhood inviting families to bring their bedding, clothing, groceries, and valuables to the school, where they would be safe. By nightfall 200 people had encamped in the classrooms on the second floor of the building,[27] feeling like Noah who had built an ark on the desert sand. There was not a sign of water anywhere. It almost seemed unreal.

As darkness fell on an uneasy city, the people in the school sat around, frightened and anxious and unable to sleep. At 12, the siren blared again, and the water hit the mission with a frightening hiss, sweeping over the sidewalks and playground, slapping the sides of the buildings with a resounding force, shaking the 40-year-old convent as if it were about to sweep it off its foundations. The sisters and priests were on their knees as were the people in the school, praying for help and protection.[28]

A half hour later the buildings stood like islands in a turbulent sea of rushing water. The mournful lowing of cows, the frightened bleating of a calf, the shrill squealing of horses being swept along in the current sent a chill through the occupants of the building.

Grateful that they were alive and safe, Father Jacobs celebrated Mass in the convent chapel at 2 a.m. and then urged the sisters to get some rest. But there was little sleep that night as they wondered in the darkness just how serious their situation was.[29]

In the morning the rising sun revealed a pathetic sight. The convent was entirely surrounded by five to six feet of water. The force of the current had ripped the railroad track from its bed and twisted its iron rails, still attached to its ties, so that it extended above the water like an upturned picket fence. Small homes of the neighborhood had been swept away. In the distance people were sitting on the roofs of their houses and screaming for help. Others were shouting from attic windows. Some were on trees. Carried by the current, horses, cows, pigs and mules, neighing, lowing, squealing and braying, were struggling for their lives among floating oil drums, cotton bales, and wood. Sitting atop some of the bales were small boys yelling for help. Boats from the army, navy, and coast guard, as well as from the bureau of lighthouses, and private motorboats were zooming back and forth, rescuing the victims and taking them to the levees.[30]

From the second floor of the convent the sisters could see the refugees in the school building, and they waved to each other across the water, grateful to be alive. People in isolated houses who hadn't known about the flood never had a chance.[31]

On the southern end of town where the land was higher, thousands of people had found shelter in government buildings and businesses. Some 3,000 of them had jammed themselves into the city hall so tightly that they couldn't even turn around, and 26 people had died through the night.[32]

As devasting and heartbreaking as the situation was, the river was not yet through with the city. Its water was still spouting through the crevasse at Mounds Landing and rising three inches an hour in Greenville. It was taking a southeasterly direction through fertile lands of a dozen counties as it sought an outlet through the Sunflower and Yazoo rivers back into its bed near Vicksburg.[33]

Sister Ambrosine took a statue of St. Joseph and placed it just above the water two steps below the front porch of the convent. By noon she had to rescue it and place it one step higher. In the evening it had to be moved again. Finally, she placed it on the doorstep and the sisters prepared to move to the second floor. Fortunately, when the water reached the edge of the step, it went no farther. It was now 8 to 10 feet deep around the mission.[34]

For the next two days refugees, from newborn babies to people in their 80's, were carried by rescue boats to the school building. The original group had shared the food they had brought with them, and the sisters, using the hastily constructed rowboat, brought over the food that they had in the convent.

When this was gone, matters looked rather bleak, but relief came on the third day when a government ship arrived with supplies of both food and clothing.[35]

Thousands of people had already left Greenville before the flood, and now the women and children who remained were urged to go. Tent cities maintained by the Red Cross and National Guard had been set up from Clarksdale to Vicksburg to accommodate the homeless and destitute. Steamers, towing two and three barges large enough to accommodate a thousand people, were plying up and down the river carrying the refugees to the safety of the camps. White men were given an option to go or to remain and help protect the city from looting, but black men were ordered to stay to help repair the levee once the water receded. Several thousand black men were on the levee waiting to board the *Sprague*, which was taking on refugees bound for Vicksburg, but the sheriff would not let them on, even though there was room. This angered many of the blacks.[36]

Fortunately for Vicksburg, the break at Scotts lowered the flood crest, causing the river to drop before it reached the city.[37] On the 21st the city had closed the sea wall gate at the foot of China Street, and that night men had patrolled the wall, placing sacks around boils as soon as they developed, to protect the business and wholesale warehouses along the waterfront.[38]

Naturally, the sisters at St. Mary's were concerned about the community at Sacred Heart. When they learned that the Mercy Sisters were coming to Vicksburg, they asked the Knights of Columbus to bring

213

their sisters also and were happy when they heard that all but three of them would be arriving by boat that very night.[39]

The Knights of Columbus were kind enough to meet the steamer when it arrived in Vicksburg and drove the sisters, shaking and tearful, to St. Mary's, where they received a warm welcome.[40] The other refugees were registered, bundled into trucks, and taken to the tent camps prepared for them. For the blacks this was in the Fort Hill area.[41]

In the days following the flood, the sisters at St. Mary's and those who had come from Sacred Heart visited the camp at Fort Hill and helped wherever they could. They found many of the people in the camp dazed and stunned, sitting motionless on their cots staring into space, unable to accept the fact that they had lost everything they owned.[42] Young men in the camp were put into trucks each morning and driven to areas around the city where they were forced to work by pistol-wielding white men, unable to protect their wives and sisters and daughters who were being raped back in camp.[43] The sisters tried to bring comfort wherever possible. Babies were still being born, and Sisters Desiderata, Josepha, and Ruth were assigned to sewing diapers and shirts from flannel furnished by the Red Cross.[44]

Meanwhile, the three sisters who had remained in Greenville—Sisters Ambrosine, Gerasina, and Basiliana—tried to make the lives of the refugees in the school as easy as possible. Each day Father Jacobs went into town by boat to bring back supplies that were being distributed in the Grand Opera House. The sisters brought them to the school building and distributed them among the people, afterward taking care of anyone who was ill.[45] Sister Gerasina was at home in the water and paddled the mission boat back and forth with ease, the two mission dogs often sitting at her feet.[46] To reach the second floor of the school she rowed through the front doors of the church, up to some planks lying across the tops of the pews that led to the stairwell.[47]

One day when she was rowing near the high school building, a current swirled her small boat around in a circle as if it were a whirling top. Try as she might, she couldn't break free and would have been taken into town or, worse, would have capsized if two men working in the high school hadn't seen her and come to her rescue.[48]

Father Jacobs offered daily Mass in the sisters' chapel,[49] and on Sundays men went around in boats to bring in anyone, including those in the school, who wanted to attend.[50] After Mass Sister Basiliana served coffee and a light lunch and distributed clothing and food to those who needed them.[51] On one of these Sundays, the four high school girls received their diplomas.[52]

During the day the missionaries were busy and had little time to think; but the nights with their sombre shadows, the howling of the wind and the lashing of the water against the house, shaking it on all sides, seemed endless. Sister Ambrosine wrote to the sisters in Techny:

It seemed like we were in a bottomless abyss and an interminable woe. How we praised the morning! Never in my life did I greet the sun with so much eagerness.[53]

On April 27 the good news came that everyone wanted to hear. The *Daily Democrat Times*, whose
215

writers were sitting in an inch of water and setting type by hand, reported that there had been no rise in the water for the past 36 hours. Now like Noah they could only wait for the water to recede.[54]

After three weeks the people in the school building at Sacred Heart were taken by the Red Cross to the levee where about 7,000 other people were encamped, along with the cattle that farmers had managed to save. Some of the unfortunate animals were standing with their back legs in the water, shivering from the cold. Occasionally, one slipped off and was carried away by the current while the people on the levee stood by helplessly.[55]

There is an interesting account of trouble on the levee in Greenville in the book *Where I Was Born and Raised* by David Cohn. According to this account, the blacks were given food, but were too lazy to take it off the ships that brought it. Senator Percy, head of the relief, *braved* the black man's anger and *courageously* went to the levee and *fearlessly* spoke to the men. Moved by his *fearlessness*, the men were *humbled* and began to work.[56] However, the black man had a different version of the event. The blacks and poor whites were being forced to work on the levee by armed guards, and some of them resented this. When one of the blacks refused to work, he was killed. Feelings ran high in the black community, and when the food boats came in, the black men refused to unload them. It was an elderly black man who called a meeting and told the story of a white man and a black man who had some property. The white man thought the black man was superstitious and made up a story, telling the black man that he had had a dream that night in which he dreamed that all

216

of his land came to be his land. "Well," said the black man, "if that's the way you dreamed it, that's the way it's going to be," and he gave the white man his property. But the black man wasn't all that dumb. After a few days, he had a dream himself. He said, "I dreamed that my land came back to me." The white man said that was all right, and he returned his property. Then the white man had another dream about the land coming to him. But the black man countered: "Last night I had a dream. I dreamed that my land came back to me and in my dream I dreamed there would be no more dreams." This story broke the tension. After he had finished it, he told the men, "I don't know what you men are going to do, but I have seven boys and we're going to help unload that boat."[57]

The three sisters made daily trips to the levee to assist the black families in every way they could. In one way, the flood helped to sweep away some of the prejudice against Catholics in the city. People who had formerly turned away when the priest or sisters passed now greeted them warmly.[58]

By May 10 the water had receded enough in the northern part of the city for cleanup to begin. But the mission property was still well under water.[59] It was not until July 6 that the sisters could put their feet on dry land.[60]

The mission was a picture of destruction. The fence around the property was flattened to the ground. Walls and roofs of houses were strewn over the premises. The carcasses of a dead cow, pigs, and chickens were lying behind the auditorium. Fish caught in the meshes of the fence wire were decomposed. There was not a blade of grass, not a weed,

nothing but mud, mud, mud. The hedges and trees
—the willows, the peaches, and the plums—were
dead.[61]

Inside the buildings the floors, swollen and warp-
ed, were covered with a sour-smelling slime and
mud. The school desks and bookshelves had fallen
apart and were useless. The piano in the auditorium
had been safe on the stage, but the furniture of the
two classrooms had been under water and was a total
loss as was the furniture of the two classrooms of the
college building. In the rectory all the furniture had
been buried in water and ruined, the plaster on the
walls was softened and loose.[62]

This picture of destitution was repeated in almost
every house and business in the city of Greenville.
But worse than this, the total flooding caused by the
Mississippi River had covered about 12,500,000 acres
of land, driving 600,000 people from their homes and
causing business losses estimated at $400,000,000.
The victims needed great courage and strength to
pick up the pieces after the flood and go on.[63]

Bishop Gerow estimated the damage of church
property in the Natchez diocese to be about $8,000,
with $5,000 of this being sustained by Sacred Heart
Mission, which had received the brunt of the river's
rampage.[64] He had sent Father Jacobs almost $2,000
immediately after the flood to help the missionaries
in their relief work.[65] With this money and that received from the Red Cross, the missionaries were
able to supply the people with beds, mattresses,
linens, stoves, tables and chairs, clothing and coal,
according to each family's needs.[66]

On July 10 the mission church bells rang out calling
the faithful to Mass for the first time since the flood.[67]

For some time the chapel had become too small for the congregation, and fund-raising events had netted a considerable sum of money for a new church. Father Jacobs had felt justified in using this money for the relief of the refugees during the flood, trusting that the Lord would provide the means later to build the church.[68]

Cleanup was still going on in August when the sisters' annual appointments were given out. To Father Jacobs' great disappointment, Sister Ambrosine was transferred to St. Margaret's Guild, a home for orphaned and neglected girls in Milwaukee, Wisconsin, and Sister Gerasina was appointed to St. Joseph School, Meridian.[69] The priest was deeply grieved to learn he was losing these two sisters because the people had come to love and esteem them for their self-giving services during the flood. Despite his protests, made even to the Bishop, the appointments remained.[70]

The new superior of Sacred Heart Convent was Sister Liobina Schikora, a strong, energetic woman of 36. Greenville was not a pretty sight when she arrived, and the basement of the convent was still buried in mud. She rolled up her sleeves and pinned up her long blue habit and began to remove the mud shovelful by shovelful. Rats and snakes were everywhere as she penetrated deeper into the wet debris in the basement, but they did not deter her from the work that had to be done.[71]

Not able to replant the trees that fell, she did lay in some pecans. In the spring, the other trees would be planted, the garden would be seeded with vegetables and flowers, and summer would find it a rainbow of color under her expert care.[72]

On November 10 Bishop Gerow attended a meeting of bishops of the flood area to discuss the distribution of $100,000 donated to flood sufferers by the Holy Father. Five bishops were concerned, and it was agreed that the money should be divided equally among them, allotting each diocese $20,000.[73]

On the same day Bishop Gerow attended a meeting of the Extension Society and requested $6,000 for the new church in Greenville and was promised the amount.[74] To that he added $4,000, contributing $10,000 toward the new building. Money also flowed in from other sources, and work on the $24,000 church, to be romanesque in style and faced with veneer brick, was begun on June 28, 1928.[75] On November 25 Bishop Gerow, in the presence of a packed church, half of whose number were white, dedicated the building and preached the homily at the morning Mass. That afternoon he confirmed a class of 15 converts who had received their first communion earlier in the day.[76]

The flood was now behind them. Life at the mission would go on as usual.

Chapter XII Footnotes: The River's Rampage

1. *Mississippi Valley Flood Disaster of 1927*, Official Report of the Relief Operations (Washington, D.C., Date unknown).

2. Robert W. Harrison, *Levee Districts and Levee Buildings in Mississippi* (hereafter cited LD), United States Department of Agriculture, October, 1951; Newspaper clipping in *Greenville Chronicle*. No date.

3. Official Report, American National Red Cross, Washington, D.C.

4. LD, op. cit., 233 ff.

5. *Delta Democrat Times* (then called *Daily Democrat Times*), April 9, 1927.

6. Interview with Sister Gerasina Kneer, 1974. *In Memoriam*, Short Account of the Life and Death of Sister Ambrosine.

7. Ibid.

8. A Missionary Sister (possibly Sister Ambrosine), "Yesterday—Today—and Tomorrow," *The Mission Auxiliary*, Techny, October, 1927, Vol. 2 (hereafter cited "Yesterday . . . .")

9. DDT, April 13, 1927.

10. JDN, April 15, 1927, and April 17, 1927.

11. DDT, April 14, 1927.

12. Ibid.

13. JDN, April 17, 1927, and April 18, 1927.

14. GHC, April 21, 1927.

15. Ibid.

16. DDT, April 18 and 19, 1927.

17. Interview with Winchester Davis, December, 1970; DDT, April 21, 1927; JDN, April 21, 1927.

18. Interview with Sister Gerasina, op. cit.; *Monarch*, March, 1965 (School paper).

19. Greenville Rectory Archives, paper written by Jacobs, no date; DDT, April 21, 1927, op. cit.

20. LD, op cit.

21. Jacobs Report, op. cit.

22. Ibid; Interview with Gladys Clark.

23. Ibid.; GHC, April 21, 1927.

24. GHC, op. cit.

25. Jacobs Report, op. cit.; GHC, op. cit.

26. GHC, op. cit.

27. Jacobs Report, op. cit.; GHC, op. cit.; Gerasina, op. cit.

28. Jacobs Report, op. cit.; "Yesterday . . .," op. cit.; GHC, op. cit.

29. Jacobs, op. cit.; GHC, op. cit.

30. Ibid. *Flood of 1927* (Mississippi River Flood Control Assoc., C. 1927); *Mississippi Valley Flood Disaster of 1927*, Office Report of Relief Operation, Red Cross.

31. "Yesterday . . .," op. cit.; Gerasina, op. cit.

32. GHC, op: cit.

33. DDT, April 21 and 23, 1927; JDN, April 21, 1927.

34. Gerasina, op. cit.; *Flood of 1927*, op. cit.; DDT, April 23, op. cit.

35. "Yesterday . . .," op. cit.

36. Flood of 1927, op. cit., 62; *Vicksburg Evening Post*, Vol. 45, 1, April 23, 1927; DDT, April 24 and 26, 1927.

37. *Vicksburg Evening Post*, Vol. 45, April 23, 1927.

38. Ibid, also April 21, 1927.

39. Interview with Sister Desiderata, April, 1973; VI IC, April, 1927; Jacobs to Gerow, no date.

40. Desiderata, op. cit.

41. *Vicksburg Evening Post*, April 22 and 23, 1927.

42. Interview with Henry Floyd, August 20, 1974; *Vicksburg Evening Post*, op. cit.

43. Greenville Public Library, Video tape, *Library on 1927 Flood*.

44. Desiderata, op. cit.

45. Jacobs Report, op. cit.

46. Gerasina, op. cit.

47. Jacobs Report, op. cit.; Gerasina, op. cit.

48. Gerasina, op. cit.

49. Jacobs Report, op. cit.

50. Ibid.

51. Ibid.

52. Jacobs, op. cit.

53. Gerasina, op. cit.; "Yesterday . . . ."

54. JDN, April 27, 1927.

55. Jacobs, op. cit.; Gerasina, op. cit.

56. Cohn, op. cit.

57. Interview with Rev. Maurice Rousseve, undated.

58. Gerasina Report, op. cit.

59. Jacobs to Gerow, May 10, 1927.

60. Gerasina, op. cit.

61. "Yesterday . . .," op. cit; Jacobs, op. cit.

62. Jacobs Report, op. cit.

63. Fred D. Beneka, *Flood of 1927* (Mississippi River Flood Control Assoc., 1927).

64. Gerow Diary, 101, July 13, 1927.

65. NJ, Gerow to Jacobs, April 28 and August 23, 1927; Gerow to Jacobs, September 1, 1927; Jacobs to Gerow, June 16, 1927.

66. Jacobs, op. cit.; Gerow to Jacobs, April 28, 1927.

67. NJ, Jacobs to Gerow, July 10, 1927.

68. Gerasina, op. cit.

69. Jacobs to Gerow, August 30, 1927.

70. Interviews with Sister Liobina Schikora, January 6, 1970, and July 3, 1974.

71. Liobina, op. cit.

72. Ibid.

73. NJ, Gerow Diary, November 11, 1927.

74. Ibid., November 10 and 25, 1927.

75. NJ, Gerow to Jacobs, January 27, 1927.

76. NJ, Gerow Diary, 113, November 25, 1928; GHC, November 25, 1928.

St. Bartholomew School Orchestra, Little Rock, AR, 1934

CHAPTER XIII
Lean and Painful Septembers

On January 1, 1933, Bishop Gerow wrote in his diary:

*Few regret the passing of 1932. It has been an exceedingly hard year. Unemployment, poverty, distress, hunger and cold have brought unprecedented suffering to the people of our country; over and above this, during the last year, an epidemic of flu seems to have added to the general distress.... As to the State of Mississippi, an article in the **Literary Digest** of May 7, 1932, says: "One-fourth of the entire area of the state went under the auctioneers' hammers. That land included twenty percent of all farms and twelve to fifteen percent of all town property."*[1]

In 1932 the per capita income of people in Mississippi was $126; the state appropriation for public schools was $19.17 per child, and the teachers' salaries of $414 a year were less than it would have cost the state to keep them in charitable or penal institutions.[2] The schools were on the verge of collapse, and only a bold move could save them: over strong opposition from the business community, a bill, the first of its kind, was passed in the state legislature and signed into law on April 21, 1932, creating a two percent sales tax on all business transactions within the state. Netting $2,000,000 in its first year, it kept the public school system alive in Mississippi.[3]

The sisters' congregation was not spared in the economic crisis crippling the nation. Beset by debt incurred in the building of a new hospital in Waukegan, Illinois, which had opened in 1929, Sister Irenaea Gier, the Provincial, wrote a letter to the sisters acknowledging their good wishes, spiritual bouquets and prayers on the occasion of the forty-third anniversary of the congregation celebrated on December 8th, adding:

> *The good will, spirit of prayer and sacrifice manifested on this occasion is also very consoling and fills us with new courage to face the many and great problems and difficulties of the present time. It makes us look into the dark future with trust and confidence. An all-wise, all-knowing and loving Providence is at the bottom of present and future difficulties and troubles. Whatever He ordains cannot be to our destruction, provided that we keep close to Him and endeavor to give Him pleasure in all that we do and say . . . . As missionary sisters, we should not forget those who are still poorer than we are, but gladly go beyond the boundaries of our province and help them by our generous gifts of prayer and sacrifices, especially during this Christmas season.*[4]

There were now sixty Holy Spirit Missionary Sisters teaching in Mississippi and Arkansas in eight elementary schools and seven high schools.[5] In September 1929 the Sisters had accepted two more

226

schools in the state of Arkansas: St. Peter's in Pine Bluff and St. Augustine's in North Little Rock.

Beginning in 1887 with a two-story frame building that served both as chapel and school, St. Peter's was the oldest black parish in Arkansas. Throughout its long history, several communities of teaching sisters had staffed its school, and at one point the enrollment had reached 300. When the Holy Spirit Missionary Sisters came in 1929, the enrollment had dropped to around thirty and lay teachers were staffing the school.[6]

The industrial courses that had been offered at the school were dropped in favor of a regular eight-grade elementary curriculum when classes began on September 16, with forty-one pupils. Sister Heribalda Baalmann, who had taught at St. Mary's in Vicksburg from 1924 until her appointment to Pine Bluff, was placed in charge of the school. Despite the depression that affected most of the other mission schools, the enrollment rose rapidly and a high school was added in 1936.[7]

The second school accepted by the sisters, St. Augustine's in North Little Rock, was started in a renovated hall. The chapel was downstairs, the convent upstairs, and both doubled as classrooms for a few months until a separate structure was built for a school. Since there were no black Catholics in the area when Sister Inviolata Krueth and Sister Susanna Rivinius arrived on August 21, 1929, their first task was to visit families and encourage parents and guardians to send their children to them. As a result of their visits, fifty children registered for classes on the first day. Again the sisters hit the dusty roads, this time accompanied by the school children, who led them to other families who had children of school age, and another fifty pupils enrolled. With no books and with desks that had been culled from three different schools, classes began with Sister Susanna teaching the first three grades in the chapel and Sister Inviolata taking the remaining children upstairs to the convent. Although several children soon joined the Church, the mission was open four years before the first adult asked for baptism.[8]

The 1930's had started out well enough for the missions across the river in Mississippi. Sacred Heart School ended the 1929-1930 term with 435 pupils. Twenty-four children had been baptized; eleven had graduated from high school and thirty-two had graduated from eighth grade.[9] That summer the first two Catholic weddings were celebrated in the parish.[10] In September 1930 the school opened with 306 pupils, a slight drop from the year before, but the enrollment in high school—eighty-eight—was the highest the school had ever had. The mission had anticipated the increase of high school students and had added on another classroom and had hired a third teacher to the staff during the summer.[11]

As the depression worsened, however, many students could not afford even the low tuition charged by the schools, and the enrollments fell drastically.[12] The loss of students added to the sisters' woes because it depleted their means of livelihood since they depended upon the tuition for their twenty-dollar a month salaries. At St. Rose the total tuition dropped to $112 a month. At St. Joseph's the enrollment remained around 300 to 340. At Holy Ghost only three seniors graduated from high school in 1933. It was a bleak time for everyone.[13]

Many of the children who did come to school were hungry and had little to wear against the cold weather. In the middle of January, Sister Joan Liebhauser looked out the window at St. Joseph's where the children were waiting for the school bell to summon them inside for classes and saw a four-year-old girl standing on the cold cement pavement barefoot. Although there were no shoes for such a small child among the second hand clothing collected for the poor, Sister discovered a large pair of bedroom slippers and wrapped these around the child's feet, pinning the material securely so it would not slip off. The four-year-old was so delighted with her warm foot gear that she walked all the way home in them.[14]

To bring some relief to the poor and the unemployed, the government distributed food and clothing to the needy. In Greenville the sisters received large quantities of basic commodities such as flour and sugar to be used for the school children. Every morning Sister Liobina mixed large batches of dough for raised doughnuts. Every afternoon she and several high school girls, who were paid by the government, went to the high school building after classes, where they fried hundreds of doughnuts in deep fat and sprinkled them with sugar as they cooled on the table. The next morning they were given to the children at recess.[15]

Some of the money for helping the unemployed and poor in the city came from waiving ordinances forbidding movie houses to open on Sundays and allowing shows for charity. The proceeds from these benefit shows went for relief work.[16]

In Greenville the money was channeled toward hot lunches for the school children, the poor, and the unemployed. Hearing that the white schools were daily receiving hot soup from the city, the sisters filled in a request. As a result, Sacred Heart School was also allotted enough soup and bread for 60 to 75 children. Daily two high school boys walked to the police station for it and the sisters and high school girls served it to the neediest children as they sat at rudely-improvised tables in a free classroom.[17]

One Saturday evening a veritable mountain of golden grapefruit was unloaded on the rectory porch by truckers from out of state, who for some reason unknown to the sisters could not distribute it and did not want to take it back with them. Scarcely able to believe their good fortune, the missionaries were only too happy to distribute it to all who came for Sunday Mass on the following morning, giving everyone as much as he or she could carry.[18]

Besides food staples the government and the Red Cross also supplied bolts of cloth for dress-making, and the sisters who could sew spent many of their free hours making simple dresses for distribution by the Red Cross. The more skilled among the sisters could cut and sew a dress an evening.

In the city of Vicksburg distribution centers were set up in strategic places, and on appointed days the government dispensed cabbage, salt pork, potatoes, apples, grapefruit, and such items as coal to the people.[19] Since the city did not supply the school children with soup and bread as in Greenville, the sisters at St. Mary's hired a woman who sold bologna sandwiches to the children for three cents apiece.[20]

People were fortunate if they had a few chickens, a pig, or a small garden. Jack Robbins, a graduate of St. Mary's and owner of a funeral parlor, often bartered his eighteen-dollar coffins for farm produce. Not having money for services, especially in the outlying rural areas, the people would take the coffins home with them and bury their dead themselves.[21]

Jobless roamed the city, and a steady stream of men, often as many as thirty a day and most of them white, found their way to St. Mary's Convent to ask for food. The sisters had little to give them—a couple of slices of bread thinly spread with homemade fig jam or butter and a cup of weak coffee; but even this little was accepted gratefully.[22]

In Bay St. Louis, where black families were earning only about three dollars a week, the city relief committee generously supplied St. Rose School with a wholesome lunch of milk, fresh fruit, bread, meat and vegetables for 116 children.[23]

At Holy Ghost School in Jackson the sisters made a little extra money for the poor by holding a rummage sale in the rectory garage every Saturday.[24]

Although these were lean Septembers, the Sisters placed their trust in God, who was Father of all. Their faith and confidence did not go unnoticed by Bishop Gerow, who commented in his diary on October 9, 1933: "These Sisters of the Holy Spirit have an excellent religious spirit."[25]

Like the schools in Mississippi, St. Bartholomew's in Little Rock, Arkansas, was having enrollment problems. A beautiful new public school in the area had drawn many children away. This, coupled with unemployment and poverty caused by the depression, brought the enrollment down to a low of eighty-seven in September 1930. The high school had to be discontinued altogether for two years. When it was reopened, a grade was added each year.[26]

There were some bright spots for the mission, however. A new convent was built for the sisters in the summer of 1925. The mission also had a new church, a simple, white structure, framed by the lush, green foliage of silver poplar and maple trees. It presented such a picturesque sight that the art students from the public school made it the frequent subject of their sketches. In 1933 the church was the setting for the confirmation of seventy converts, the large number surprising many of the clergy who were present for the ceremony.[27]

On May 23, 1934, the event that the missionaries had been awaiting for over a decade took place in Bay St. Louis in the presence of more than 700 visitors. In an improvised, tastefully decorated outdoor chapel, the first four black priests of the Society of the Divine Word were ordained: Vincent Smith of Lebanon, Kentucky; Maurice Rousseve of New Orleans; Anthony Bourges of Lafayette, Louisiana; and Francis Wade of Washington, D.C. The ordaining bishop was Bishop Jules B. Jeanmard, Bishop of Lafayette.[28] His diocese of 60,000 black Catholics embraced more black Catholics than any other diocese of the United States; and he was confident that they would welcome the ministry of the newly ordained priests with open arms.[29]

Meanwhile, across the ocean a man named Adolph Hitler had moved into power in Germany, and in 1935 he declared that the Versailles Treaty no longer existed. He had begun to prepare his country to cast off the treaty's shackles, determined to humiliate and conquer the world which had imposed its mortifying terms upon the German people. The United States scarcely took notice of his morbid, torrential speeches, his aggressive anti-Jew, anti-intellectual, and anti-communist propaganda, simplistically thinking it could refrain from entering into another war by simply declining to become involved in foreign affairs. It waited, unprepared, while Hitler swept Austria, Czechoslovakia, Poland, and a host of other countries into his pocket and then turned on Great Britain.[30]

On December 7, 1941, Hitler, deeming that his war plans were on target and that the moment had come to launch the third phase of his grandiose scheme for world conquest, gave the nod, and Japan attacked the American Fleet at Pearl Harbor, sinking or putting out of action eight battleships, three cruisers, and three destroyers. A bewildered, shocked United States realized, too late, Hitler's far-reaching plans and hastily mobilized its forces for war.[31]

Color made no difference when the country called its able-bodied men into the Armed Forces, and Mississippi blacks, deprived of equal opportunities in jobs and education, served their country well, many laying down their lives for their homeland.

Decorated in red, white, and blue bunting, St. Rose's gym became the registration area for blacks in the Bay area.[32] One registrant, a grade school dropout from St. Rose, applied for service in the air force and dumbfounded the administrator who tested him with his high score. He was asked to take the test over because the administrator could not believe that a grade school dropout could make the score that he made. The young man obliged and did just as well the second time.

"You're one of those smart niggers," the administrator said contemptuously.

Angry, but not wanting to spoil his chances of being accepted, the young man controlled himself and gave a polite answer, "I didn't finish eighth grade, it's true, but I had good teachers," he said. The administrator grunted his acceptance.[33]

By February 1943 St. Rose had 25 young men in the army, three in the navy, four in the marines, one in the air force and several working in other defense-related jobs. Since there was no USO recreation center between Mobile, Alabama, and New Orleans, Louisiana, provided for the black divisions of the armed forces, the parish opened its gym to the men, and St. Augustine seminary offered its ball field, tennis courts, and swimming facilities.[34]

In Meridian the army had claimed a great number of students from St. Joseph's. By December 1942, except for five old men and a handful of high school students, all male members of the parish had been inducted into the army. In 1943 there were only nine high school graduates. The others were in the service, one having been called the day before his graduation.[35]

Two high school students at Sacred Heart completed their studies and received their diplomas while in the army.[36]

The school children participated in walk-to-school programs, scrap metal drives and victory clubs, and saved their pennies to purchase war bonds in the nation's all-out effort to end the war.[37]

As members of an international congregation, the sisters were experiencing the effect of the war on all fronts. About seventy percent of the Holy Spirit Missionary Sisters in Mississippi and Arkansas were from Germany and were living under the same roofs with their American, Polish, Czech, Dutch, and Austrian sisters, united in a common bond of love while their brothers and uncles and nephews were killing one another in a fruitless war of conquest. In their youth, some of the younger German sisters had been members of Hitler's Youth Movement, which had started out with organized learning and leadership development activities similar to the British-born Scout program, and they were appalled when its true purpose became manifest. As children of the same loving Father who wanted His sons and daughters to live in peace and harmony, the missionaries refrained from discussing the war and united in fervent prayer for its cessation, each one remembering her own loved ones in her heart.

The little country of Holland, the birthplace of the congregation, had tried to remain neutral, but in May 1941 the Germans swept across its border and invaded its towns, abetted by German spies, often long-time residents of the country, who had set up machine gun posts.[38] As a stern lesson to the rest of the world, the German Luftwaffe pounded the defenseless city of Rotterdam unmercifully, and within five days the little country surrendered.

On May 9, 1941, the German army moved into Steyl and appropriated an entire wing of the Mother House of the Holy Spirit Missionary Sisters as barracks for the soldiers and the spacious grounds for their drilling exercises. Night after night the frightened community and terrified civilians from neighboring villages who had fled to the sisters for protection hurried to air raid shelters and basement rooms in the opposite wing of the convent, while American

235

and English planes roared overhead, dropping deadly explosives in an effort to dislodge the enemy. After one such night, the chronicler wrote:

Es knatterte und ratterte, es summte und brummte, es blitzte und donnerte, es sauste und brauste. Es schien als ob alle boesen Geister am Werke seien in der Luft.

(There was such rattling and battling, whizzing and buzzing, lightning and thundering that the convent trembled and shook. It seemed as though all hell broke loose in the air.)

For four years the community lived with the enemy close to them, never knowing when death and destruction would rain down from the skies. Finally, on March 1, 1945, amidst a hail of bombs, anti-aircraft fire and grenades, the American and British fliers succeeded in routing the Germans from their redoubt. It took two more months before the German army in Holland surrendered to the Allied Forces and the community could return to normal and assess the damages done to the buildings.

By 1945 the war had enveloped the entire world, and where least expected, sisters of the congregation became casualties of fierce and bloody battles.

At Holy Ghost College in Manila, Sister Sebastiana Saar, her feet swollen from malnutrition, had become too ill to be carried in and out of the air-raid shelter when the bombs fell upon the city. The sisters made her as comfortable and as safe as possible by placing a bed in the basement hall of the convent where she died peacefully on April 4, 1945, at the age of 69. A quiet, prayerful religious, she had begun her mission life at St. Mary's in Vicksburg after violence had prevented the opening of a school in Merigold and had ended it in Manila amidst the violence of nations at war with one another.[39]

As the Americans and Japanese struggled for control of the Philippines, no one could predict which city was the safest on the bomb-ridden island of Luzon.[40] In Santo Tomas, a small town about thirty miles from Manila, the congregation conducted a kindergarten, elementary and high school. The eight sisters who were living there had built a dugout with seats carved along its sides and considered it to be reasonably safe in case of an air raid on the town. When conditions became more critical and food supplies more scarce at Holy Ghost College in Manila, the superiors assigned seven sisters to Santo Tomas to relieve the community in Manila as well as to secure better and safer living conditions for them. When the sisters from Manila joined the community in Santo Tomas in the autumn of 1944, they represented five nations—Germany, Austria, Czechoslovakia, Mexico, and the Philippines. Sometime during air raids on the town between March 16 and 19, 1945, a bomb made a direct hit on the dugout where the sisters had gone for shelter and all perished together instantly. Their deaths were but a shadow of what was happening in the larger world where the innocent blood of peoples of all nations was being spilled out in a senseless conflict that brought no one any good.

Even more tragic news for the Holy Spirit Missionary Sisters came from the remote islands of New Guinea in the South Seas.[41] Despite Japanese occupation of the islands, the missionaries—Protestant and Catholic—had been able to continue their work among the people along the coast. Their bush schools and hospitals remained open, and the work went on unhampered. The converts were comparatively new, without native priests and sisters, and depended upon their missionaries for religious guidance and strength. For this reason, the priests, brothers, sisters, and Protestant ministers declined an offer of the Australian government to take them away from the islands to the safety of Australia.

Little did the missionaries realize then what the future had in store for them. As the Japanese retreated before the advance of the American and Australian armies in March, 1943, they forced the missionaries and half-castes to go with them into their jungle hideout, thus cutting them off from all contact with their people. Among the prisoners were Sister Theophane Maier and Sister Ottonia Ruholl, both of whom had taught at schools in Mississippi. On February 5, 1944, the prisoners and their captors, 250 in all, boarded a Japanese warship bound for Hollandia. In early dawn, as the ship, unable to reach port in the cover of darkness, sailed in the open waters, it was sighted by American bombers who were unaware of the precious cargo aboard. In the strafing that followed, nine Protestant missionaries, seven half-castes, seven children, twenty-seven sisters, thirteen brothers, and seven priests were killed instantly. So gruesome was the mayhem on deck after the planes trailed off that those living half-wished they were dead themselves. Sister Theophane had been killed instantly. Sister Ottonia had the tip of her finger shot off. Forty of the missionaries were wounded so seriously that they died in the weeks following the strafing. Those who survived were forced to retreat into the jungle with their captors as the American planes continued to pursue them. Finally, realizing that there was no advantage in keeping the weakened, defenseless captives with them any longer, the Japanese soldiers took leave of them and fled for their lives. The weary, famished remnant of missionaries was found by astonished American soldiers on April 15, 1944.

After the war, new mission fields around the world would open for the Holy Spirit Missionary Sisters and the superiors would be hard pressed for personnel. The lives of those that had been lost would be keenly felt. Even the missions of Mississippi and Arkansas would experience a shortage of teaching sisters because of the deaths and the lack of vocations resulting from the war.

School children on back porches, Sr. Pauline, Sr. Otgera, Sr. Rosata, Sr. Dulcinea, St. Peters School, Pine Bluff, AR

Chapter XIII Footnotes: Lean and Painful Septembers

1. NJ, Gerow Diary, 212, January 1, 1933.

2. Richard Aubrey McLemore, ed., *A History of Mississippi*, Vol. II (Hattiesburg, 1973); Bishop, op. cit., Chapter 4.

3. Bishop, op. cit., Chapter 4.

4. PP, Irenaea Gier to Sisters, December 15, 1932.

5. "Statistics," *St. Augustine Messenger*, January, 1931; *Master's Work* (hereafter cited MW), house organ of the Paraclete Province, Vol. 3 (September, 1935).

6. "History of Pine Bluff," *St. Augustine Messenger*, August, 1940; Report by Sister Aelicia Hess, not dated; Telephone conversation, Spring, 1983.

7. Ibid.

8. Golden Jubilee booklet of St. Augustine Church, North Little Rock, October 21, 1979.

9. GHC, May 28, 1930.

10. Ibid.

11. SVD, Jacobs to Provincial, September 22, 1930.

12. GHC, September, 1931.

13. Bay St. Louis Rectory Archives, 1935; JHSC, May 29, 1933; Meridian School Records for 1934-35.

14. Sister Joan Liebhauser, "Meridian," MW, Vol. 1, January, 1933.

15. Gladys L. Clark, December 8, 1970, and Liobina, January 9, 1970.

16. *Vicksburg Evening Post*, 1932.

17. GHC, February 13, 1933, "Greenville," MW, Vol. 1, May-June, 1933.

18. Liobina, op. cit.

19. Ibid.; Interview with Jack Robbins, August 21, 1974.

20. Interview with Sister Desiderata Ramb, November 8, 1971.

21. Robbins, op. cit.

22. Liobina, op. cit.; Desiderata, op. cit.

23. Interview with Sister Matutina Holle, January 23, 1974; Bay St. Louis Rectory archives.

24. Interview with Dock and Alice Gordon, June 22, 1971.

25. NJ, Gerow Diary, op. cit. 228, October 9, 1933.

26. Aelicia, op. cit.

27. Ibid.; Sister Eulogia von Vondern, MW, Vol. 2, January, 1934.

28. NJ, Gerow Diary, op. cit., May 23, 1934; "St. Augustine," *Christian Family*, 357, September, 1936.

29. Ibid.

30. H. G. Wells, *The Outline of History*, 917, ff.

31. Ibid., 931.

32. Bay St. Louis House Chronicle, October 16, 1940.

33. *St. Augustine Messenger*, February, 1943; Interview with Ridgley Curry, May 4, 1970.

34. "USO," *St. Augustine Messenger*, September, 1942, and May 20, 1943.

35. Jacobs to Eckert, September 21, 1941, and December 7, 1942; Meridian School Chronicle, May 26, 1943.

36. GHC, May 23, 1943.

37. DAH, *Biennial Report of the Department of Education 1941-42 and 1942-43*; GHC, September, 1942 and October 5, 1942; January 31, 1945; Interview with Lillian Courtney.

38. PP, *A Detailed Account of Events in the Motherhouse during World War II 1940-45*, an unpublished manuscript translated from the German (November, 1945).

39. PP, *In Memoriam*; An account of Sister Sebastian Saar written after her death as an obituary.

40. PP, *Our Deceased Sisters* No. 43, "Our War Victims," A. Philippines; An unpublished manuscript by Sister Siglinde.

41. PP, *A Glorious Page in the Annals of the SSpS*, "My Captivity Experiences 1943-44," translated from the German, Techny, November 18, 1954.

CHAPTER XIV
Lush Septembers

Before 1900 more than ninety percent of all blacks in the United States lived in the South, and eighty percent of these were classified as rural dwellers. The first spectacular urbanization of blacks, brought about by the wartime prosperity in the North and the depressed cotton industry in the South, took place during the time of World War I. By 1920 thirty-four percent of the black population were urbanized, although eighty-five and two-tenths percent remained in the South. This trend continued through the 1930's and 40's as blacks left the plantations and migrated to the cities in ever increasing numbers.[1]

Illiterate parents and guardians saw education as something good and wanted their children to have it even though they didn't quite know what it meant.

"I'd see the kids coming home from school and I'd say, 'I sure hope my daughter would graduate,' " said one mother in Meridian who only learned to read herself when her daughter was in high school. "Didn't really know what graduation meant, but knew it would be good for mine."[2]

With the improvement in the economy and the expansion of the job market, money became more plentiful in the 1940's and people could afford to send their children to school. Since the schools staffed by the Holy Spirit Missionary Sisters were in the major urban areas of Mississippi and Arkansas, their enrollments mushroomed almost overnight.

In the fall of 1941 Holy Ghost School registered more than 500 students, the highest enrollment in its thirty-two year old history.[3] Fortunately, during the summer of 1940 a one-story high school had been put up across the street from the original two-story building. The grades in the elementary school had been separated, and the children in grades five through eight had spilled into the four rooms on the second floor vacated by the high school, leaving the ground floor to the first four grades.[4] By 1941 the high school was already too small to accommodate the ninety-two students that registered that year, and a sewing room was transformed into a classroom for forty-one freshmen, two-thirds of whom had never set foot into a Catholic school before. Sister Florence Henry, their homeroom teacher, was deeply impressed with their sincere appreciation for even the slightest personal attention she gave them in the classroom. Here were young people serious about their education and their future.[5]

In September 1942 the school registered 618 students.[6]

The same summer that Jackson put up its new high school, the pastor and students at Sacred Heart School razed their old high school building, being careful to save any materials that were reusable, and under the supervision of an inspector provided by the lumber company which supplemented the building materials, the boys built a new school. They mixed the concrete for the new foundations and steps and raised walls of tarred gypsum boards over the floor of the old gym. They transformed old doors into tables, and crates, cake boxes, old pipes, and bricks into equipment for a library, two classrooms and a recreation room. They installed gas heat in all of the classrooms and running water where needed, not forgetting the laboratory, where water was required for experiments. Many of the boys earned their tuition for the year by working on this project.[7]

With a registration of 556 pupils in September 1941, Sacred Heart School far exceeded any of its previous enrollments. Although an additional classroom had been made from an old storeroom, there still wasn't enough room to accommodate all who came. It seemed as if there was no end to the third grade pupils asking for admission to the school. At one point there were thirty more children than seats and still they kept coming. Lillian Cober, the second grade teacher, generously squeezed fifteen of them into her already crowded classroom, but others were reluctantly turned away.[8] In 1942, with the enrollment of 579, about 120 more children had to be refused admission.[9]

Every corner of every classroom was packed with pupils sitting on chairs and using apple boxes for their desks.[10] From their corner each morning, they kept a vigilant eye on the regular desks, and the first child to note a vacancy because of absenteeism slid quickly into the empty seat for that day.[11]

The sisters dreaded the sight of parents entering

their classrooms with two, three, and even six youngsters in tow, asking to have them enrolled in their respective grades. Sometimes parents cried openly.

"Yo' say, M'am, no room for my chile?"

"Ma'm, I'll gladly buy a chair for my son to bring to school, jus' let 'im stay."

But even if he brought a chair, where would he put it? That was the question. Some rooms were so crammed with chairs that they had to be pushed back or packed before the children could pass from the room.

One morning, as Sister Marie Jogues Coors remonstrated with a woman who wanted to enroll her son in her first grade, showing her the already overfilled classroom, the woman's eye caught sight of a step leading to the blackboard.

"Sit him down right hyere on this step," she cried triumphantly. "He don't go to any other school, but this hyere Catholic school. I wants him in this school." Sister bowed to her wishes.[12]

Meanwhile, Sister Petronia Biener, another first grade teacher, was having a similar problem in her room. As she was demonstrating to the mother that there was no room, the child squeezed into a seat with another boy, pulled out his tablet and began scribbling away as fast as he could. Finally, realizing that there really was no room, the mother sadly called her son, "Come, Jasper, there is no room for you."

The boy refused to budge and had to be forcefully removed by his mother.

"Why do them people chase me away from the school I like best?" he wailed as she pulled him from the classroom.[13]

246

One day after Sister DePazzi Zurowski had given the answer "No room," she heard sobs coming from under the classroom window. Upon investigating, she found Gayle, a child she had just turned away. But there was nothing Sister could do since the only places left in her classroom were the window sills and the teacher's desk. Three times that week, Gayle returned to the playground to ask the children if there wasn't an empty seat yet. The fourth time she came with her aunt. "Sistuh, you just have to do something. This chile hyere cries every morning and evening the kids come from school, and she just won't go to de public school, on account she wants to hear stories about Jesus, and she says she wants to be baptized in the Catholic religion, like her ma was."

What could the young sister do? She placed Gayle on the teacher's platform and gave her a box for a desk.[14]

In September 1943 St. Mary's School in Vicksburg began with 530 children and here, too, many had to be turned away for lack of room.[15] Some children were walking five and six miles one way in rain and shine to attend classes. Others, parents were driving into the city from twenty miles away. Some came in well-used cabs stuffed with bodies that spilled out on to the playground like the uncurling of a large snake once the doors swung open. One day a sister counted fourteen children unraveling from this mass of squeezed-in humanity. One family, whose only support was the meager wages of a father with a seasonal job, managed to send eight children to St. Mary's although it meant, in the words of the mother, "a tough time pulling."[16]

At St. Mary's the pupils were paying $1.00 a

month tuition in kindergarten; $1.10 in first grade, with an additional ten cents for each succeeding grade. The first year high students were paying $2.00 monthly tuition; the senior, $2.25.[17]

St. Joseph's in Meridian was having similar problems with enrollment.[18] In 1942 it reached the 500 mark, and in 1943 it rose to 560.[19] Of these, 58 students were in high school and 80 in kindergarten. Some sisters had 65-70 pupils in a room, and eventually children in the elementary school had to be turned away for lack of space.[20]

The kindergarten children were taught in a small six-room bungalow across the street from the convent. By 1944 the little house played host to 98 tots. Desks were made for them by placing two see-saw boards on apple boxes, and seats by resting boards between two chairs.[21]

At St. Rose School the classrooms were so overcrowded that children had to climb over each other to get to their places or be excused from the room. To reach a child who needed help, teachers had to walk sideways in the one narrow aisle that ran down the middle of the room. The situation was relieved somewhat when two classrooms were added to the gym.[22]

While it is true that the public schools for blacks in the cities were facing the same problems from overcrowding, as was shown in a report from Jackson, where the average teaching load was 63,[23] one may ask why black parents, many of whom were devout Baptists and did not want their children to join the Catholic Church, were so insistent on enrolling them in the mission schools. Although no study was actually made, the excellence of the teaching, the professionalism of the teachers could well be two important reasons. In his 1943-44 and 1944-45 biennial report, the state superintendant of schools reported that of the 6,547 black teachers in the public schools, only 600 were college graduates; 2,400 were high school trained and 3,547 (more than half) were less than high school graduates. Of the 3,737 black schools in Mississippi, 1,500 were housed in churches, tenant houses, and any other available building.[24] No one appeared to notice that the sisters were white, nor that the faculty was fully integrated, since, by this time, most of the mission schools were employing black lay teachers.

In an article for *The Master's Work*, a magazine published by the Holy Spirit Missionary Sisters, Sister Charitosa Klug wrote that she believed that parents were bringing their children to the mission schools because of the religious training and personal interest given to each child.[25]

Religion classes were an important part of the curriculum, and a four-year high school course of study had been approved by the state for credit toward graduation. Two units of credit could be granted from among the sixteen required for graduation, or four if the school required eighteen credit units for graduation. The first year course centered on the Fatherhood of God, trust in and cooperation with Him as Father; the second year dwelt on spiritualized interpretation of the material environment and the reality of the sacraments; the third year concentrated on Christ and His mother as models for imitation; and the fourth year, Christlikeness as demonstrated by showing concern for the poor, sick, and elderly.[26]

Works of charity toward the poor were encouraged and, as a result, the students became frequent visitors at the hospitals and county homes in the area, where they sang and talked and prayed with the people and gave out fruit, candy, cookies, and small gifts bought with money donated by themselves. They also participated in drives for the Bishops' Relief, the Red Cross, March of Dimes, and European Relief.[27]

A number of these students in the 1940's were children of former pupils or graduates of the mission schools who had found good-paying jobs and were becoming lower middle class. At one time they had gratefully accepted food and second-hand clothing from the sisters. Now they were able to help others less fortunate than they themselves.

A sister at St. Mary's wrote to Techny in 1940:

How conditions have improved! Parents, non-Catholic as well as Catholic, dress their children who are receiving their first communion or being confirmed in white. Formerly, the mission had to provide the entire communion and confirmation outfits. Furthermore, in the majority of cases of children receiving these sacraments, one or both parents are Catholic. Among those confirmed this spring were several mothers whose children were likewise receiving the sacrament.[28]

Not only were the mission schools prospering in the 1940's, but church life was also flourishing. Week-long missions given by the newly-ordained Divine Word Fathers were well received.[29] The churches were crowded on feastdays and on other special days of the year like Thanksgiving.[30] The choirs were singing two-part Latin Masses, Latin songs such as *Transeamus*, and three-part Christmas carols.[31] Baptisms were many. At Sacred Heart Church as many as 26 were baptized on Easter Sunday in 1943.[32] Of the fifteen high school graduates at Holy Ghost School, eleven were Catholics.[33] Of the 456 pupils in school, 169 were members of the Church.[34]

The people, especially the children, became apostles and spoke to others about the Church or encouraged the sisters to visit their relatives who were ill or dying. A fifteen-year-old boy talked to an older brother who was near death and convinced him to call a priest and receive baptism.[35] A servant girl was responsible for the conversion of the seriously ill daughter of her employer. The twelve-year-old girl had noticed the servant studying her catechism and had asked to see it. She was captivated by the prayers and she memorized them and prayed them frequently. When the servant girl was baptized, the sick girl asked her parents, devout Baptists, to let her be baptized in the Catholic Church also. Shocked by their daughter's request, the parents at first refused; but as the child persisted and her death seemed imminent, they finally gave their consent. After the baptism, the two girls embraced each other. The next day the girl died as the servant knelt at her bedside praying and weeping, more for joy that her friend had been baptized a Catholic than from sorrow.[36]

Vocations were also appearing among the students. Two sisters from Bay St. Louis who had attended St. Rose School joined the Sisters of the Holy Family in New Orleans: Marie Hazeur became Sister Mary Rose de Lima and Felice Hazeur became Sister Mary Bertille. Sister Mary Rose was later elected the Mother General of her congregation.[37] Maxine Williams, also a graduate of St. Rose, was ordained a Divine Word priest in 1941,[38] and Herman Porter, a

251

member of Sacred Heart Church, Greenville, was ordained a priest of the Sacred Heart. He was a graduate of Coleman High and a close friend of the Millers. Daisy Miller Greene had taught him English in high school.[39]

The Holy Spirit Missionary Sisters did not accept black women into their congregation until 1946.[40] The congregation was founded as a foreign missionary community, and any woman asking to join it had to have a vocation for foreign missionary work. The sisters in Mississippi and Arkansas had been working with first and second generation Catholics who could hardly be expected to go abroad and preach the gospel. Rather than accept these newly formed Catholics into their congregation, it seemed better to encourage them to enter an order that was dedicated to the work at home.[41] There were several religious communities open to black women in the United States. Some were started for and by black women. Vocation directors of these communities were welcomed at the mission schools and given opportunities to talk to the girls about religious life.

In 1949 Bishop Gerow celebrated his silver jubilee as bishop of the diocese. According to an October edition of *Catholic Action of the South*, the Catholic population of the diocese had increased about fifty percent during the quarter century he was bishop, with the greater increase among blacks. Their number had increased by sixty percent. In 1924 there were 31,387 white Catholics in the diocese as compared to 48,103 in 1949, and 3,478 black Catholics in 1924 as compared to 5,407 in 1949.[42]

Of the twenty-three churches for blacks, nine were under the care of the Josephites, nine under the

Divine Word Fathers, and five under the Missionaries of the Most Holy Trinity. Schools were staffed by sisters of nine communities: fifty-one Holy Spirit Missionary Sisters, twenty-one Holy Ghost Sisters, eight Blessed Sacrament Sisters, four Sisters of Charity, twelve Franciscans, four Ursulines, four Franciscans of Perpetual Adoration, three Franciscans Regular, and two Missionary Servants of the Most Blessed Trinity.[43]

On the day of Bishop Gerow's jubilee celebration in Jackson, Sister Leonardine, the principal at Holy Ghost School, dismissed the children early because Samuel Cardinal Stritch was scheduled to address the people from the balcony of the chancery in the morning and she thought it would be good for the students to be present for this special event. Shortly after the talk, she was dismayed to find the Cardinal, Archbishop Moses Kiley of Milwaukee, and Bishop Gerow appear at the convent door asking to visit the classes. Upon learning that the children had been dismissed for the day in the bishop's honor, the three prelates spent the time with the sisters and then talked with a few stray children whom they found on the playground, offering them medals blessed by the Pope.[44]

Despite their heavy classloads, the sisters continued to visit the sick and elderly, encouraging people to receive the sacraments, to return to the Church if they had strayed or to accept the faith if they were not Catholic.

In Jackson Sister Florence visited a gray-haired, semi-paralyzed man who told her that he had been wanting to be baptized since he was fourteen. Sister began at once to give him instructions in his one-room hut. But this wasn't enough for him. One Sunday morning he surprised the congregation by appearing at the church door. He had dragged himself to church by holding on to his chair. When the chair slipped from his grasp, he would, as he put it, "hit the ground." But he was full of joy as one of the boys helped him up the steps and into church.[45]

Sometimes it seemed that God directed the sisters' steps in mysterious ways. Sister Pudentia Tschiderer missed one of her pupils at St. Mary's for a few days and learned that he was in the hospital for appendicitis and was asking for her. Knowing that the boy was an orphan, Sister expected him to be in Charity Hospital. But when she went there, he was not listed as a patient. As she was about to leave, a doctor met her and invited her to see a boy who had run into a tree with his bicycle and was in a dying condition. To Sister Pudentia's surprise, he was one of her previous year's pupils. She remembered him saying to her, "I'se nevah been taught how to pray befo'; nobody at mah home evah sed a pray'r. But since ah'se learned how to pray, ah loves it; but mos' of all ah loves de Hail Mary."

Recalling his love for the Hail Mary, Sister believed that it was Mary who had directed her steps to Charity Hospital that day. The doctor handed her a glass of water and a towel, saying, "Baptize him, Sister; he cannot live." The boy died that same day.[46]

Others who were ill called for the sisters through friends, school children, and relatives. The sisters would prepare them for baptism and when they were ready Father would administer the sacraments to them.

One day the sisters at Holy Ghost Convent received a written message from a woman who was ill and about to undergo surgery. She was not a Catholic, but often attended Mass, she said. For some years she also worked for a Catholic family and admired their good religious spirit. But most of all, she told the sisters, she owed her desire for baptism to her dead baby:

Last night, my dead baby appeared to me in my dream and said: "Mama, you must be baptized when you want to go to heaven." The baby wasn't my child. She came to me on a cold winter morning, very early. Her mother knocked at my door, and when I saw the two children she held by the hand, shivering with cold, I bade them come in. She begged me to take the girl, who had a slight deformity, since she wasn't able to support her. She was going to give the boy to some other person. I accepted the child whose large, beautiful eyes wandered to the fire in the stove and then to the breakfast on the table. I sent her to the kindergarten of the sisters, where I knew she would learn well. From the first day she repeated to me whatever she learned in class, especially about Jesus and the Blessed Mother. Every afternoon I learned something new from her, and then she taught me the lesson that made me call you Sisters today. "Sister told us that we must be baptized when we want to go to heaven. Mama, please, may I be baptized?" I needed time to think this over. In the meantime, I had saved enough money for an operation to have her deformity straightened. On the way to the hospital, she asked again for baptism, and I assured her she could be baptized; but she died before the operation was begun. Now she appeared to me in a dream repeating her words.

The sisters reassured her that they would be back

to begin her instructions.[47]

In Jackson, Sister John Hemesath regularly visited a 94-year-old former slave known as Aunt Lucy to see that she wanted for nothing. On one of the early visits the woman told the nun quite emphatically, "I've been here a heap of years, and I could never change my belief."

"I'm not asking you to," Sister replied, "but if you change your mind, let me know."

One day, Sister John received word through a neighbor that Aunt Lucy wanted to see her.

The woman smiled when Sister came into the house.

"Are you sick?"

"No, I'm not sick. I called you to tell you that I want to become a Catholic."

Sister began the instructions, and by the time Aunt Lucy was ready to receive the sacraments of Baptism, Holy Eucharist, and Reconciliation, she had fallen and seriously injured herself, and so she received the Sacrament of the Anointing of the Sick as well. After a slow recovery, she said that she had one more desire and that was to attend Mass "just once." This was arranged for her on Pentecost Sunday. As Aunt Lucy watched the priest at the altar during the celebration of the Mass, tears of joy streamed unashamedly down her worn face. She had come home, and it felt so good.[48]

Often in their visits to the sick, the sisters found deplorable conditions. According to the 1960 census, in the country as a whole, 18.8 percent of all dwellings were "dilapidated or lacking plumbing facilities." The percentages were 49.2% in Mississippi and 44.9% in Arkansas. In the cities the sisters found such dilapidated shacks, and inside a sick child or mother lying on rags and covered with an old coat, sometimes one that the sisters themselves had given them earlier. The homes might have a single chair, a stove, and a table in a room whose walls and ceilings were black and peeling, scarcely seen in the dim light coming through a single small window. Through their visits the sisters were able to help many sick and dying to receive admittance into the charity hospital or county home.

The sisters found similar conditions on the plantations surrounding the cities, often an eight-hour walk through miles and miles of cotton fields on narrow, dusty, or muddy roads depending upon the season.[49]

When Sister Meline Karasz visited a parishioner in Greenville who was very ill and living a long distance from the convent, she saw a "For Rent" sign on the post outside the woman's door. Entering, she found the poor old woman lying in bed in a cold, bare room with no one to look after her. She explained that the "For Rent" sign was there because she hadn't been able to pick cotton and pay her $1.50 a week rent for the two-room shack. A wall was missing on one side of the house, exposing the room that she called her kitchen to the inclement weather. It was no wonder that she had contracted a severe cold and complications had set in. Sister Meline made her as comfortable as possible and later was instrumental in having her moved to better surroundings where she soon recovered her health.[50]

People who had been slaves often found their freedom more deplorable than their bondage, especially those who had been house servants. This was the case of Lillie's grandmother, who lived with the child and the child's mother in a two-room shanty on the outskirts of the city of Meridian. On a cold, damp day in November on the way to visit them, the sisters walked through mud that was sometimes over their ankles. They found Granny sitting before a fireplace void of fire, writhing with rheumatic pains. Lillie was not home, but was out looking for wood to start a fire. When the sisters inquired about Lillie's mother, the woman pointed with a deep groan toward the other room. The sisters went in and found a corpse of a young woman, a pool of water caused by a leak in the roof beside her bed. Although the girl had told her grandmother that her mother didn't answer and was very cold, the grandmother was too weak to get up and see.

As the sisters spoke to the grandmother, she punctuated her conversation with lamentations and sighs for the days of slavery when the master and the lady of the house had been father and mother to her. She had never known a day of want in her life until she was given her freedom. After the funeral the grandmother was placed in the county home and Lillie was sent to live with relatives.[51]

The sisters did not neglect to visit the county and city jails. Occasionally, they were grieved to find a former pupil there. One day Sister Desiderata heard that a young Vicksburg man whom she had taught in kindergarten was condemned to death. When she visited him in jail, it was a sad encounter for both teacher and pupil.

"Is this the way I find you?" she asked, disappointment seeping through her voice. Tears came into the youth's eyes as he hung his head in shame.

Sister kept in frequent touch with him until the day of his execution, encouraging him to turn to the Lord.[52]

One day while stopping by the women's ward to talk to a woman who was being held for killing her husband, Sister Desiderata and her companion, Sister Jucunda Kuettinger, a high school teacher at St. Mary's, spoke to another woman in the ward who was watching them curiously.

"What did *you* do?" asked Sister Desiderata. The woman's powerful frame seemed to shrink the slight form of the little missionary.

"I killed somebody," the woman answered simply, adding when asked that her name was Mildred. She had been condemned to die in the electric chair, she said; but her case was being appealed to the Mississippi Supreme Court.

Sister spoke a few words to her about God's enduring love and invited her to be sorry for her sins and ask God for His pardon and mercy.

Her words met with a mute response. At home the two sisters couldn't stop thinking about the woman and asked the other members of the community to join them in a novena to St. Jude. Soon after the novena ended, the telephone rang. It was a message from Mildred, who wanted the little "low" sister to tell her more about her religion.[53] From then on Sister Desiderata visited her weekly and gave her instructions.

The other three women in the ward, one of them a juvenile, also listened to the lessons as Sister Desiderata and Mildred went through the main truths of the Catholic faith. Sister Desiderata taught them the Memorare, and Mildred developed a special love for it. Sister also left her a book of prayers.

At first Mildred had some hope that her sentence would be changed. She had been found guilty of brutally beating her 70-year-old landlady to death.[54]

The woman lived alone in a rambling house set back in the yard and hidden by shrubbery and magnolia trees in the area where Vicksburg High School now stands. Mildred had gone to the house in the evening of May 25 on the pretext of paying her rent. She handed her landlady a twenty-dollar bill, and when the woman brought in her money to make change, the attacker picked up a walking stick and struck her on the head. The elderly woman fell across her bed, begging for her life.

"Please, don't kill me. Take the little money I have, but spare my life."

But Mildred picked up the fire poker and a pair of tongs and beat the defenseless woman to death. Her clothes spattered with the victim's blood, she grabbed the money and went to a tavern where she became drunk and began talking about the murder.[55]

Her trial had been held in July, and Mildred was sentenced to die in the electric chair on September 17, 1943; but her case had been appealed to the Mississippi Supreme Court. On April 10, 1944, the lower court's decision was upheld and a new execution date was set for May 19.[56] Mildred resigned herself to her death, accepting it as a penance for her sins, especially for the murder of her landlady.[57]

"You're 33, just as old as Our Lord was when He died," Sister Desiderata told her one day when they were discussing the Passion of Christ.

"If I knew before what I know now," Mildred said, "I wouldn't have been that way. But I had nothing.

My father drank and my mother drank. Everybody drank, and so I drank, too.''[58]

As Mildred's baptismal day approached, the sisters discussed her baptismal dress. Since she was such a large woman, it wasn't going to be easy for them to find a dress to fit her. Sister Amantia Schulien solved their dilemma by offering to sew the dress, and Sister Desiderata chose a spring color, a pastel green gingham, to which were added a few touches of lace. The little missionary thought her protegee looked beautiful for her baptism, the lovely green dress matching her gentle repentant disposition. Father Robert O'Leary, pastor of St. Mary's, baptized her the day before her execution, with Sister Desiderata serving as her godmother.[59]

A middle-aged man was to follow Mildred to the electric chair. Waiving the custom of having the deaths take place at 12 midnight, the sheriff changed the time to early morning to make it easier for the two sisters to be present with Mildred to the end.[60]

This was also the newly-baptized Christian's first communion day, her first encounter with her God under the forms of bread and wine. Sister Desiderata and Sister Jucunda went with Father O'Leary early enough to conduct the communion service and have time for prayer.

When they arrived at the jail, light was pouring from every window, giving an impression of celebration rather than sorrow. The sisters walked into the ward where Mildred, her head shaven, was in the process of dressing. She appeared calm and greeted her visitors with a smile.[61]

"Father is here and brings you Jesus," Sister Desiderata told her. "Hurry."

While Sister Desiderata helped her with the finishing touches of her toilette, Sister Jucunda opened the suitcase they had brought with them and laid out altar linens, a crucifix, and two candles which she lighted. The other women in the ward were up, too, and sitting on their beds. No one spoke. When Mildred was ready, she took a place on the bench with the sisters and all began to pray. Since all knew the Our Father and the Memorare, they recited these prayers together.[62]

When Father O'Leary came in with the Sacred Host and laid it on the table, they knelt on the hard floor of the cell. But noticing that Mildred appeared strained, Sister motioned her to sit. The condemned woman was very quiet and devout, following the priest's actions with reverence and devotion.[63]

After communion the group made a thanksgiving together. Then for a quarter of an hour they sat in silence, each one praying in her own words. There was a solemn stillness in the ward. Mildred kept her eyes on the crucifix that she held tightly in her hands. Shortly before four o'clock they began to pray for the dying.

May Christ Jesus, who was crucified for you, deliver you from torments. May He deliver you from everlasting death, who died for you. May Christ, the Son of the living God, give you a home in the never-fading garden of His heights, and may He, the true Shepherd, count you as one of His flock. May He absolve you from all your sins and place you at His right hand in the midst of His elect. May you have the joy of seeing your Redeemer face to face; of standing forever in enraptured vision before Him, who is the Truth made manifest. And thus, happily numbered among the spirits of the blessed, may you enjoy the sweetness of God's love forever and ever. Amen.

As the prayers ended, the big steel doors swung open.[64] At the sight Mildred panicked and grasped the frail frame of the missionary by the arm, but quickly composed herself again.[65] They rose from the bench and began the march of death, first the officers of the jail, then Father O'Leary praying aloud, then Mildred with Sister Desiderata.[66] The convicted woman had told Sister all about the chair. She knew what was going to happen, she said. Three volumes would be pumped into her body; then it would be over, and she would be dead.[67]

At the door of the execution chamber the warden informed Sister that this was as far as she could go. Mildred said good-bye to her, smiled, and thanked her again for all that she had done for her.

"I hope to see you again in heaven," Mildred told her.

Then unaided she walked to the chair and sat down. When they fastened the straps around her waist, she asked that they be moved slightly because they were pinching her.[68]

Suddenly an attendant rushed over to Sister Desiderata.

"Does she have any medals on?" he asked.

Sister Desiderata called to Mildred, "Mildred, do you have your medal on?"

"No, Sister. I took it off," she answered. These were her last words.[69]

As they prepared to place the death cap and eye guards over her shaven head, she smiled faintly at the priest who was praying beside her, then settled back into her chair to await the first shock which was applied at 4:14, followed by a second and final one at 4:16½. Mildred gave only one quick start as the current hit her for the first time, and then her body slumped slightly down into the chair. She was pronounced dead by Dr. A. J. Podesta, the official county physician, who told the sisters afterwards that she still had a smile on her face.[70]

Mildred's execution was followed by that of the middle-aged white man who had been convicted of slaying a deputy sheriff. He, too, was very calm and professed his faith in Christ before the death cap and eye guards were placed on him.[71]

Mildred's body was placed in a plain wooden box, a little too small for her huge frame. When the lid was closed, a part of her pastel green dress hung out along the side, a sign of her eternal spring that would never end.[72]

For almost forty years the missions in Mississippi and Arkansas had received priority status by the American province of the congregation. Probably not more than twenty to twenty-five American sisters had been assigned to the foreign missions during this period. Now, however, mission fields were opening to the Holy Spirit Missionary Sisters in Ghana (West Africa) and Australia, both English-speaking territories, and the Mother General of the congregation was looking to the United States for sisters. It was difficult for the American provincial, Sister Margarethis Bischopink, to break this news to Rev. Joseph Eckert, the provincial of the Society of the Divine Word. In a letter dated December 7, 1944, but not sent until January 4 in order not to spoil his Christmas, she wrote that her council was considering withdrawing the sisters from the three missions in

Arkansas. She quoted from a letter from the Mother General of the congregation, reminding her that the congregation was founded for foreign mission work:

It would be better to limit your activities in your province in order to send more sisters into the missions.

Sister Margarethis continued:

Yesterday, I received another letter from Mother General, exhorting the council to do all within our power for the African mission. She wrote: "The number of sisters needed by Msgr. Adolph Noser (Ghana) is thirty-one: fifteen for teaching, four for medical work, and twelve for social work and evangelization."

Then, there is an urgent request for American sisters on the part of the Apostolic Delegate in Australia, who wants our congregation to establish a novitiate there soon.

By the time she sent the letter off on January 4, she had received a cable from Australia:

Needed urgently fifteen American Sisters.

She also suggested the hiring of more lay teachers in order to keep the schools open in Arkansas.[73]

In his reply the priest admitted to his distress upon reading her letter; but, since he shared the same missionary goals as she, he suggested that they sit down together and discuss the problem. He didn't think the sisters should withdraw from Arkansas, but by using one or two more lay teachers in each of the schools, perhaps enough sisters could be freed for the foreign missions. "Do not worry too much about it," he replied to Sister Margarethis.[74]

There was no longer any possibility of the congregation's accepting additional missions in Mississippi. In 1945, when the sisters were approached about staffing a new school to be opened in West Jackson, the superiors reluctantly turned it down.[75]

Bishop Gerow was very understanding, and on August 19 he wrote to Sister Margarethis:

Father Eckert has just written to me telling me that you have written to him and definitely stated that it will not be possible for you to take the West Jackson school. I appreciate the difficulties under which you are laboring, particularly in view of the fact that you are being called upon to furnish a large number of missionaries for war-stricken countries.

Your sisters in this diocese have worked hard and faithfully in the various schools in which they have been teaching, and I have always admired their fine religious spirit. It is really a sort of spiritual tonic to me to visit these sisters.[76]

It was a very difficult time for the superiors of the congregation because not all were as understanding as the provincial of the Divine Word Society and the bishop of the diocese. When the first German sisters came to the United States in 1901, the country was considered by Rome to be a mission territory. This was not the case in the 1940's, and American sisters, who had entered the congregation for foreign mission work, were becoming restless. When the provincial asked for volunteers for the missions in Ghana and Australia, her desk was buried under letters.[77] But there were others who thought the work in Mississippi was not finished and still deserved priority treatment from the American province.

Chapter XIV Footnotes: Lush Septembers

1. *Americana Encyclopedia*, Vol. 20, 1972.

2. Interview with Polly Heidelberg, May 21, 1970.

3. Sister Florence Henry, "Holy Ghost School," MW, January, 1942, Vol. 10, No. 1.

4. JHSC, May 29, 1940.

5. Florence, op. cit. ·

6. JHSC, September 18, 1942.

7. Florence, op. cit.; Greenville Rectory files: Virden Lumber Company to Rev. Richard Lyons, November 8, 1939.

8. GHC, September 15, 1941.

9. Ibid., November, 1942.

10. Sister Marie Jogues Coors, "Greenville," MW, 10, February, 1942.

11. GHC, November, 1942.

12. Jogues, op. cit.

13. Sister Joanna Latz, "Greenville," MW, 11, January, 1943.

14. Sister DePazzi Zurowski, "Greenville," MW, 11, December, 1943.

15. SVD, Rev. Francis Tetzlaf to Rev. Joseph Eckert, December 3, 1943.

16. Sister Charitosa Klug, "Vicksburg," MW, 9, October, 1941.

17. Meridian School Chronicle, September 13, 1945. There was an effort to unify the tuition in all the schools.

18. MHC, October, 1941.

19. SVD, Rev. Anthony Jacobs to his Provincial, October 25, 1942; Rev. John Gasper to Eckert, September 26, 1943.

20. Gasper to Eckert, op. cit.; MHC, September 11, 1944.

21. Sister Maris Stella Carr, "Vicksburg," MW, 12, November, 1944.

22. Sister Cherubina Kruchen, note written in 1974.

23. Two papers in vertical file in the Department of Education, Jackson.

24. *Biennial Report 1943-44 and 1944 and 1945*, 21.

25. Charitosa, op. cit.

26. Rev. Geoffrey O'Connell, Superintendent of Diocesan Schools, to Jacobs, October 22, 1941.

27. Sister Joanna Latz, "Greenville," MW, 10, June, 1942; Sister Elaine LeBeau, "Vicksburg," MW, 12, January, 1944; Meridian School Record Book 1922.

28. Sister Rosette Kubicki, "Vicksburg," MW, 8, September, 1940.

29. Sister Florence Henry, "Greenville," MW, 6, June, 1938; Sister Michaeline Willsch, "Vicksburg," MW, 8, June, 1940.

30. SVD, Rev. Theodore Koeller to Provincial, November 27, 1942.

31. GHC, December 25, 1940.

32. SVD, Eckert to Koeller, January 25, 1943.

33. JHSC, June 19, 1942.

34. Ibid.

35. Sister Florence Henry, "Greenville," MW, 8, September, 1940.

36. Sister Eleanore, "Jackson," MW, 9, May, 1941.

37. Bay House Chronicle, September 8, 1942, and March 19, 1943; Interview with Sister Matutina Holle, January 24, 1970.

38. Matutina, op. cit.; Bay St. Louis Chronicle, January 12, 1941.

39. Greenville High School Monarch, March, 1966; GHC, June 29, 1947; St. Augustine Messenger, September, 1947; Interview with Greene, December 5, 1970.

40. Bernardine to Sisters, Feast of St. Augustine, 1946.

41. JHSC, February 21, 1949.

42. Catholic Action of the South, Mississippi Today, October 13, 1949.

43. "Rev. Oliver Gerow," St. Augustine Messenger, October, 1949.

44. JHSC, October 19, 1949.

45. Sister Florence Henry, "Jackson," MW, 1, July, 1933.

46. Sister Pudentia Tschiderer, "Vicksburg," MW, 12, February, 1944.

47. Sister Dulcinea Mrasz, "Jackson," MW, 13, April, 1945.

48. Sister John Hemesath, "Jackson," MW, 17, October, 1949.

49. Sister Joan Liebhauser, "Bay St. Louis," MW, 8, April 1940; Sister Jucunda Kuettingen, "Vicksburg," MW, 12, January, 1944; Interview with Sister Desiderata Ramb, January 20, 1970.

50. Sister Meline Karasz, "Greenville," MW, 9, April, 1941.

51. Sister Elaine LeBeau, "Meridian," MW, 9, February, 1941.

52. Interview with Sister Desiderata Ramb, April, 1973.

53. Ibid.

54. VHC, An insert in 1944.

55. "Funeral of Annie Laurie Conkline," *Vicksburg Evening Post*, No. 125, May 26, 1943, and No. 126, May 27, 1954, front page.

56. Warren County Attorney Chancery, County Courthouse in Vicksburg; Johnson v. State, No. 35467, April 10, 1944; Vicksburg Public Library, *Vicksburg Evening Post*, No. 176, 1, July 31, 1943.

57. VHC, insert.

58. Desiderata, April, 1973.

59. Ibid.

60. Ibid.

61. VHC, op. cit.

62. Desiderata, op. cit.

63. Ibid.

64. VHC, op. cit.

65. Desiderata, op. cit.

66. VHC, op. cit.

67. Desiderata, op. cit.

68. Public Library, *Vicksburg Evening Post*, No. 120, May 19, 1944.

69. Ibid.

70. Ibid.

71. Ibid.

72. Desiderata, op. cit.

73. SVD, Sister Margarethis Bischopink to Rev. Joseph Eckert, December 7, 1944.

74. Eckert to Margarethis, January 10, 1945.

75. SVD, Folder, SSpS; Margarethis to Eckert (Joseph), August 24, 1945.

76. NJ, Gerow Diary, Vol. III, 665, 1942-48; Gerow to Margarethis, August 29, 1945.

77. PP, Margarethis to Sisters, January 18, 1945.

CHAPTER XV
Into the Diocesan Mainstream

From 1937 until 1950 Msgr. Geoffrey O'Connell, a pastor residing in Clarksdale and later in Biloxi, one of the largest parishes in the diocese, was head of the Catholic school office for the diocese of Jackson. Each school was an independent unit, its pastor and principal (often the same person) making all decisions and rules regarding school policies.[1]

In 1950 Msgr. O'Connell was given an assistant, Rev. Joseph Koury. The office of education was centralized in Jackson and a diocesan school board was named to serve in an advisory capacity to the bishop. The board's principal function was to meet once, sometimes twice, a year with the bishop and the superintendent to hear a report on the state of the diocesan school system and to offer criticism or suggestions for improvement.[2]

On May 2, 1950, the board, composed of eight priests of the diocese, one of them Msgr. Joseph B. Brunini, a native son of Vicksburg and the future bishop of the Jackson diocese; a visitor, Msgr. Leo

Byrnes, superintendent of schools in the diocese of Mobile, Alabama; Msgr. O'Connell and Bishop Gerow met with S. A. Brasfield, supervisor of Mississippi public high schools, and Clyde McKee, supervisor of Mississippi public elementary schools. At the meeting the two public school supervisors presented a brief history on the accreditation of schools in Mississippi.[3]

Brasfield told the assembled priests:

Prior to 1912 there was no accrediting agency for the Mississippi school system, and students entered college only by examination. Then James C. Fant of the University of Mississippi visited the high schools in the state and drew up a list of schools whose graduates would not be required to take a college entrance examination to enter the university. Other colleges soon accepted this list.

Brasfield went on to explain that in 1918 Fant persuaded the Mississippi Education Association, which had no connection with the state, to form an accrediting commission composed of representatives from each college and superintendents from selected public schools.

In 1919 the state appointed a high school supervisor who was invited by the accrediting commission to serve as its secretary. Thus the State Department of Education became associated with the commission although these two institutions remained distinct from one another. Membership in the accrediting commission was entirely voluntary.

"A college can accept students from a non-accredited school, but de facto they do not," Brasfield said.

In 1932 the commission required that a high school

have an average daily attendance of fifty students, and for grades nine through twelve, a minimum of three teachers. In September 1950 the number of high school students in average daily attendance was raised to sixty. Although the standards had been on the books for almost twenty years, the commission had only begun to enforce them in the last four, resulting in about seventy public high schools losing their accreditation on the point of insufficient enrollment alone. While never actually voted on by the commission, in practice parochial schools were classified as isolated schools in which an enrollment of only thirty pupils in average daily attendance was required. Only if two parochial schools were located within the same territory were they not to be treated as isolated schools.

Brasfield then pointed out that the commission had not borne down on the parochial and mission high schools as they had on the public schools. The deficiency, for example, of having a teacher who was teaching in three fields was pointed out; but nothing else was done about it. There was also an unusually large number of teachers in the parochial high schools who did not have the required number of credit hours in the subjects they were teaching. He said:

> We expect three out of four of your high school teachers to be graduates of standard colleges and to have twenty-seven quarter hours in psychology, education, and the like. We do not expect this all at once, but we do not expect to continue to warn and to advise you.

Another difficulty, he pointed out, was the qualifications of some of the principals. A principal was expected to have three semester hours in school administration and twelve quarter hours in the various fields of school supervision. He concluded:

Some of your schools are on probation. If it is not demonstrated that an effort is being made to correct the deficiencies that have been noted, these schools will be dropped from the list of accredited schools. In the past we have not done this . . .from now on, we are going to have to do it.

Following Brasfield's talk Clyde McKee spoke on the history of the elementary school accreditation.

He pointed out that the Elementary Accrediting Association was formed around 1920 and was distinct from the high school commission. From 1926 to 1947 a point system for accrediting, worked out by the elementary school supervisor in a Master's degree program at Columbia University, was used in the elementary schools of the state.

Points were assigned based on the number of years a teacher had taught, the years of college education, and the physical accommodations of the schools, such as classroom space, water and toilet facilities.

Under this system the schools improved for a time, but then began to decline. The Elementary Accrediting Association decided to take drastic action. It abandoned the point system in 1946 and adopted a rating somewhat similar to the A, B, C rating used for the high schools. All schools whether rated A, B, or C were fully accredited, but the standards were different in degree. In each class, two-thirds of the teachers had to meet the minimum requirements: 4 years of college for A schools; 3 years for B schools; and 2 years for C schools.

On July 1, 1949, the elementary association and the

high school association, which had been independent and distinct from one another, united to form the present Mississippi Accrediting Commission.

Then turning his attention to the elementary Catholic schools in the diocese, Mr. McKee commented:

The greatest weakness in your schools is in the qualifications of new teachers. A number of teachers who come in each year do not meet the minimum requirements. No exceptions have been made. When the standards are not met, the rating of a school has been lowered.

In the high schools the problem with the enrollment was too few students and in the elementary schools it was too many: forty pupils per teacher was the absolute maximum allowed.

In the afternoon following the talks by the two public school officials, the diocesan school board and Msgr. Byrne returned to the conference room to draw up plans to raise the standards of the diocesan schools.

There was no doubt in the minds of Msgr. O'Connell and Father Koury that the schools needed upgrading.[4] In 1944, in cooperation with Dr. T. G. Foran from the Catholic University of Washington, D.C., the Jackson Diocesan Office of Education had requested the teachers in all the Catholic schools of the diocese to administer a battery of Achievement and IQ Tests to their pupils, correct them (which they had done manually), and mail the results to Washington. Although the teachers knew the scores of their individual schools, they had waited for a full report from the diocesan office; but they had waited in vain.[5] Perhaps this was because the report had been so devastating: it had exposed some buildings

as firetraps and unsuited for schools; it had complained of inadequate illumination; it had revealed
poor sanitary facilities; it had brought to light the lack
of the most routine equipment such as chalk, blackboards, maps, globes, and the like.[6]

In the section on the black schools, the report had
stated that the black children were older than the
white children in the same grades, and in many
instances the difference was considerable, especially
in the seventh and eighth grades; that the average IQ
based on the results of the tests was substantially
below 100 among the black children; that after grade
four the number of pupils per class dropped dra-
matically.[7]

The section on the white schools had stated that
work in the first three grades was average, but beginning with grade four there was a steady decline until
grade seven.[8]

The report of Dr. Foran had not been released and
would not be released for yet another two years. At
that time Father Koury could say:

*After a survey, Dr. Foran in 1943 (sic) made a report
on our diocesan school system with regard to educational achievement of pupils and with regard to the
physical facilities. The survey was very critical. To
enter into details on the criticisms of the educational
achievement of pupils would now be impractical since
these students are no longer in the elementary grades.*

*However, the survey does show the need for constant
supervision of our teachers and for the constant testing of our pupils, so that such criticism will not be
forthcoming in the future.[9]*

Not even the diocesan school board was privy to
the report at the time of the May 1950 meeting with

the representatives from the Mississippi Accrediting Commission. Its greatest concern after listening to the public school officials was the qualifications of the teachers in the Catholic schools of the diocese. Enrollment numbers could be reduced on the day of registration; maps, charts, and books could be purchased; but academic degrees were not earned overnight. The board noted that one summer school for teachers was already scheduled for Vicksburg: it proposed a second to be held in Biloxi, if needed.[10] Provincials of the congregations having schools in the diocese were to be notified not to send any new teachers into the classrooms who were not properly qualified according to the Mississippi Accrediting Commission.[11]

A month after this meeting the Mississippi Accrediting Commission scheduled a two-week conference for white educators at the University of Mississippi, Oxford, beginning on July 10, and another for black educators at Rust College, Holly Springs, beginning on July 12, for the purpose of rewriting the standards governing the accrediting of both elementary and high schools.[12] Sister Leonardine from Jackson and Sister Victoria Grosse-Beckman were the bishop's choice to represent the black Catholic schools in Mississippi, and Sister Leonardine was elected secretary of the conference.[13]

As a result of these meetings, definite and unified regulations were issued for all Mississippi schools, and teachers' qualifications were standardized. Instead of the A, B, C system, the schools would be classified as Accredited Schools, Class A Schools or Class AA Schools. Included in the qualifications for these ratings were a central library in grades one through six in addition to individual classroom libraries for grades one through three; a payment of seventy-five cents per year per child for library books as opposed to the then required fifty cents; a teacher load of not more than three grades and not more than forty pupils. Thirty-five pupils per teacher was the recommended ratio.

What was behind this sudden interest in the schools in the late 1940's and the early 1950's? Civic and public school leaders of Mississippi could see the handwriting on the wall. For years, the state had carried on a dual educational system under the banner of "Separate but equal," but the slogan was fooling no one. Public schools for blacks and those for whites were far from equal.

In June 1953 the Mississippi Economic Council published a booklet entitled *Education: A Challenge and an Answer for Mississippians*. The challenge, the pamphlet stated, was the low level of public education in Mississippi when compared to other states in the South. More immediate were the unequal levels of educational opportunity between the races in the different areas. The report went on to say that while Louisiana, which ranked first in aid to public education, paid $1.50 per child per day, Mississippi paid only fifty cents. It added that since 1940 all other Southern states had increased aid to their public schools by over 200% while Mississippi had lagged with 159%. The report revealed that Mississippi was annually spending only $30 per black child per year compared to $125 per white child. Compared to the taxpayers in all other Southern states, taxpayers in Mississippi were paying the smallest percentage of their personal income for the support of schools.[14]

The pamphlet went on to say that a recent public opinion survey showed that citizens overwhelmingly approved expanding and equalizing the public school system. To accomplish this, in 1952 the Citizens' Council on Education recommended to the legislature a sixty-nine million dollar biennial appropriation plus fourteen million dollars from local funds, but the governing body decided to await action until it made a complete investigation. Accordingly, it appointed a recess committee composed of eight members of the Senate and ten from the House to further study the situation. In March 1953 the committee in its report recommended constitutional amendments and legislation to reorganize the school system, finance a minimum program of education, and construct needed new facilities.[15]

Accordingly, in an effort to equalize the educational opportunities for the races, the legislature in an extraordinary session voted to contribute twelve dollars annually for each child in average daily attendance plus an additional three dollars for ten years, effective July 1, 1954, for each black child.[16]

A frenzied building program was already in progress—blank walls with little or no equipment. In his 1951-52 Biennial Report to the legislature, the superintendent of education stated that $36,212,054.34 had been spent on white schools and $15,943,256.20 for black schools during this period, with most of the schools for blacks being constructed during the past two years at a cost of nine million dollars. The county and local districts had spent $29,000,000, almost half of this going to black schools.

One can point with pride at the improvement made for both races in the past seven years. Still, many have to attend school in uncomfortable and poorly-equipped school houses.[17]

Prior to 1945 over half of the 3,159 black public schools were one-teacher "log cabin" schools, and only 153 were recognized by the accrediting commission.[18] A 1950 report issued by the superintendent of public education in Mississippi showed that the total number of black one-teacher schools dropped from 2,015 in 1945 to 1,077 in 1952; two-teacher schools from 850 to 612; and three-teacher schools from 184 to 160.[19]

Despite its being the lowest state on the educational totem pole, Mississippi felt comfortable as the testing time for desegregation approached. When the Supreme Court issued its May 17, 1954, desegregation ruling, state officials dared the federal government to enforce it in Mississippi, confident that it would not even try.

On the evening of June 1, 1954, J. P. Coleman, attorney general of Mississippi, addressed the state over WLBT Jackson.

I sincerely believe that we can maintain our separate schools. A system of education which we know from experience to be best for all concerned has been challenged by individuals of whom not a one ever lived in our state. We don't need any outside assistance to solve this problem.

After reviewing the history of court decisions on desegregation, he continued:

On May 18, 1896, we have the well-known case of Plessy v. Ferguson which was written by a Justice from Michigan. So it was the North who agreed to this type of thing. Then in recent years, agitated by sources completely outside the states involved, suits were filed in behalf of a few colored children against school districts in South Carolina, Virginia, Delaware and Kansas, seeking to overthrow that which had been the law of the land for over a hundred years.

...As Senator Stennis has pointed out, these nine judges have seen fit to destroy the holdings and doctrines approved and reaffirmed by that same court in at least five of its own previous decisions.

Coleman went on to say that Mississippians were almost unanimous in their desire to preserve and improve their public school system and pointed out that the court didn't say how or when schools should be integrated. He went on to say that in 1930-40 Mississippi spent $7.34 on public education for each black child in average daily attendance. In 1953-54, it increased this to $51.25. In the same period, the increase for white children was less than three times that for blacks.

It will be interesting to see whether the colored race will make a fruitless attempt to fall off after agitators who pay no taxes in Mississippi, who have no voice in Mississippi government, who are interested in their own personal gain, who contribute not a thin dime to the operation of the public schools of this state. Will the colored people spurn the recent laws which give the teachers salary equalization? Will they reject the new buildings for them as a result of the new program? Will they have the good judgment to accept these benefits from the only source whence they can be received or will they exchange a bird in hand for nothing in the bush?

He concluded by pointing out that Mississippi would be the most seriously affected of all the states if the decision of the Supreme Court were to be enforced since 48% of its school children were colored as compared to six percent in Kentucky, seven percent in Oklahoma, and fourteen percent in Texas.[20]

On June 23 five hundred Mississippi lawyers unanimously endorsed an address by Hugh V. Wal from Brookhaven before the Mississippi State Bar Association.

On May 17, he had said, *the form of our government was changed by the order of nine men, none of whom were elected by the people. For more than 160 years the U.S. has been a government by the people, and this has been taken away now. . . . They think they are better qualified than the parents of children or the local community or the state to say how our public schools should be run. . . . They have usurped the sacred right to educate our own children in our own way.[21]*

How did the Catholic Church in the South meet the announcement? In November 1953 at a meeting of all Catholic superintendents held in Washington, D.C., the superintendents of the Southern dioceses met to discuss common problems. Anticipating the decision of the Supreme Court on desegregation, they agreed not to make any public comments on it themselves, but to let the statements come from the hierarchy. As far as the ruling was concerned, all agreed that the "law must be followed." It was a comfortable stand to take.[22]

When the Supreme Court decision was announced six months later, Bishop Gerow sealed the lips of the clergy by sending them a letter enjoining them to refrain from entering into any public controversy over the racial situation in Mississippi without his express approval.[23]

The activity of the Mississippi legislature to improve the public schools for blacks was bound to have an effect on the schools staffed by the Holy Spirit Missionary Sisters. To meet the new standards for teaching qualifications, the requirements for buildings and equipment, and the regulations regarding enrollments without the aid of the kind of money the state was pouring into the public school system was a tremendous challenge. Could the excellent reputation of the schools which had been established over the years continue to attract pupils despite the new public schools nearby? The sisters could recall one instance in Jackson in September of 1925. That year a new public high school had been built near the mission school, and all but one student from Holy Ghost High School, a daughter of a minister, transferred to the new school. Only three of its eighth grade graduates had decided to enter its ninth grade and as a consequence the high school was dropped. The sisters were heartsick, but by the end of the term, their former students had become disillusioned with their new school and were ready to return.[24] Despite its low budget and no-frills curriculum, the school offered a quality of education that compared favorably with any public school in the state. Would this be true in the 50's?

Fortunately, in the struggles of the 1950's the mission schools could count on their alumni and parishioners to support the schools. Many of them had better-paying jobs than their parents had had, and they wanted to support their alma mater. True, many of them had moved to the North where job opportunities were better, but those who remained became the pillars of the parishes and schools. In 1950 Holy Ghost School netted twelve hundred dollars at their annual "Spring Festival," and in 1951 the house chronicle noted that a Christmas shower was given the sisters by the parishioners. "A reversal of the past when we were the givers," she commented.[25] In October 1953 a bazaar at Sacred Heart School netted fourteen hundred dollars; and in 1956 one at St. Mary's raised eleven hundred dollars.[26]

The school buildings were still among the best in the diocese. In 1949 Ernest Boykins, Sr., a 1927 graduate of St. Mary's and now a building contractor with a son who was a senior at the school, supervised the building of a one-story, brick high school. Some materials he salvaged from the old hall. The remainder he donated. The completed building had four classrooms, a library, a laboratory, and a principal's office.[27] Bishop Gerow dedicated a new St. Rose de Lima Elementary School (for which he had donated $5,000) in Bay St. Louis on September 25, 1955.[28] On September 1, 1957, he was in Greenville to dedicate the new Sacred Heart Elementary School.[29]

For the sisters the biggest problem caused by the 1955 standards of the accrediting commission was the qualifications demanded of the teachers, although time had been allowed the communities to achieve these goals.

From 1906, when the Holy Spirit Missionary Sisters first came to Mississippi, until 1938 a normal school training consisting of two years of college was the prerequisite for qualifying one to teach. In 1938 the standards were raised to include a degree plus eighteen semester hours of college credits in education. In 1954 the standards were raised again requiring a qualified teacher to major in elementary education to teach in elementary school or major in a particular subject with eighteen semester hours in secondary education to teach in high school. The teacher also had to have a degree.[30]

As we have seen in earlier chapters, most of the sisters in Mississippi had gone through the normal course in Steyl, Holland, before coming to the United States. Mother Leonarda had also engaged a professor from St. Ignatius College and later from Loyola University to teach classes for credit at the mother house in Techny. In 1923 the congregation had opened a Home for the Aged in Hyattsville, Maryland, a ten-minute ride from the Catholic University of America. This made it possible for sisters to live with their own community while pursuing higher studies at the university. In 1938, when the accreditation standards required teachers to have degrees, many of the sisters had been teaching twenty, even thirty years. Some, of course, had already earned their degrees, but for others who had to return to the classroom it was a struggle.

When the accrediting commission raised the teacher qualifictions in 1954, the change came at a time when bishops in foreign countries were also asking for degreed teachers.

To meet all the demands placed on the sisters, it became necessary for the superiors of the congregation to withdraw sisters from the schools for full-time studies. In a letter dated June 1, 1954, after reviewing the qualifications expected of the teachers, Sister Provincial Bernardine Roesner wrote to Father Francis Baltes, the pastor of St. Mary's:

We are obliged to keep our young sisters in the provin-

*cial mother house for further studies . . . . The sisters,
perhaps, could have been more advanced in their
studies if the difficulty of remaining in the Southern
stations during the summer vacation time could have
been eliminated. Now we must ask the pastors kindly
to employ at least one more lay teacher in their schools
because we will have to withdraw one sister from every
station.[31]*

She concluded her letter by reminding him of the
high cost of food and requesting that the sisters'
stipends be raised to fifty dollars a month. Since they
had to return to Techny in the summer for studies,
they could no longer maintain a garden nor chickens,
but had to purchase all their food.[32]

In 1955 Father Koury reported that all of the
schools conducted by the Holy Spirit Missionary Sisters in Mississippi had been accredited. A few teachers were missing credit hours and the high schools
lacked library funds and qualified librarians, but all
other deficiencies had been eliminated.[33]

In 1960, of the eleven black Catholic high schools
and nineteen black elementary schools in the diocese
seeking accreditation, twenty were listed with no
deficiencies. St. Rose and St. Joseph high and elementary schools were all clear as was Holy Ghost
High. The elementary school had one substandard
teacher and four overloaded ones. St. Mary's High
School was all clear except for one substandard
teacher who was excused because she had over thirty
years of teaching experience. The high school also
had an inadequate library budget. Sacred Heart High
School lacked scheduled library periods, and the elementary school had four overloaded teachers. By
1961, all of the schools staffed by the Holy Spirit

Missionary Sisters were free of deficiencies except for one overloaded teacher at Sacred Heart Elementary School. Slowly, painfully, the schools inched their way to the head of the class.[34]

There were some missionaries, both among the priests and sisters, however, who were concerned about the emphasis being placed upon accreditation. Through all of this, they saw the schools losing their missionary character. In the 1940's all children had been accepted into the elementary school even when the classrooms were overcrowded, so as not to turn away any potential convert. If the enrollment were limited to thirty-five or forty according to the present school standards, would there by any high school students, since the dropout rate increased with each succeeding grade? Would tuition have to be raised to make up for the loss in numbers, and would the schools then become schools for the middle class and well-to-do? Where did the poor fit into the picture?

In 1953 Rev. Amos F. Gaudette, a priest of the Society of St. Joseph, pastor of Holy Family parish in Natchez and a member of the diocesan school board, explored these questions through a survey of priests and teachers conducting black diocesan schools.[35] In his report, which he submitted to the school board, he listed fifteen areas that were common problem areas to the priests and teachers he had interviewed. He began the report by reemphasizing the missionary character of the schools, giving this as their "raison d'etre." The black parochial schools were the main source of converts, he stated. Every pastor engaged in the Negro apostolate for any length of time is forced to admit that his school is the source of his future parish because it is the main supply of his converts. He continued:

I would dare to hazard this statement: eighty percent of the Negro converts in our parishes are school children or parents of school children who have come under the influence of the priests or sisters. Non-Catholic children must attend catechism classes and weekly weekday Mass celebrated in most parishes.

Using Holy Family parish as an example, he pointed out that about six hundred children were attending the school. Of these, two hundred were Catholics in September.

Since the opening of school we have had about thirty-five to forty converts from the school. In the senior class alone we had five converts, students who have been attending our school since they were small, but because of someone at home refusing to allow them to be baptized or for some other reason known only to Divine Providence, they have not asked for baptism until now. This point is very important in any consideration that will affect the attendance because it is difficult to choose at the beginning who will be Catholics later on and who not.

This was a very serious point for many missionaries who agonized over the possibility of sending someone away who might have become a Catholic.

The priest's findings seemed to be confirmed by a 1958 report of the Commission on Negro and Indian Catholics:

The work in the interest of blacks is not only pastoral, but also missionary. Most of the establishments are dominantly missionary in aim and function. These churches and schools are located in almost entirely non-Catholic black neighborhoods. The main and often exclusive objective is to bring the knowledge of

Faith to the people within their reach and to win them to the Church. Mission schools are helpful and an important part of the program. They instruct thousands of non-Catholics in religion and establish favorable contacts with their parents and relatives. Thus they serve to breach the barrier of aloofness that ignorance of the Church, prejudice, or indifference puts in the way of the missionary.[36]

Father Gaudette's report went on to explain other points that were disturbing some of the missionaries in Mississippi.

In most instances, the missionaries engaged in the Negro apostolate are also concerned with the poorest class of people in the community. In this present day and age, with the many conveniences, there is a difference working with children from homes without even the bare necessities. Recent examinations have shown so many children in need of glasses, for example, a fact due to trying to study with a 25-watt bulb. A fact due also to poor diet where it is so common. Crowded conditions in the homes, four or five children sleeping in one stuffy room which is often used as parlor, dining room, etc., make many of the children extremely nervous and restless.

The evident lack of home life and consequent lack of home supervision seems like a condemnation of the Negro people, but rather, it is a condemnation of a society which makes such demands on the parents that they have no time for their children. Demands in this sense, mothers must work eight to ten hours for a pittance, trying to complement the low salary of the father. The parents are not home when the children should be getting a bit of affection and direction. As in all cases where this condition exists, in white slum

289

areas as well as Negro ghettos, there is little discipline in the children, oftentimes lack of respect for elders and superiors and authority. Consequently, much of the teacher's time is spent in trying to quiet the youngster down and trying to win his or her confidence.

In many schools there is a grading of students and courses are taught accordingly, adapted to the talents of the children. This is possible where a school can provide sufficient facilities and teachers. The majority of our Negro schools are struggling for existence, swapping school funds and church funds back and forth when an emergency arises, which arise daily. A boy or girl reaches a point of complete frustration when made to expose themselves to the languages and sciences when they at best can get their English and religion and history. It has been suggested that such students would be better off working, but that same boy or girl is a potential convert, and possibly one of the best. The school then is using a course of studies suitable for 10% of its children and leaves the 90% to struggle as best they can. Public schools have much to offer in the way of vocational training for both boys and girls. In the past few years diversified occupations as used in the public schools have done much in complementing the school work. The parochial schools, due to lack of funds, are in no position to compete, except in the academic courses, which it provides in a far superior way. In several instances where an attempt has been made to provide shop work for the boys and more home economics courses for the girls, absenteeism has decreased and the children did better in the subjects required to take. This was done with capable instructors but unqualified ones.

The report continued with a discussion on the difficulty that the black schools had in hiring credited lay teachers because of their limited incomes.

Then he added:

It is asked many times why our schools seem to shrink as the grades get higher, and what can be done about it. First of all, the reason is that many of our children must get to work as soon as they are old enough, or others find the studies too much for them, or others have to leave the South with their families who, rightly or not, are searching for a better way of life. In many, many instances the children have been left with aunts or grandmothers, who agree to raise the children until they get older. Consequently, as the children approach their middle teens, they go to join their parents. Now, the matter of the crowded classrooms—should the rule be observed to the letter in regard to the limited number of students per room, it is obvious that the higher grades would be empty. A practical fact to be added to this is that if the lower classes were made smaller, the income would be cut further, thus making existence of the school almost an impossibility.

Then he addressed another difficulty:

We are teaching our children the same Catechism and the same faith that is being taught in any Catholic school in the world. There has been an element of doubt on the part of many of the children, as they grow older, in regard to our sincerity. The question is asked: If, as you teach, and you are a Catholic priest, the Catholic Church has for its founder Christ Himself, and there are no grades of Catholics other than those excommunicated, those fallen away, or those in good standing, how is it that there is allowed in so many churches the attitude that Negroes are second-class Catholics? It is only recently that signs have been taken down in the churches; Catholics about to go to Communion will turn their backs on us in the churches; there are black and white sodalities; and so on.[37]

There was no doubt that the survey reflected the thinking of many of the priests and teachers engaged in the black apostolate who feared the changes taking place in the schools, and the diocesan office of education gave it serious consideration. Then following the recommendtion of the school board, it submitted a reply to the points in the report that dealt with education and therefore within its competency. However, before discussing each point individually, the office stated at the very beginning of its reply:

The primary function of the diocesan school office is to see and to help our Catholic schools maintain the highest professional standards as outlined by the Catholic philosophy of education. Its primary function is not the apostolate. If our schools have been so successful in the black apostolate, it is for the reason that they have been superior to all other schools in every phase of educational activities available to the blacks. The school office is trying to help our schools maintain their superiority.

Responding to the criticism that the curriculum of the schools was for the 10% who may attend college, not for the 90% who must go to work immediately after graduating, the school office replied that in 1953 thirty percent of the graduates from black schools went to college and forty-nine percent from the white schools. It went on to say that it recommends to all schools that they follow a three-track curriculum: General—based on four years of history, English, basic courses in science and mathematics, and courses in home economics and shop; Academic—preparation of those who intend to and are capable of going to college; and Business—the same as the General curriculum with business courses instead of home economics and shop.

Discussing the need for lay teachers and the limited funds of the parishes for hiring qualified teachers, the diocesan report pointed out that this was a burden of every parish and that if accreditation of a school were in danger, it would be necessary for the better reputation of the school that the enrollment be limited.

In response to the statement that if the rules in regard to the number of children in the classrooms were followed, few of the schools would have a high school, the report stated:

Some schools who have a strict policy on numbers to a classroom and on attendance have a very high holding power of their children. Usually unrestricted and unreasonable classroom loads have these effects: the teacher can hardly teach the class since she is spending most of her time trying to control the class. The children do not receive the attention they need with their learning problems, so the parents withdraw them and put them in other schools. The school population is never stable; consequently, the school lacks the essential Christian atmosphere among the students which is essential for love and religion and love of God and Church. The teachers are always at a loss with their classes. Some children are prepared for a certain class work, others are not. A class may have children of many different ages, which is bad socially and morally for them.[38]

The Holy Spirit Missionary Sisters were caught up in the dilemma facing all the missionaries in the black apostolate. What was best for the students? Although there was no express policy issued by the major superiors in Techny, the academic training of the sisters influenced their thinking. If their schools were of inferior quality, the graduates would not be helped, nor would the other students who did not go to college. Although Mississippi was entrenched in segregation, the Supreme Court had spoken. Segregation was doomed. It was only a matter of time. Some of their present students would surely graduate from integrated high schools and would have to compete in a white/black world. Gradually, this kind of thinking prevailed, and the policies of the school board were implemented in the schools. It wasn't easy for some teachers and some parents to accept. A former graduate of St. Mary's complained:

Our principal at St. Mary's was one of the nicest sisters we've had, but she carried on the policy that was already begun. If you were not at least an average student, you had no place at St. Mary's. That's what destroyed the school. They sent so many away. No action stands alone. Word gets around. One tells another, "The sisters are no longer interested in us."[39]

To some it seemed that way; but, in reality their decision showed a different kind of caring. Time never stands still. To hold on to what was good in the past without seeking what was best for the future was to fail their students.

As the 1960's approached, the sisters could sense the restlessness and tensions mounting among the students in their classrooms, and as the dangers of riot and bloodshed appeared more and more likely in Mississippi, they increased their prayers, adding the Litany of the Blessed Mother to their night prayers. The young, educated blacks wanted what rightfully belonged to them but didn't know quite how to achieve it. Unknown to them, their peers in the North had seen their plight and were preparing themselves to show them the way and support them in their struggle. The characters of the mid-sixties in both the North and the South were beginning to take their places upon the stage for a knockdown, drag-out drama that would shake Mississippi to its very core and break its solid chain of segregation.

In Meridian on March 20, 1955, two fifth graders of Sister Gertrudina Morbach, Ruby Ramsey and James Chaney, were baptized. They received their first communion on April 17 with seven other children. The following year, on November 4, James and his sister, Barbara, who had been baptized on December 8, 1953, were among twenty-six children confirmed by Bishop Gerow. Eight years later James Chaney would lay down his life in the cause of freedom.

Greenville, MS, 1987

Chapter XV Footnotes: Into the Diocesan Mainstream

1. Interviews with Msgr. Josiah Chatham, November 19, 1971, and Msgr. John Scanlon, June 2, 1970.

2. Scanlon, op. cit.; Diocesan Education Office, (hereafter cited DEO) folder March 6, 1953.

3. DEO, Minutes of the Meeting of the School Board of the Diocese of Natchez, Jackson, May 2, 1950.

4. DEO, *Foran's Survey*, handwritten report in folder: School Board Meeting, May 29, 1952.

5. Greenville Chronicle, January 15, 16 and 17, 1944.

6. DEO, *Foran's Survey*, "Schools and Equipment."

7. Ibid., "Colored Schools."

8. Ibid., "White Schools."

9. Ibid.

10. Minutes, May 2, 1950, op. cit.

11. Ibid.

12. DEO, Diocesan School Board Bulletin No. 1, June 10, 1950.

13. JHSC, July, 1950.

14. DAH, *Education a Challenge and an Answer for Mississippians*, pamphlet by Mississippi Economic Council, June, 1953.

15. Ibid.

16. Library of Law, General Laws of Mississippi, Extraordinary Sessions of 1954-55, 137.

17. *Biennial Report of the Superintendent of Education, 1951-52 and 1952-53, January 1, 1954.*

18. Bishop, op. cit.

19. Department of Education, *Public Schools for Negro Children*, a paper prepared by Division of Administration and Finance and G. F. Cain and issued by J. M. Tubb, Superintendent.

20. J. P. Coleman, Attorney General of Mississippi, An address delivered over WLBT-TV, June 1, 1954.

21. DAH, Hugh V. Wal, Brookhaven, June 23, 1955, address before the Mississippi Bar Association, Edgewater, Mississippi.

22. DEO, *Southern Catholic Superintendents—Enrollment of Elementary Schools in the Southern Association's Committee for Improvement of Elementary Education*, in folder: School Board Meeting, March 23, 1954.

23. Greenville Rectory files: Brunini to priests in diocese, October 3, 1962.

24. Interview with Sister Desiderata, op. cit.; Heick Chronicle, September 16, 1925; NJ, Heick to Gerow, July 12, 1927.

25. JHSC, April 27, 1950; December 23, 1951.

26. GHC, October 19, 1953; VHC, November 2, 3, 4, 1956.

27. VHC, Fall of 1949; Sister Therese Marie McNeeley, *St. Augustine Messenger*, April, 1956; DOE, Ms. Accrediting Commission Report for 1954-55; Made December 11.

28. Bay House Chronicle, August 31, 1954; Septembr 25, 1955.

29. GHC, November 28, 1956, and September 1, 1957.

30. DEO, ''Teaching Service,'' folder: School Board Meeting May 1965, Administrators Manual, a mimeo booklet of 66 pages.

31. Sister Provincial Bernardine Roesner to Rev. Francis Baltes, June 1, 1954.

32. Ibid.

33. DEO, Copied from Report to Sisters for 1955-56.

34. DOE, Lamar Fortenberry, Mississippi Negro Accrediting Commission, February 18, 1961, to Rev. John Scanlon, Superintendent.

35. DEO, *Results of a Survey Made in Regard to Problems Peculiar to Our Negro Parochial Schools*, folder: School Board Meeting, March 23, 1954.

36. *Our Negro and Indian Missions*, pamphlet, 1958, 5.

37. Results of Survey, op. cit.

38. DEO, *Report of the Office of Education on Father Gaudette's Survey*, in folder: School Board Meeting March 23, 1954.

39. Interview with Henry J. Floyd, July 15, 1970.

CHAPTER XVI
Ground Rules

On January 29, 1957, Joseph B. Brunini, a native son of Vicksburg, was named auxiliary bishop of the Natchez-Jackson diocese, the hyphenated name resulting from Bishop Gerow's having moved his offices to the capital of the state. Born on July 24, 1909, Bishop Brunini was the fourth son of John and Blanche Brunini, who were living on Cherry Street at Magnolia when the Holy Spirit Missionary Sisters arrived in Vicksburg in 1906. After graduating from St. Aloysius High School, he entered the diocesan seminary and pursued his studies at Georgetown University, Washington, D.C., and the North American College in Rome. He was ordained December 5, 1933, and continued his studies, receiving a doctorate in canon law from Catholic University, Washington, D.C., in 1937.[1]

Growing up in Vicksburg, the young Brunini knew that St. Mary's Mission existed since his mother often went there for weekday Masses, and St. Aloysius School on First North was only three blocks away. But in Vicksburg, as in other areas of the South, the division between the black and white communities was well defined. According to his own words, his contact with black people was limited to servants, carpenters, and country people who delivered fresh produce and live chickens to his mother.[2]

Of Sicilian and Jewish background, it was natural for him to compare the progress made by his parents and the white minorities in Vicksburg, such as the Italians, Lebanese, and Jews, who had come to America with only a few pennies and the packs on their backs, with that of the blacks who had enjoyed almost a century of "freedom." He liked to recall that his father, whom he regarded as an example of hard work, discipline, and strong faith,[3] had a doctor friend in Vicksburg, one of a group of wealthy Protestant people with plantations in the Delta. One day, the story goes, the doctor came into his father's law office and said that he was quite happy with the new Italian immigrants who were working for him. They weren't like the blacks: they were hard working and industrious and did things on their own. But fifteen years later, the friend was in his father's office again; and this time he felt differently about the immigrants. He didn't like the Italians because they didn't buy from his store; they had a flower garden on one side of the house and a vegetable garden on the other; they had their own pigs and cows.[4] The inference drawn by the bishop from this illustration was simply that the immigrants were ambitious and too smart to get caught up in the credit business of the commissaries as had been the case with the blacks.[5]

He saw the Italians—and white people, in general—as willing to make lifelong sacrifices in order to give their children a better life than they had had. He didn't see this as being true for the "poor blacks." They found it easier to get into their "ring-around-the-rosie bit."[6]

No doubt, the bishop was expressing the sincere and honest beliefs of many other God-fearing Mississippi whites whose contact with black people was *limited mostly to servants, carpenters, and some people from the country who came to the house to sell chickens and fresh vegetables.* They accepted the status quo as the normal way of life, not questioning how it happened or what forces were keeping it in existence. But was getting ahead simply a matter of diligence and discipline, a prerogative to be found in the white immigrant, but lacking in the black American?

We have already seen in an earlier chapter how blacks were deprived of educational opportunities on the plantations in order to keep them subjugated to the white man's rule. We have also seen how the white community in the cities controlled the wages for black employees and determined on-the-job promotions and other job-related privileges. As late as the 1960's, many were working for their wealthy employers for fifteen to twenty-five dollars a week. As incredible as it may seem, a seamstress working in the mill in Greenville was making only 75¢ an hour.[7] In Mississippi the black man was truly tied to the white man for his daily sustenance: if he displeased his employer and was fired, or if conditions on the job became unbearable and he quit, word would be passed along and wherever he went looking for a new job, he would find himself turned away.[8]

Those who tried to start businesses of their own

301

soon learned that they lacked the necessary money and knowledge to compete with white-owned businesses.[9] Except for barbershops that catered to clientele of either race and funeral parlors and insurance companies for blacks only, there were few other black-owned enterprises.

In contrast to the entrepreneur and the day laborer, there were many blacks, males especially, who really had no ambition to make something of themselves. They felt that it was useless to try: in the end, the whites would take it all away from them anyway. In a paper by Laurence C. Jones, founder of Piney Woods School, the author notes:

Before 1940 the average black householder was afraid to paint his house and fix up his premises because of the attitude of some white man that he was becoming too "uppity." Sometimes they were even driven from their home or had it burned. This was not always the case, of course, but the fact remained that a Negro didn't always feel as safe in a neat cottage with attractive surroundings as he did in a tumbledown shack.[10]

The black Mississippian had been made to understand that everything he did, everything he had, even life itself, was only through the good graces of the white ruling power which could revoke it all at their whim. Even in seeking legal redress in the courts, he was at the mercy of white supremacy. This lesson of submission to the white man's rule began as far back as 1876, when President Rutherford B. Hayes withdrew the federal troops from the South at the end of the Reconstruction period. Free from the interference of the Northern sympathizers, the Southern states united in a concerted effort to restore white supremacy in their jurisdictions. First and foremost, this meant the disfranchisement of the Negro freedman: before they could be subjugated, they had to be stripped of the power given them by the Fourteenth and Fifteenth amendments and be driven from the ballot box. By using simple terror-beatings, lynchings, arson, and torture, Mississippi and the white South accomplished this goal in less than twenty years. Paralyzed by the fear of the night riding Klansmen, murder, and the burning of their homes, Negro voters in Mississippi became all but extinct.[11]

Less frightening than the swift descent of the night riders upon their homes, but just as devastating, were the economic pressures leveled on blacks living in the more populated areas to assure the entrenchment of white supremacy. An account of this kind of tactic is given in the Bay St. Louis *Gazette* under July 4, 1868. The paper listed the names of *six scalawags who voted at Thompson's Mill for the degradation of the white race.* Then the *Gazette* listed seven names, adding,

> These colored gentlemen at the Bay voted the white man's ticket and have proved themselves sensible and well-behaved and trustworthy people. Don't let them suffer. If you have any work, let them only have it. Assist them with your counsel and advice and if they get sick or in trouble, remember that they stood up for you in the hour of trial.

The paper then added the names of those who had voted Republican and

> thereby proved that they would gladly trample the white race under foot if they could. White people who employ servants and laborers, here are the names of those who attempted to ruin you.

There followed a list of names and a promise that more would be added the next week.[12]

Along with terror tactics and economic pressures, white Mississippians turned to the legislature to legalize their gains and to assure them perpetuity. The legislative process to deprive the blacks of their right to vote reached its climax in the 1890 Constitutional Convention. After a lengthy debate, the Convention passed the franchise section of the Constitution which provided an educational qualification, required the payment of all taxes for the two years preceding the election, and included a poll tax of two dollars on every male inhabitant of the state. Carefully couched in terms that appeared on the surface to treat both races equally, these sections of the Constitution, especially the one on the educational requirement, became the instrument of the white power structure to practically do as it pleased in the registrar's office.[13]

As some politicians had feared, soon after the 1890 Constitution went into effect, the number of voters dwindled ostensibly, more because of the poll tax than for any other reason.[14] This was understandable since in some years cash income of white farm families in Mississippi was not more than a few hundred dollars.[15] But the white Democratic power structure was now fully in control of the government, and on June 22, 1903, the State Democratic Executive Committee met in Jackson and adopted a resolution permitting every white Democrat to vote at the general election to be held in November.[16]

A year earlier a paper read before the Alumni Association of the University of Mississippi by the noted historian, Dunbar Roland, justified the electorates' actions in depriving the black male of the right to vote. The paper stated that during the Reconstruction era, ignorant and vicious Negroes had filled the most important positions of honor and trust, placed there by extreme radicals of the Republican party. At that time every white man swore a solemn oath under heaven that he would free himself and his posterity from the disgrace of Negro rule or die in the attempt. He felt that the peace of his home, the safety of his wife, the happiness of his children depended upon it.

During this time of intense feeling and excitement many mistakes were made, the paper acknowledged. Many irreparable wrongs were committed; innocent lives were lost; frequent armed conflicts occurred between the races; and the Negroes always suffered the most. But the Negro had proven himself unworthy of the suffrage and it was to be taken from him.[17] Roland's statements were not challenged by his listeners: it was what they wanted to hear.

Once the black body politic was destroyed, the way was clear to build, under the wing of the state government, a society in which black "arragance and aspiration" would be impossible. Lily-white legislatures passed bill after bill, enforcing the new system of fear and coercion in every conceivable area of life.[18]

Always preoccupied with the maintenance of its iron grip on the Negro, the state never had time or interest to work toward eradicating the poverty within its borders. Instead of solving their inequities, opposing factions such as the poor rednecks (farmers) and the rich Delta planters united against the black to avoid giving him even the spectre of power.

The politician who could shout the word "nigger" the longest and loudest, the candidate who could appeal most eloquently for Mississippi's way of life, always came out the winner on election day. Solidarity became the keynote of Mississippi politics, and whites forgot their differences in economics, nationality and religion to close ranks against a common foe. The immigrant was wooed into this show of solidarity. Blacks who objected to the system either buried their grievances, left for the North, or died protesting it.[19]

When women began campaigning for voting privileges, the spectre of Negro suffrage again came up in the debates going on around the state. The chief argument in the Mississippi legislature against ratification of the Woman's Suffrage Amendment was that it would permit Negro women to go to the polls.

Wrote the editor of the Jackson *Daily News*:

This is just an excuse....We know there's no more danger of Negro women in this state attempting to vote than there is of Negro men. Any assertion to the contrary is an insult to the supremacy of the Anglo-Saxon race. The Negro is finally and forever out of politics in Mississippi and nobody knows it better than Negroes themselves.

In common with all of our other Southern states, Mississippi offers no apology for barring Negroes from the polls. Our conscience suffers no twinges. We know our actions are fully justified. Our position is permanent. It will endure for all time to come. The door of hope is forever barred to Sambo in so far as suffrage is concerned.[20]

And so it seemed that it was. While the children of white immigrants were encouraged to go to the polls, the children of black Americans whose sons had fought in two wars to save democracy were threatened with death if they even tried to exercise this right.

If there was one obstacle to success as a race that the blacks could have removed, it would have to be the lack of loyalty they showed one another.

Unfortunately, they were often their own worst enemies. To the utter disgust of some of their own people, they informed on one another and drove one another on the job to win favors and token rewards for good behavior from their white benefactors and employers, not realizing they were being used by the white power structure to undercut others of their own race, preventing them from uniting under strong leadership. In return for affection and paltry favors the recipients, often servants, cooks, even ministers, closed their eyes and ears to the plight of their race. To understand how this could happen, however, it must be borne in mind that often members of the black communities were more white than black and had strong ties with the white community.[21]

"We should be called 'Mixicans,' suggested one black, "because we are all mixed up with almost every nationality flowing in our veins."[22]

Often a mulatto living in the black community had a father who was a prominent white man in the area who sent him to a private school and opened doors for him to better-paying jobs. In return, the child was expected to keep his or her eyes and ears open for the father's interests.

A mulatto graduate of Holy Ghost School remembers hearing his father say to somebody: "Now the same blood that's in my veins is in his, so don't bother him or you'll have to see me." So he and his brothers and sisters were always treated well by his father's friends. But being close to the white power structure, he saw how unjustly other blacks were treated. "I have to say it," he said, "but they cheated the colored people, treating them wrong and taking their earnings away from them. It was rough."[23]

Stripped of any legal redress, the "smart black" learned to latch on to a "friend," a protector, a white man who would plead his case if he got into trouble or would help him if he needed assistance. During a Ku Klux Klan meeting, the protector would say "He's my friend. Don't touch him." When a hospital in Vicksburg wanted to fleece an elderly parishioner of St. Mary's from her health insurance money, she was fortunate to have worked for a woman who later married Bishop Brunini's brother. After several unsuccessful attempts by her friends to get the money for her, she went to her former employer who asked her husband to make inquiries at the hospital. As soon as he appeared, he was assured that the money would be sent to the woman promptly.[24]

Without a friend in the white community, the black person was like a stranded, defenseless pilot walking through a hostile jungle. He could easily be turned into an "example" for other blacks to remind them to keep their place and not to get "too uppity." Life was never safe. Many a mother lay awake at night fearing lest something that her son had said or done that day would bring the wrath of the white man down upon him. A slight error or indiscretion could mean torture or death.[25]

One mother who had graduated from St. Joseph's

Elementary School was shocked when her son came home from the public playground one evening and told her what he had said to a white woman. The family had missed a hatchet and she accused the boy and his playmates of taking it, calling them "niggers."

"What if I called you a Caucasian?" her son asked. When the woman complained about their playing in the area, he told her that according to the Fourteenth Amendment they had as much right on that playground as her child had.

Talking back to a white woman was a terrible crime punishable by death, and the mother lay awake all night, fearing that someone would come for her son.

"They would have had to kill me to do it," she said, "because I would have fought as long as I could." She added sadly, "That was the kind of fear that I raised my children under. It's hard to tell a child 'You leave the white person alone. Don't have anything to do with a white girl and don't say anything to them.' At the same time, I've been approached many times by white men."[26]

A mistake made by the boyfriend of a light-skinned student at St. Joseph's High School in Meridian almost cost him his life. His crime was waving to a white woman on the street, thinking she was his girl friend. That same day, his friends had to scuttle him out of the state in a trunk of a car to keep him from being lynched.[27]

Two instances that occurred in Bay St. Louis in the 1940's clearly illustrate the climate in which the black man in Mississippi moved. Although both tragedies were regarded with horror by the inhabitants of the Catholic town where race relations were probably the best in the state, neither murderer was brought to justice.

Albert Raboteau and his wife, Mable, were faithful parishioners of St. Rose Church and were expecting their third child on the fateful morning when he went to the ice house for the day's supply of ice. There he met another parishioner, Andre Lizana, who handed the ice clerk, the owner's son, a five-dollar bill for her ten cents worth of ice and received only 90¢ in change. When both she and Raboteau pointed out the error, the clerk angrily knocked the woman to the floor and threatened her defender with worse punishment. That afternoon, as Raboteau was working in his accustomed place in the vegetable section of Schaff's grocery store on the corner of Maine and Toulme, the father of the ice clerk came in and shot him on the spot. On the way out, the gun still in his hand, he grunted to the owner of the grocery, "If the police want me, you know where I live." He was never brought to justice.[28]

"But," as one elderly gentleman in the Bay noted, without malice, thirty years later, "the Lord takes care of his own. The man who did the killing is all crippled up now and is shaking all the time. And his son went to the service and came back with no legs and no arms. Yea, the Lord takes care of his own. He don't need us."[29]

On October 13, 1942, another senseless murder shook the Bay, and again the victim, Louis Cleggett, Jr., was a faithful parishioner of St. Rose. The father of two children, Cleggett was coming home from work around 11:15 p.m. with two fellow workers when a white man, slightly retarded and under the influence of liquor, accosted them at the corner of

Necaise Avenue and Esterbrook Street and demanded that Cleggett open his coat. When the young man complied, the assailant fired a double barrel shotgun fully charged into the victim's abdomen and legs. The murderer said that he had mistaken his victim for someone else and after spending a few days in jail, he was allowed to go free.[30]

No one in the Church spoke on behalf of these innocent victims. Unfortunately, even the white Catholic Church was part of the solidarity wall that said: You keep your place. Don't ever think that you will be accepted as an equal. It would be the black Catholics, however, who would turn on the Church in the 1960's in love and confront it with its hypocrisy. *You* taught us in school that in the eyes of God *all* are created equal. Yet *you* do not accept *us* as equals. This new black who was emerging did not depend upon the patronage of a white father to get ahead in the world. He was educated, well-read, and conscious of his rights as an American citizen, and he would demand these rights in government, and if he were Catholic, in his Church.

Students at Holy Ghost High School in Jackson were participating in Black Power meetings being held at Tougaloo College, and one student who had gone to New York for summer school had returned competely indoctrinated in the Black Power movement. Discipline in the classrooms often turned into a black-white confrontation as students suddenly realized for the first time that their teachers were white. Parents became upset when a few girls showed up in American-Afro costumes at the senior banquet. Many of them were professional people who lived in beautiful homes on Jackson's north side and were inclined to be conservative and didn't want their children to do anything foolish that would destroy everything they had worked for. Neither did they want them to get hurt. A father serving in Vietnam wrote to the principal of the high school that he had heard that his daughter was wearing an Afro and was going to Black Power meetings and that he had sent her to Holy Ghost School so that she wouldn't get involved in anything like this.[31]

But nothing would stop the students now. James Jackson Kilpatrick wrote in *The Southern Case for School Segregation*:

> *A new Negro is emerging and is unrecognized by many staunch Southern segregationists, the bright young high school senior, the serious college student, the impatient middle-class Negro couple who are struggling for respectability and status.*[32]

The white power structure of Mississippi only flexed its coercive muscles and prepared to deliver to these emerging educated blacks the same hard-core lessons that had worked for almost a hundred years and, in their opinion, would work a hundred more.

Meanwhile, the Catholic Church in Mississippi hovered in the sidelines, two wings covering its eyes, two wings covering its ears, and two wings covering its feet. Once in a while, it peeked out to see which group was winning the battle.

Chapter XVI Footnotes: Ground Rules

1. NJ, Life Sketch of the Most Rev. Joseph B. Brunini; Conversation with Bishop Brunini.

2. Interview with Bishop Brunini, May 31, 1971.

3. Ibid.

4. Ibid.

5. Ibid.

6. Ibid.

7. Interview with an unknown parishioner in the vestibule of Sacred Heart Church on November 20, 1970. She asked what it meant to give an hour's wage for the bishop's poverty campaign. When I told her, she smiled and said that she could do that. She was earning seventy-five cents an hour; Interview with Connie Moore, June 6, 1970.

8. Interview with DeWitt Webster, June 7, 1970.

9. Interviews with James A. Stewart, Jr., June, 1971; Rev. R. S. Porter, June 5, 1970.

10. DAH, Laurence C. Jones, *The Bottom Rail*, Addresses and Papers on the Negro in the lowlands of Mississippi and on interracial relations in the South during 25 years (Revelle, 1936); Cohn, op. cit.

11. Greenville Rectory Archives, Challenge of the Mississippi Freedom Democrat Party (hereafter cited MFDP).

12. Bay St. Louis Gazette, July 4, 1868.

13. Albert D. Kirwan, *Revolt of the Rednecks* (Lexington, 1951), "Mississippi Politics: 1876-1925," 66.

14. Ibid., 73, 75.

15. Ibid., 75, 76.

16. Ibid., 131.

17. Dunbar Rowland, "A Mississippi View of Race Relations in the South," a paper read before the Alumni Association of the University of Mississippi. (Jackson, 1903).

18. Greenville Rectory files, Challenge of the MFDP; op. cit.

19. Ibid.

20. *Jackson Daily News*, January 18, 1920.

21. Interviews with Connie Moore and Mr. and Mrs. Joseph Williams, in June and July, 1960; Rev. Carl Wolf to Gerow, January 16, 1933.

22. Williams, op. cit.

23. Interview with John H. Grisham, June 20, 1971.

24. Interview with Luella Mallet, June 21, 1970.

25. Interview with Mamie Sudbury, June 3, 1970.

26. Ibid.

27. Interview with Sister Liobina Schikora, January 6, 1970.

28. Interviews with Rosalie Piernas Gauff, April 29, 1970; Sister Matutina Holle, no date; Ridgley Curry, no date.

29. Curry, op. cit.

30. Bay House Chronicle, October 13, 1942; *Seacoast Echo*, October 13, 1942, and October 16, 1942.

31. Interview with Sister Claudette Burkel, September 1, 1969.

32. James Jackson Kilpatrick, *The Southern Case for School Segregation* (Crowell-Collier Press, 1962) 97.

CHAPTER XVII
Secondary Education Reevaluated

Despite the drain on its tax dollars, Mississippi continued to build new schools for blacks in a determined effort to keep its "separate but equal" educational system. Each year new public schools were opened, offering a variety of courses and athletic programs never offered to blacks in the state before. The Holy Spirit Missionary Sisters were the first to recognize that their high schools were in no position to compete with the newly-funded government schools and programs, especially in areas of finance and personnel. Each year their high school enrollments dropped a little more as non-Catholics who had been coming to their institutions for more than forty years because of the quality education they offered left them for the newly-built public schools. It seemed that the mission high schools had served their purpose. They had offered blacks the best in secondary education at a time when it was not available to them. Now that the state was providing this service, even though the motives were reprehensible, some sisters thought it was time for the congregation to withdraw from secondary education in the South.[1]

The enrollment at St. Joseph's High School in Meridian had always been the lowest of all the sisters' high schools in Mississippi. Since its first graduating class of two in 1919, the number of seniors graduating in any one year had never exceeded twenty. The people in Meridian, for the most part, were poor and the majority of the students left before graduation to help support the family.[2] In September 1960 there were only sixteen Catholic students in the entire high school, and it was thought that the religious atmosphere in the school could be replaced by a strong Catholic youth program, using the parish facilities as a meeting center.[3]

Thus as quietly as it had opened, St. Joseph's High School closed its doors in May 1961 with a graduating class of ten, two of whom received scholarships to Tougaloo College, one a scholarship to Dillard University and another to Haven Rust College.[4] By that time, half of its 291 alumni had left the state to seek jobs and fortunes in other parts of the country.[5]

Apparently the parents of the students had not been sufficiently forewarned about the closing of the school because the announcement was met with a flurry of excitement as they attempted to organize parish associations to raise money and have the school reopened in the fall.[6]

James Finlay, a 1924 graduate, wrote to Sister Michael Zatopa, the provincial of the Holy Spirit Missionary Sisters in Techny:

Today, as our entire nation celebrates its own independence with parades and fireworks, for one small

*city, Meridian, there hovers a pall of gloom. Many
hearts are sad because of a very sudden and unexpected
ultimatum, namely, the discontinuance of St. Joseph's High School. . . .A good Catholic education,
for which our grandparents and parents have so ar-
dently worked, hoped, wept, and prayed is now taken
away from our youth of today. Why?[7]*

But a sudden burst of enthusiasm would not supply funds and teachers, Sister Michael pointed out in
a letter to another parishioner who wrote to her begging to keep the school open. The number of pioneer
sisters retiring because of age or ill health was three
to four times as great as the number of young girls
joining the congregation and the sisters were no
longer receiving recruitments from Europe as they
had formerly.[8]

Realizing that funds were not available to hire all
lay teachers to staff the school, the parents finally
accepted the inevitable and dropped their plans to
have the high school reopened.[9]

That same year, St. Peter's High School in Pine
Bluff also closed because of decreasing enrollment
and lack of teaching sisters. In the final graduation
class there were only eight seniors.[10]

Sister Kathleen Kane, Directress of Studies for the
sisters, was assigned by the provincial council to visit
the remaining high schools and reevaluate the role
they played in their communities in the light of
government-sponsored schools and the needs of the
Catholic students. A graduate of DePaul University,
Chicago, with a Master's Degree in Education, Sister
Kathleen had taught at Holy Ghost and St. Rose
schools before assuming her duties as directress.[11]

In her report to the provincial council,[12] she noted that the minimum number of courses in high school was twenty-six units of work. There was no way that the four teachers in each of the high schools could handle the twenty-six courses even with six classes a day, the report stated. It was one thing to teach six periods a day when the teacher had two or three sections of the same class and quite another when she had six different preparations and presentations to make. There weren't enough hours in the day to prepare adequately for so many classes, to say nothing of grading papers and maintaining records. In addition to the teaching load, the report continued, teachers had to monitor extra-curricular activities such as the student council, honor society, glee club, school paper and yearbook, the sodality and Red Cross. Added to these were clerical duties, parent interviews, home visits, convent duties and religious exercises.

Even if the teachers could carry this impossible load, the report pointed out, the high schools were failing to fulfill their objectives of providing *for students having different talents, intellectual capabilities, and future interests*. This was an injustice to the students, who were entitled to a choice of courses in business, industrial arts, homemaking, and agriculture if they were to become worthwhile members of the technological society in which they were living. The high schools could not offer opportunities to the students for music, art, and dramatics. No provision was made for the areas of health and physical education. According to the report, the better type of student was not satisfied with minimum offerings which allowed him no choice of subjects and which did not prepare him as he wished for future studies. Such a student would leave for the school offering broader opportunities, and the small school would be left with the poorly-talented children.

In regard to the buildings, the report stated that improved facilities would lessen to some extent the burden of the present teachers, but would not eliminate the above-mentioned problems. Then, too, the financial outlay necessary to provide needed new buildings would preclude money for adequate equipment in science rooms, libraries, audio-visual aids and the like.

The report concluded:

From an educational point of view, it seems inadvisable to continue the high schools. They are such in name only. From the missionary point of view, it also seems unnecessary to provide four well-qualified, degreed sisters to teach secular subjects to sixty or seventy students of whom only thirty or forty are Catholics. Would not the suggestion of assigning two sisters for regular home visiting be of much greater value for missionary work than this waste of personnel in a phase of the apostolate which is no longer effective, and, we may say, is no longer needed?

A second report submitted by the principals of the high schools also raised the question of the effectiveness and timeliness of the schools.[13]

Unless the high school curriculum offered more subjects than it was presently doing, the students would not be able to fully cope with the stiff competition in college, one principal wrote. This was especially true in regard to science and mathematics, but it was precisely in these fields that the teachers were overloaded in the preparation and number of classes.

319

To add more sisters would be impossible in the light of the dwindling enrollment. To add lay help was another great drain on parish funds. Besides, she wrote, the new impetus toward integration was changing the picture rapidly. Students were no longer satisfied. They wanted the best. To them, this meant seeking admission into white schools. If and when this came through, the better black students would leave the mission schools.

Several principals complained of dilapidated buildings: one because of large cracks in the wall and serious troubles with water pipes; another of rotting foundations, loose ceiling tiles, walls separating from each other. Equipment was inadequate, and in one school students were bringing their own typewriters to class; in another, there was only one microscope for twenty-five to thirty students.

Another principal wrote:

Integration will have to come to the Catholic schools soon. Our Catholics will then be taken care of. We have fulfilled our purpose in giving secondary education to the blacks when no one else cared to do so. Our purpose has been accomplished. It is up to us to realize that we are no longer needed and make a graceful departure.

The fact that half of the students were not Catholic posed a special problem for the schools. It was not fair to ask the parishioners to bear their full cost as was customary in most parishes in the United States where the school children were all Catholic; but if the schools raised the tuition of the non-Catholic students, these students would leave. Either way, the schools could not exist much longer under their present circumstances.

Sister Provincial Michael forwarded copies of the two reports to the provincial of the Society of the Divine Word, Father Robert Hunter, and Bishop Gerow. She added that there were six sisters with master's degrees and thirteen sisters with bachelor's degrees teaching some 365 students of whom only one-half were Catholics. She wrote:

With our shortage of vocations and with the much greater needs of our foreign missions, these sisters are certainly not being used to the fullest advantage for the Church.

She reemphasized that the schools no longer adequately provided for the education of the students according to modern standards and suggested that other arrangements could be made to advance the apostolate in the parishes.[14]

It was not easy for the pastors to accept the sisters' decision to withdraw from the high schools. After listening to his priests, Father Hunter shared his thoughts with Sister Michael in a letter dated June 27, 1963:

I do not think we can judge these schools solely on educational standards or policies. It is the missionary element that must be preserved, and I can only go by the repeated and emphasized thought of the old priests and present pastors that the schools—both elementary and high—are absolutely essential to the missiology of Mississippi. It is our only approach to the Negro people of better class. It is the proven way to establish the Church, as the past shows, although numbers do not figure in the success.[15]

Then writing about the small numbers in the high schools, he pointed out that this was no different from the small white Catholic high schools in the diocese,

> . . .and so we see this is the Catholic situation in Mississippi, and we must sow so that others later on may reap. Besides, if numbers alone will save the schools, I believe we could round up one hundred students in each place.[16]

In a letter on July 10, he added the following:

> Father Bourges at Holy Ghost writes: "We had fourteen graduates, and fourteen are going on to college, and the same fourteen received some nineteen scholarships." Now that sounds like genuine education to me. We can get lost in some of the educational frills. But, maybe, instead of judging a school by pupils per sister, let us look to the greater achievement of students going on to college and leadership, and there our small enrollments and meagre but well-selected courses will stand the test of success.[17]

The response from Bishop Gerow was to ask the sisters to wait a few years until the schools in Mississippi were integrated before closing their high schools. In a letter to Sister Michael on July 18, 1963, he wrote:

> At the present time we are not prepared for the peaceable and friendly entrance of our colored boys and girls into the general schools. Unfortunately, this is true. I look forward to the time in the not too distant future when this is going to be possible, but at the present time it is absolutely impossible. If, therefore, these high schools are closed now, it will mean that there will be no alternative other than that the students go to the public schools. I had hoped that these schools would be kept open until such time as we will be able to take care of these children. It is true that in the high school departments this may take some years because

my own thought in the matter is that when we do start the mixing, it should be in the first grade and from there grow up, each year including another grade; but even that at the present time has not yet been made possible. We are trying our best to create an atmosphere which will make it possible. In fact, I've sent sample sermons around to the pastors to help them in creating this atmosphere.[18]

The bishop's response was disappointing to the sisters. It was now nine years since the Supreme Court's ruling on desegregating the schools, and he was still talking about ten or fifteen years down the road for it to actually happen in the diocesan high schools. But Sister Kathleen's study had convinced the provincial council that the schools, so very important when they were started in the South, were no longer serving a need. It was better for the students, and consequently for the apostolate, to close them.

In the spring of 1961 the Sacred Heart High School building in Greenville had been condemned by the city. The south wall had pulled away several inches from the adjoining wall, a result of the pressure of the newer construction built in 1952 onto the old part built in 1917.[19] The roof leaked and the plaster on the walls and ceiling was cracked and falling. The five classrooms and library were impossible to heat.[20]

It was estimated that a new high school would cost $150,000 and several articles were carried in the *Delta Democrat Times* appealing for assistance from the business community. The response was nil.[21] Since it was impossible for the 300 parishioners to take on another debt because they were already burdened with a $52,000 debt on a new elementary school and a rectory, the first four-year Catholic high school for blacks in Mississippi closed its doors in the spring of 1963. The last graduating class numbered only twelve, but several had won scholarships to Mississippi colleges and one had received a scholarship to Loyola University, Chicago.[22]

A newspaper clipping reports that among the 466 alumni, there were twenty teachers, seven registered nurses, three laboratory technicians, two pharmacists, one band leader, seven postmen, an army officer, a Peace Corp volunteer, and a priest.[23] The band leader was Wyn Davis, who had returned to his alma mater after graduation to teach music to any student willing to learn. His marching band, using as a basis for their formations the drills he had learned under the tutelage of Colonel Reilly, had won award after award.[24] The priest was Father Charles Burns, who had offered his first solemn High Mass in the church before a full congregation of relatives and parishioners on March 25, 1962.[25] The homilist for the Mass was another black priest from Sacred Heart, Father Herman Porter.[26] The first graduate, Mayme Upshaw Foster, had received a Master of Arts degree from the Catholic University of America and was acting dean of women at Howard University.[27]

In the last years of the high school's existence, about one-half of the students were Catholic, and it was believed that at least twenty converts had been led into the Church through its influence in the two years before it closed.[28]

Even though the public schools in Greenville were not integrated, the black Catholic parents were shocked into disbelief when they realized that the all-white St. Joseph High School in Greenville would not accept the Catholic students from Sacred Heart, giving lack of room as their reason. The Church had taught them that it was their duty to send their children to a Catholic school, and now a parish school was refusing to take them. Letters addressed to the bishop had no effect.[29]

Sister Mary Grace Dusheck, the principal of Sacred Heart, wrote to her provincial in Techny:

None of us realized how really in earnest many parents were to get a Catholic education for their children. Many are planning to send the children to other cities having Catholic high schools. Some families may even move away for this purpose. But the hot issue right now is St. Joseph High School in Greenville. Several parents have written letters to Bishop Gerow asking for permission to register their children in the white Catholic high school. The situation is quite tense over at St. Joseph's. They have politely said that there is no room. Yet the black Catholics would be satisfied if only the five black seniors can get in. What a magnificent opportunity for our Catholic Church in Mississippi![30]

It was an opportunity that the Church would miss. St. Joseph refused to open its doors to the Catholic students from Sacred Heart, and the bishop abided by their decision.[31]

St. Mary's High School in Vicksburg closed the year after Sacred Heart.[32] Of the sixty-five students in the high school, eighteen were in the graduating class.[33] As in Greenville, the black Catholic parents were deeply wounded when their children were not accepted into the two all-white private Catholic schools in Vicksburg, St. Francis Xavier for girls, and St. Aloysius for boys, and plans were made by the pastor of St. Mary's to send the Catholic students to

St. Francis High School in Yazoo City, fifty miles away. Some parents made this trip twice a day, morning and evening, for several years, determined to give their children a Catholic education at all costs.[34]

In 1964 Father Anthony Bourges, one of the first four Divine Word Fathers ordained at St. Augustine's Seminary in Bay St. Louis, was pastor of Holy Ghost parish in Jackson. The parish numbered 461 Catholics and that year it reported sixty-eight baptisms, forty-eight converts, and thirty-eight catechumens taking instructions.[35] The parishioners were proud of their first black pastor. In the school yearbook, *Veritas*, the class of '63 wrote:

Just as you, Rev. Father, were among the first Negro priests in the United States, so now you have come as the first Negro pastor at Holy Ghost Church. We are happy to have you in school as our instructor in religion and trust that we shall in the years to come carry out your teachings in our daily lives.[36]

Holy Ghost High School had also been singled out to close, but after consultation with the bishop and the provincial of the Society of the Divine Word, Sister Michael was able to tell Father Bourges on Feburary 11, 1964, that the school would remain open for probably another four or five years, and the sisters would supply two teachers and the principal. He would be required to hire lay teachers to complete the high school faculty.[37]

Both bishops had assured Sister Michael that they would help financially with needed repairs for both the high school and the elementary school and would provide necessary equipment for the high school if it remained open. Bishop Brunini came himself with the repairmen to see what needed to be done.[38] Leaky roofs were patched; classrooms were painted; light bulbs replaced by fluorescent lights; and the open high school porch along the front of the building was enclosed, giving the school a neater appearance and the students some protection from the cold when changing classes in winter.[39] One day twenty-four new typewriters arrived at the school through the courtesy of Bishop Gerow. When school opened that September there were 140 students in high school and 320 students in the elementary school.[40]

In 1964 the pastor of St. Rose in Bay St. Louis was Father Francis Wade, a classmate of Father Bourges.[41] The high school had been losing students even though the black high school, Mother of Sorrows in Gulfport, had closed and some of its students were coming to St. Rose.[42] Because there were so many Catholic students involved, it seemed important to do everything possible to keep St. Rose School open. Bishop Gerow called a meeting to which he invited Father Koury, the provincials of the Holy Spirit Missionary Sisters and the Society of the Divine Word, the pastors of St. Rose, Mother of Sorrows, and Mother of Mercy in Pass Christian, and the St. Rose faculty. He sent his auxiliary, Bishop Brunini, to preside over the discussions.[43] At the meeting the priests of Mother of Sorrows and Mother of Mercy were encouraged to send their high school students to St. Rose. The group hammered out a means of transportation for them, Father Harold Perry, the Divine Word provincial, promising to furnish a brother from St. Augustine's Seminary to drive the bus to and from the Pass for the students of Our Mother of Mercy, and the pastor of Mother of Sorrows offering to arrange transportation with the public school bus for his students. Bishop Brunini offered to pay the tuition of Catholic students who had gone to the public schools if inability to pay the tuition at St. Rose was the problem. As in Jackson, Bishop Brunini offered to assist the school in acquiring necessary science equipment and typewriters.[44]

When the schools opened in September 1964, the Holy Spirit Missionary Sisters were conducting three high schools in the South: Holy Ghost and St. Rose high schools in Mississippi and St. Bartholomew's in Arkansas. How much longer they should remain open was still uncertain. Should the sisters be thinking about closing their elementary schools also? These were questions that they would continue to ask as they saw both state and Church in Mississippi refusing to move toward integration.

Chapter XVII Footnotes: Secondary Education Reevaluated

1. Sister Michael Zatopa to Bishop Gerow, July 3, 1964.
2. Meridian School Records from 1922; Interview with Mamie Sudbury, June 3, 1970.
3. Robert C. Hunter to Bishop Gerow, June 16, 1971.
4. Meridian School Records.
5. 1960 Meridian Alumni Record.
6. Elizabeth Godette Washington to Michael, July 16, 1961.
7. James H. Finley to Michael, July 4, 1961.
8. Muriel Webster to Michael, July 11, 1961; Michael to Webster, July 12, 1961.
9. PP, Rev. Clement Mathis to Michael, June 25, 1961.
10. PBC, May 28, 1961.
11. PP, Sister Kathleen Kane's Personal Data Sheet.
12. PP, Kathleen, *Report on the Situation of our Southern High Schools*, undated; succeeding paragraphs are based on this report.
13. PP, Paper beginning with words: *The following are reports of the Principals of the High Schools in the South:* No names are given, but the reports are separately numbered. No date.
14. Michael to Hunter, July 3, 1963.
15. Hunter to Michael, June 27, 1963.
16. Ibid.
17. Hunter to Michael, July 10, 1963.
18. Gerow to Michael, July 18, 1963; Greenville School Files.
19. Report on Greenville facilities sent to Diocesan school office for Accreditation.
20. *Delta Democrat Times*, April 6 and 20, 1961. Newspaper clippings.
21. Ibid.
22. Greenville School Records; Gerow to Michael, July 26, 1963.
23. Newspaper Clipping, "Sacred Heart School, Greenville, Has Closed." Undated.
24. Interview with Winchester Davis, December, 1970.

25. Greenville House Chronicles, March 25, 1962.

26. Ibid.

27. Newspaper clipping on school closing, op. cit.

28. Ibid.

29. Interview with Daisy Miller Greene, December 5, 1970, and Mrs. Courtney, December 28, 1970.

30. PP, Sister Mary Grace Duschek to Michael, August 6, 1963.

31. Courtney and Greene interviews, op. cit.

32. Vicksburg House Chronicle, 1931 ff., March 22, 1964; May 25, 1964; St. Mary's Secondary Report to the Accrediting Commission, 1964.

33. Ibid.

34. Interview with Sister Priscilla Burke, June 16, 1970.

35. Jackson House/School Chronicle 1957/58, January 1, 1964.

36. Katie Jenkins, *1963 Year Book Veritas*.

37. JHSC, February 11, 1964.

38. Ibid.

39. Ibid., September 3 and 4, 1964.

40. Ibid., March 21, 1964.

41. Sister Leonardine Huettemann to Michael, March 14, 1964.

42. Bay School Chronicle, September 5, 6, 1961; *Mississippi Catholic Schools News Notes*, 1-68, "School Board Data and Education Programming."

43. Ibid., March 13, 1964.

44. Leonardine to Michael, op. cit.

CHAPTER XVIII
Summer Storm

As the Holy Spirit Missionary Sisters wrestled with the closing of their high schools, changes were taking place in the state that would drastically affect the direction of their apostolate in Mississippi. Blacks and whites together had begun the process of chipping away at the iron-and-steel foundations of the state's segregated way of life. In the spring of 1961 the first Freedom Riders, a mix of black and white college students trained in nonviolent techniques under the auspices of the Congress of Racial Equality (CORE), headed for the South to test its compliance with the federal court's orders to desegregate facilities on buses and terminals for passengers traveling between states. Though they were beaten, pistol-whipped, stamped upon, the tires of their buses slashed, their buses burned, nothing could stop them.[1] After desegregating the bus terminals, they went on to lunch counters, stores, and restaurants.[2] As shocking and spectacular as the Freedom Riders were, as effective as they proved to be in other states, the leaders of the movement soon saw that they were no more a threat to the Mississippi status quo than a gnat to an elephant.[3] Secure in the knowledge that the more vigorous and brutal its attacks, the better its chances for reelection, the hard-core power structure, impervious to even a thought of a change in race relations, could wield heavy-handed assaults upon the Freedom Riders with impunity.[4] It soon became clear to the leaders of the movement that it would make no headway in Mississippi until the racial power structure was altered, which would only happen when the composition of the electorate was more balanced between the races.[5]

The Student Nonviolent Coordinating Committee (SNCC) under the leadership of Robert Moses was already teaching blacks how to register to vote in McComb, a town in Pike County about seventy-five miles south of Jackson. After each trip to the registrar's office, the whites retaliated with economic sanctions, beatings, jailings, and finally murder.[6]

In the winter of 1962 SNCC and CORE united with the National Association for the Advancement of Colored People (NAACP) under the name of the Council of Federated Organization of Workers (COFO) with the purpose of organizing a comprehensive voter registration drive to encompass the entire state.[7] After the regular election for the U.S. Representatives, the Freedom Democratic Party it had formed held a mock election to demonstrate the disfranchisement of blacks in Mississippi, the winners challenging the right of the regular Mississippi Democrats to be seated in Congress. Though the case was dismissed in the House of Representatives eight months later, it accomplished its goal: it focused the eyes of the nation on the plight of Mississippi's disfranchised blacks.[8]

From this awareness grew the Freedom Summer of 1964. Hundreds of Northern college students volunteered to come to Mississippi at their own expense and assist COFO, some as voter registration workers, others as teachers in freedom schools where they would encourage the development of black leadership among the youth while giving them an opportunity to experience democracy on a small scale, and others as organizers of community centers to provide a place for the people to gather for recreation and fellowship. In addition to the college volunteers, there was a smaller group of professional men and women—doctors, lawyers, social workers, and ministers—who also offered their skills and time to the movement.[9]

Indicative of the new climate in the South among the young people, a cluster of white students from ten Southern colleges met in Nashville, Tennessee, in April 1964, and issued a statement to show their solidarity with the Freedom Movement. It read in part:

The Freedom Movement for an end to segregation inspires us all to make our voices heard for the beginning of a true democracy in the South for all people . . .not only an end to segregation and racism but the rise of full and equal opportunity for all . . . .[10]

The white power structure of Mississippi, embodied in the state legislature, prepared itself for the summer "invasion" by pushing through a series of clearly unconstitutional laws which included the outlawing of picketing and the banning of distributing economic boycott literature. It proposed legislation that would prohibit the entry of the volunteers of the summer project into the state, the establishment of freedom schools and community centers, the boycotting of white businesses by blacks, using passive resistance in civil rights demonstrations; and if the impossible happened and the bulwark of segregation did topple, there was a bill pending to provide funds to private schools.[11]

The mayor of Jackson boasted that he could easily take care of 25,000 prisoners. His riot-trained police force of 450 men was backed by a reserve pool of deputies, state troopers, civilian city employees and neighborhood citizen patrols. Let them come, was the loud and clear message. We'll be ready for them.[12]

Meanwhile, the student volunteers were in Oxford, Ohio, for an orientation period. They were being drilled in the techniques of nonviolence and being taught that their job was to bring love where hatred and fear resided:

We who are Christians are obliged to pray for the oppressor, even as he kicks us in the stomach and knocks our teeth out. This kind of loving sacrifice will transform Mississippi.[13]

To drive the lessons home, blacks who had been beaten and jailed, living witnesses of what the students could expect for their commitment to the movement, addressed the volunteers. One of the students' favorites was Fannie Lou Hamer, a political activist from Ruleville, Sunflower County, who had been a candidate of the U.S. House of Representatives in the mock elections.[14] She and five companions had been held in jail for four days and beaten by the nightsticks of policemen and the leather straps

334

of prison trustees.[15] COFO repeatedly warned the volunteers that Mississippi was dangerous territory and it wasn't too late for them to change their minds.[16] But the students felt that if Fannie Hamer and others like her could do it, they could, too. Their courage would be put to the test sooner than anyone expected.

In the early part of 1964 a young man in his early twenties, wearing a gray sweat shirt, baggy pants, sneakers, and a visor cap pushed carelessly back on his sandy hair, became a familiar sight on the Meridian streets. His name was Michael Schwerner, and he had come to Meridian with his wife, Rita, bent on making changes.

A 1957 graduate of Cornell University, Schwerner had pursued graduate studies at the Columbia School of Social Work and was employed in New York City when he decided to leave the typical social worker scene to join CORE. He had been deeply affected by photographs of blacks sprawling under dogs and fire hoses, shaken by the slaying of Medgar Evers, the NAACP leader in Jackson in 1963. When four little girls were murdered in church on September 15, 1963, nothing short of complete commitment to the movement would satisfy him.[17]

Soon a frequent companion of Schwerner was 20-year-old James Chaney, a former student of St. Joseph's School who had left after eighth grade to support his mother, his sisters—Barbara, Janie, and Julia—and his brother Ben, as a carpenter's or painter's helper like his father, who had deserted the family.[18] In school he had been an average student, a little better in mathematics and grammar than in reading and spelling.[19] He had been baptized and

335

confirmed at St. Joseph's and had served as an altar boy.[20] But as he grew older, he slipped away from the Church although he attended Mass on occasions at the urging of the pastor.[21] His former teachers and classmates remembered him as being quiet and shy in the classroom, and most of them expressed surprise when they learned that he had joined the Freedom Movement.[22] Ben Chaney often absented himself from school to be out with his older brother knocking on doors and passing out voter registration leaflets.[23] In time the entire family, including the mother, became involved in the movement.[24]

The Schwerners were assigned a six-county area in the east-central part of the state: Lauderdale, where Meridian is located, Kemper and Neshoba to the north and northwest, Newton directly west, and Jasper and Clarke counties to the south and southwest.[25]

Meridian had about 17,000 blacks in 1964. One of the first tasks for Schwerner was to organize voter registration workshops in churches and in any other place which would open its doors to them in order to assure a continuous flow of persons to the courthouse for registering.[26]

They also opened a community center in a five-room flat on the second floor of a building at 2505½ Fifth Street, owned by a black pharmacist who was behind the movement. In time the center collected about 10,000 books for a library and developed programs for each age group: a weekly Saturday afternoon story hour for five- to ten-year olds; ping-pong, movies, parties, and classes in arithmetic, reading, black history, and sewing for teens; job-training classes for clerical and sales positions for adults.[27]

Chaney often went hungry just to stay around the center, where he felt that something was happening, never asking for as much as a cup of coffee. He built bookshelves, unloaded and shelved books, canvassed the neighborhood for voters, and set up meetings, going out to some of the roughest rural counties to make contacts for Schwerner. The shy, quiet youth could even stand up and speak at meetings as well as organize them and keep them moving quietly along. Before long, Schwerner had him named a staff member by the central office in Jackson and brought him in on all major decision-making deliberations.[28]

Mindful of Bishop Gerow's exhortation that the priests and religious refrain from any public controversy over the racial situation in Mississippi without his express approval, the pastor of St. Joseph's, Father Clement Matthis, visited the center quietly and promised the leaders he would encourage his parishioners to make use of it.[29] One evening at their request he opened the parish hall for a meeting which was packed with the city's blacks. Also present were the faculty of St. Joseph School, the priests from the all-white St. Patrick's parish in Meridian and the naval air base outside of town. The speakers dwelt on the importance of each person present exercising his or her right to vote and the way to go about doing it. Finally, Chaney, who had organized the meeting, spoke briefly, and the sisters admired his courage as well as the fearless commitment of the other speakers. But they could also measure the tenseness in the hall and the air of an impending crisis, and it was frightening. How would it all end?[30]

Sometime in March, Chaney, driving a blue Ford station wagon that belonged to COFO, began to search out rural groups in Neshoba county, hoping to persuade them to sign up for voter registration classes.[31] No black had registered to vote in the rural areas of Neshoba county since 1955,[32] and in 1961 COFO had given up the territory as impossible and too dangerous. Young blacks in these parts were disappearing mysteriously every day, and worried parents were told by police that they had probably run away from home and gone north.[33] Neshoba County Sheriff Lawrence Rainey had been voted into office on the boast that he could keep the blacks in line, and he had already killed two since he had taken office.[34]

At Chaney's urging the people in the Longdale farming community near Philadelphia, a town of 6,000, agreed to open the Mt. Zion Methodist Church for voter registration classes. When news of this reached Rainey, he decided to make an example of Schwerner. Told by some Meridian men that the civil rights worker would be at the church to talk on the evening of June 16, the sheriff with some of his own men and some from Meridian drove to the site with the intent to kill him. This was the day that the State Democratic Party had set for precinct meetings, and COFO had urged all registered black voters and those trying to register to attend them and help select the delegates to the county conventions. The following week was to be the beginning of the summer "invasion" of Mississippi by the Northern college students. Rainey hoped that the murder of Schwerner would scare the blacks from voting and the do-good college kids from coming to Mississippi.[35]

Unknown to Rainey, Mickey and Rita Schwerner were not even in Mississippi the evening of June 16 because they had left Meridian before dawn to drive to Oxford, Ohio, to meet with the summer volunteers who were preparing to come to the state the following week.[36] What the posse found at Longdale was a twenty-four hour guard posted to protect the church after it was designated as a site for voter registration classes.[37]

Angered on finding their plans thwarted and blaming the Meridian crew for sending them on a useless quest, the Neshoba band withdrew, while the knot of Meridian men stood around drinking and passing the time, perhaps still expecting Schwerner to appear. When they decided to leave, they beat up the three guards, threw diesel fuel into the church, struck a match, and left the building in flames.[38]

Rita Schwerner remained in Ohio while Mickey returned to Meridian on June 20 with six volunteers,[39] among them a young man named Andrew Goodman, who thought it unfair for him to have so many good things in life while others were suffering.[40] When Schwerner learned about the incident in Longdale, he resolved to go there the next day to inquire about the men who had suffered so courageously for the movement and to investigate the damages done to the church. Taking the blue station wagon and promising to be back in Meridian by 4 p.m., Schwerner, accompanied by James Chaney and Andy Goodman, left the next morning for Longdale. They never returned. Like so many others in the area, they mysteriously disappeared, their burnt-out station wagon discovered in a swamp outside Philadelphia.[41] Had Chaney been alone, many blacks believe, nothing would have been done about his disappearance, but because two of the missing men were white, question of what happened to them made national and international headlines. The FBI were sent to the state, and 400 sailors from the naval air base were dispatched to the swampy, wooded area in east Neshoba County and its neighboring counties to search every inch of ground. But there was no sign of the men, and no one was talking.[42]

A *Meridian Star* editorial wailed:

If three people not connected with Negro revolution came up missing, would President Johnson ask Allen Dulles to investigate? Would Bobby Kennedy postpone a trip abroad? Would newspapers around the world send reporters to the place where they were last seen? Would FBI send in a large contingent of its topflight personnel? We know this wouldn't happen. Isn't it quite evident that all of Mississippi is being made the whipping boy for political reasons . . . . Our law enforcement officers are fully capable of handling any problems and they will come up with the answers in due time. Let us rely on their training and judgment.[43]

Despite the shocking disappearance of the three civil rights workers, the summer "invasion" began on schedule, and voter registration classes were started throughout the state.

Community centers and freedom schools dotted the cities, most of them housed in rented rooms or houses.

Vicksburg's only freedom school was a former Baptist academy, a two-story frame building situated on the top of a cliff, under the constant surveillance of the Vicksburg police, who staked out the foot of the hill in their squad cars.[44] The mayor had instructed the people to leave the workers alone and

340

not bring upon the city any adverse publicity; but a local black man who spoke favorably about the summer project everywhere he went was murdered, his body discovered a week later.[45] Black people didn't count. People outside Mississippi would not make a hue and cry about the murder of a black as they would if a Northern freedom worker were slain. Nevertheless, the workers were surprised to find that their phone at the freedom school was tapped and letters received from home were delivered to them open.[46] One day someone in a passing car fired into the community center just a few houses down the hill from the freedom school; but fortunately no one was injured.[47]

The freedom workers were allowed to use St. Mary's rectory to wash their clothes and mimeograph their materials, but the pastor did not consider it safe to open the gym for meetings, not even when Martin Luther King came to Vicksburg to speak. He did, however, lend the parish loudspeaking equipment to the church where King was welcomed.[48]

The pastor's fear of reprisals stemmed from several bombings and burnings of Vicksburg's churches and stores that had been housing voter registration classes during the summer. One rainy morning at about 2 a.m., the freedom school became the target of a bomb, which injured at least one person. Somebody said later that if the dynamite had been set right, the entire hill would have disappeared.[49]

The bombings, fires and harrassments in Vicksburg were mild compared to the beatings and jailings experienced by freedom workers in other cities and towns in the state. The volunteers had been warned about the dangers attached to their work; but even

341

the older, professional workers were surprised at the amount of violence and hatred they encountered. There was fear everywhere. One lawyer wrote home in disbelief.

> *Mississippi is a police state. I've been accustomed to the invisible shield of law all my life. When it is removed, the feeling is really indescribable. The kids are so brave; one has to listen carefully to sense the fear, but only a little carefully. It shows. For that matter, everyone is afraid and I'm no exception.*[50]

Every day workers experienced jailings, obscenities, and threats; blacks in the movement lost their jobs. By the end of the summer of 1964 at least twenty-five COFO workers had been seriously beaten and seventeen churches burned. There had been shootings and bombings in the state every day. Thirteen blacks had disappeared in Mississippi since January.[51]

In his book, *Our Town*, Hodding Carter, Greenville's Pulitzer prize-winner for distinguished editorial writing, claimed that Greenville was the only major city in Mississippi that summer not to have bombings, church burnings, beatings, or harrassment arrests. Qualified educated blacks had been voting since 1930, he wrote. Blacks were on the police force. The airport and railroad depot had been integrated without incident at a time when blacks in Jackson were being beaten and arrested for challenging the old taboos.[52] According to a freedom worker in Greenville, the local police even provided them with protection.[53] One day he noticed Klansmen filing down Main Street distributing leaflets, and right behind them were the police officers picking them up

342

and snatching them away from pedestrians.[54]

On another occasion a cross was burned on the levee at night, and the sheriff had the instigators jailed.[55] Unlike St. Mary's in Vicksburg, Sacred Heart parish felt safe in opening its gym to COFO for a series of meetings on voter registration, at least one of them drawing as many as 300 people.[56]

On August 4 through the help of an informer, members of the FBI were led to the grave of the three civil rights workers killed in Neshoba county in June. The site was a dam about 250 feet long, 30 feet wide and 18 feet high on a farm outside Philadelphia.[57] It was a typical "cattle pond" dam, common in the county. After the trench was dug, the base was packed with red clay which hardened like cement, preventing water from seeping underneath. Upon this floor dirt was piled sometimes to 60 feet high with sloping sides that eventually were planted with grass. From such a dam the bodies were unearthed by bulldozers and found fully clothed, lying face downward on the floor of the trench. All had been shot, Chaney three times. He had been inhumanly beaten.[58]

James Bishop, a 1927 graduate of St. Joseph's and owner of the Enterprise Funeral Home at Lithe Street and 32nd Avenue in Meridian, was called to the University of Mississippi Medical Center in Jackson where the FBI had taken the three bodies for examination and was given the responsibility for their funeral arrangements. The remains of Schwerner and Goodman were flown to New York, and Chaney's body was returned to Meridian.[59] Accompanied by his parents, brothers and sisters, a few close friends, and about 25 newspaper reporters, his body was taken to the Resthaven Memorial Park in Mount Barton, southwest of the city, for burial. After a graveside service with several clergy present, including Father James Kuepers, a young Dutch priest who was at St. Joseph's for the summer, the slain civil rights worker was laid to rest in the only grave in a new cemetery, nothing more than a large weed-blown field.[60] He had celebrated his twenty-first birthday on May 30.

On September 4 FBI agents rounded up twenty-one men, including Sheriff Lawrence Rainey and his deputy, Cecil Price, and eleven men from Meridian.[61] As the story of the fate of the three civil rights workers unraveled, it became clear that the trio had been arrested for speeding by Price in the afternoon of June 21 and had been jailed in Philadelphia. Released about 10:30 p.m., they were waylaid on the road and murdered, their bodies thrown into the dam, then under construction on a farm outside Philadelphia.[62]

Although the Meridian blacks packed the courtroom during the ensuing trial of the men, few expected the legally-protected arm of the white power structure to be convicted and sentenced.[63] But when Rainey and Price and five others were sentenced to prison for violating the civil rights of their victims, the mood of the blacks of the city changed completely from one of deep anger and dejection to that of satisfaction and self-confidence: Justice was possible in Mississippi after all.[64]

According to prominent black leaders, COFO had definitely made an impact in Mississippi. It had dispelled the Mississippi black's well-founded belief that the rest of the country didn't care what happened to them.[65] It had demonstrated to the more timid local leaders what could be done when people worked together for freedom.[66] Leaders said that they could not have made the changes without the help of the Northern college students. They needed the incentives and the assistance the courageous young people had given them.[67]

Said a Vicksburg man:

The Northern people didn't take no for an answer and once they started, they died for the cause. White leaders still tried to go back to where we were before, but now people protest so quickly, they don't have a chance to do anything.[68]

Although the majority of white Mississippians continued to cling to segregation, it was no longer at any price, and politicians were finding it expedient to take a more moderate line for the first time since the post Reconstruction era.[69]

On January 21, 1965, the Greenville Separate School District Board voted unanimously to desegregate the public schools under its jurisdiction.[70] It was probably the first public school district in the state to do so, and it was the moment for which the Catholic parents of Greenville were waiting. They immediately wrote to Bishop Gerow:

We sorely feel the need for, and the loss of, Sacred Heart High School. The CCD is unable to cope with the lack of Catholic atmosphere in the classroom; lukewarmness and estrangement have come earlier to our youths as a result of the closing of Sacred Heart High School. It is because of this that we write to you.

Now that seventy Negro children of Greenville have registered in white public schools without incident, now that the racial climate is more favorable, we, the

345

*undersigned parents of Sacred Heart Parish, ask per-
mission for our high school pupils to enter St. Joseph's
High this fall.*[71]

This time the response from the bishop was af-
firmative, and the first five black Catholics entered
the all-white St. Joseph's High School without any
problems.[72]

That same September the first four black students
entered the all-white St. Joseph's High School in
Jackson.[73] According to a sister's report, two of the
girls were the only students in the school to make the
Math Honor Society that year.[74]

Chapter XVIII Footnotes: Summer Storm

1. "Freedom Riders," *Life*, May 25, 1961.

2. Interview with Doris Tharp Hall, June 20, 1971.

3. Greenville Rectory Archives, MFDP, "Historical Background."

4. Ibid.

5. Ibid.

6. Aickin, Mary R., Thesis, contained in Civil Rights Collection at the Wisconsin State Historical Society (hereafter cited WSHS and CRC), Madison. Used with special permission from Polly Heidelberg; Folder, Charles Stewart.

7. "Long Hot Summer 1964," *U.S. News and World Report*.

8. WSHS, "MFDP," Reel 1, Section 6, *Clarion-Ledger*, Jackson, August 25, 1965; *Meridian Star*, September 18, 1965.

9. WSCH, Aicken, op. cit.; WSHS, COFO Memo, Reel 1, Section 13.

10. WSHS, Civil Rights Collection, folder Martin Nicolaus.

11. CRC, under MFDP, Micro Reel 2, no. 25, "Mississippi Legislature 1964;" Mississippi Code 1942, Jackson Law Library.

12. CRC, reprint from *Newsweek*, February 24, 1964.

13. CRC, Richard Gould folder.

14. Greenville Rectory files, flier "The Congressional Challenge," MFDP, undated.

15. CRC, MFDP Reel 1, Section 6.

16. WSHS, David Haspel folder, "Letter for summer volunteers."

17. William Bradford Huie, *Three Lives for Mississippi* (New York, 1965). CRC, folder Walter Kaufmann, contained news release quoting Michael Schwerner. *Meridian Star*, chronology of missing men, December 10, 1964.

18. Meridian School Records.

19. Ibid.

20. Meridian School Chronicle, March 20, 1955, and October 7, 1956; Interview with Sister Xavier Ann Schwacha, June 2, 1970.

21. Ibid. Rev. Clement Mathis, Interview on May 16, 1970.

22. Interview with Ina Glass, May 29, 1970.

23. Terence Shea, *Witness*, October 3, 1965, Vol. 2, no. 1, paper given author by Polly Heidelberg.

24. Interview with Polly Heidelberg, May 22, 1970; WSHS, MFDP, Reel 13, Affidavits; Micro Reel 2, Nos. 29 "Mass Meetings" and 52 "Reports."

25. WSHS, Micro Reel 2, MFDP No. 52, "Reports."

26. CRC, MFDP Reel 1, Section 8, January 9, 1964.

27. Huie, op. cit., 70; CRC, MFDP Microfilm Reel 2, No. 52; Leaflet describing Community Center; Rita Schwerner's Weekly Report, 52, op. cit.

28. Huie, op. cit. 93-94.

29. CRC, 52, op. cit.; Interviews with Dock Gordon, June 22, 1971, and Msgr. Josiah Chatham, November 19, 1924.

30. Xavier Ann, op. cit.

31. Huie, op. cit., 119.

32. CRC, Report by Michael Schwerner, March 28, 1964, 52, op. cit.

33. CRC, Folder Walter Kaufman.

34. CRC, 52, op. cit.

35. Huie, op. cit., 136.

36. Ibid , 124.

37. Ibid., 139.

38. Ibid.

39. CRC, MFDP, 52, op. cit.

40. Huie, op. cit., 143.

41. *Witness*, op. cit. quoting Fannie Chaney; *Meridian Star*, op. cit.

42. *Meridian Star*, August 5, 1964, "Bodies."

43. *Meridian Star* Editorial, newspaper clipping in Meridian files.

44. CRC, folder Jan Louise Handke.

45. Ibid.; Gould folder, op. cit.

46. Ibid.

47. Interview with Joseph Williams, July 29, 1970.

48. CRC, Handke, op. cit.; Williams interview, op. cit.

49. WSHS, MFDP, Reel 1, Section 6, October 3, 1964.

50. CRC, Letters by Kenneth Griswold, August 21, 1964.

51. CRC, MFDP, Reel 1, Section 8, Correspondence.

52. *Current Biography, 1946*, 95-97; Carter, *Our Town*, op. cit.

53. CRC, Folder SC 626, Russell Allan.

54. CRC, Russell to mother, op. cit.

55. Ibid.

56. Interview with Rev. Louis Benoit, December, 1971.

57. *Meridian Star*, August 5, 1964, op. cit.

58. Huie, op cit., 188-190.

59. Interview with James E. Bishop, November 7, 1974; *Meridian Star*, August 6, 1964, "FBI Sifting Information."

60. St. Joseph (Meridian) Church Register, 105; Meridian House Chronicle, August 7, 1964, 195; *Meridian Star*, "Burial," August 8, 1964.

61. *Meridian Star*, op. cit.; September 4, 1964. Chronology.

62. Huie, op. cit., 162, 41; WSHS, "COFO Report," June 22, 1964, 52, op. cit.

63. Interviews with Connie Moore, June 6, 1970, and Heidelberg, op. cit.

64. Ibid., DDJ, October 20, 1967.

65. Mississippi Black Paper.

66. Ibid.

67. Interview with Leonard Rose, August 14, 1974.

68. Ibid.

69. Mississippi Black Paper, op. cit.; Gordon, op. cit. (June 22, 1971).

70. Carter, "Our Town is Conservative," *The Virginia Quarterly Review*, Spring, 1965.

71. Greenville Convent files, Letter of Greenville parents to Bishop Gerow, June 18, 1965.

72. Sacred Heart School paper, *Monarch*, November, 1965.

73. Interview with Gladys Garrett Clark, December 8, 1970; Sacred Heart School Records for September, 1965.

74. *Paraclete Chronicle*, op. cit., Winter, 1965.

Sr. Marie Angela, Greenville, MS

CHAPTER XIX
Septembers of Confrontation

Following the aftermath of the Freedom Summer when public schools reluctantly began to integrate, many Holy Spirit Missionary Sisters in Mississippi were becoming convinced that their all-black schools were being used as excuses by those wanting to prevent integration in the Mississippi Catholic school system. Perhaps by closing them they would be doing a greater service for the black people than by keeping them open. There were other reasons, too, for relinquishing their schools. Despite the assistance from the diocese, the facilities of Holy Ghost and St. Rose high schools were inadequate. The elementary schools were burdens on the parishes, and the financially-undernourished school board were grossly underpaying their faithful lay teachers, thus perpetrating an injustice to black teachers.[1] The missionaries themselves were only receiving forty-five to fifty dollars a month remuneration for their service in the mission schools, and the lack of vocations as well as the high cost of the sisters' higher education were becoming acute problems for the community, which had one hundred sisters over the age of sixty-five, at least one hundred twenty between sixty-five and fifty, and twenty-five sisters in studies.[2] With integration of the diocesan schools just a few years ahead, hopefully, it seemed unwise to seek additional funding for channeling into new schools, modern equipment, and salaries of increasing numbers of lay teachers. But neither could the sisters continue operating the schools as they were if they were to maintain the same excellence in education that they had given blacks for more than half a century.

On October 18, 1966, Sister Marilyn Dobberstein, Provincial of the Holy Spirit Missionary Sisters, sent a letter to Bishop Brunini and Father John Bowman, Provincial of the Society of the Divine Word, requesting a meeting to discuss these and other problems facing their schools in the South.

She added,

Since relatively few children in our schools are Catholic and in general conversions are few, we have been wondering if another type of apostolate would not be more effective and less expensive.[3]

The date for the meeting was set for November 10 and the place the Heidelberg Hotel in Jackson. In his letter of confirmation to Sister Marilyn, Bishop Brunini assured her that the Church in Mississippi was definitely committed to integration:

Actually, the question here in Mississippi is that the government will now permit us to integrate as we have always desired according to Christian principles.

About 20 students from Holy Ghost and Christ the King high schools are now enrolled in St. Joseph High

School in Jackson. Integration is also proceeding on the elementary level, but we simply do not have space available for full integration of our Catholic Negro children in Jackson at the present time.[4]

On November 10 Bishop Brunini arrived at the Heidelberg Hotel with Msgr. Koury; Sister Marilyn was accompanied by Sister Kathleen; and Father Bowman had invited the pastors of the Southern missions.[5]

The summit meeting got off to a good start. Bishop Brunini and Father Bowman readily admitted that the sisters' remuneration of $45 to $50 a month was meager. Msgr. Koury said that he couldn't see how their present salary even provided the necessities of life, and being professional women, their life style required more than the mere necessities. The diocesan school board recommended an annual salary of $1,200 for religious teachers with a Bachelor's Degree and $1,500 for one having a Master's Degree. Although the cost of their sisters' higher education was the same as that of other communities, the Holy Spirit Missionary Sisters were not expecting the priests to compensate them in accordance with the diocesan salary scale. The difference was their contribution to the black apostolate and a sign of their love for poverty, the constant companion of Christ, as their religious constitution decribed it. When the pastors hesitated about naming a definite figure for the raise, Bishop Brunini suggested raising it from $45 and $50 to $75 a month for ten months, which was acceptable to Sister Marilyn, and he told the priests present to let him know before they left the meeting if their parish budgets could support the increase, adding that he would help any parish having difficulty with it.

When addressing the missionary aspect of the schools, Father Leonard Hoefler of St. Mary's in Vicksburg said that almost every member of his parish who had joined the Church had been brought in by the sisters through the schools. Father Louis Benoit, pastor of Sacred Heart Parish in Greenville, confirmed his observation, adding that all the converts in one way or another were traced back to the schools.

Msgr. Koury pointed out that forty percent of the diocesan schools in Mississippi were mission schools educating over 3,500 non-Catholic children. For half a century this had been the most effective means in bringing blacks into the church. If the sisters closed their schools, they would be giving up this apostolate. He thought this would be disastrous and emphasized the importance of thoroughly evaluating any new programs before allowing them to replace their present school system.

At the end of the meeting it was clear to the sisters that the pastors and superintendent wanted to keep the schools open despite the shabby condition of some of the facilities and the difficulty of raising funds to meet the day-to-day expenses. They were disappointed that the clergy appeared to have no program for the future and seemed to be satisfied to settle back comfortably into the status quo and simply face decisions when they were thrust upon them.[6] This left the sisters with a very uncertain future. If they were to specialize in other fields, they would need education and training in their areas of competence and this could not be accomplished overnight.

In Rome the sisters' major superiors were also regarding the future of the Southern missions with interest, and at their request Sister Marilyn sent Sister Kathleen on a fact-finding mission to discover the kinds of apostolates that would be open to the sisters if integration came and their schools closed.[7] After interviewing a number of key persons in Jackson, including the Director of Diocesan Renewal, a Catholic Civil Rights worker of Christ the King Parish and a prominent member of Holy Ghost Parish, Sister Kathleen's response to her superiors revealed a variety of missionary opportunities that would be available to the sisters. The list included leadership training programs, family life and adult education, social work, counseling and catechetics, home care instructions, secretarial schools for girls and trade schools for boys, education on how to register and vote, teaching in public schools and the whole area of human relations.[8]

From Sister Kathleen's report it appeared that the possibilities were endless and, for the most part, would be dependent upon each sister's individual preference in the light of her education, talents, and physical health. The next step, then, was to hear from the sisters. This meeting of all the Holy Spirit Missionary Sisters teaching in Mississippi and Arkansas was held at Holy Ghost Convent in Jackson on March 15, 1969, and proved to be so beneficial that it became an annual affair.

In addition to Sister Kathleeen's list of apostolates there were added day nurseries and headstart, home visiting, instructing school drop-outs (a very important area since Mississippi had dropped its compulsory education law), prison work, and projects for the poor. In the discussions that took place during the full-day session the sisters pointed out that little was being said or done in the diocese about integrating the Catholic elementary schools, yet they believed that it had to come soon. They expressed an uncertainty about their future in the South when this happened and said that it was very important to hear what the parents of the school children and the parishioners were saying about the sisters' role in any future programs that would involve the black people. They proposed that a sister be freed to make this study and that a definite statement follow from it on the future direction of the Southern apostolate.[9]

The proposal was accepted by the Provincial Chapter in Techny in the summer, and Sister Engratia Gales was assigned to make the study. She had just completed a two-year assignment in the San Diego (California) Diocese, instructing teachers in religious education, and was free at the moment to accept another assignment.[10] It would be her task to hear from the greater community where the sisters taught in order to make the transition from the classroom to other apostolates go smoothly.

Sister Engratia's first stop was at Holy Ghost Convent, Jackson, where she remained from October until November 8, interviewing parishioners, superintendents of both the Catholic and public schools, Catholic Charities, public school principals, civic agencies, the bishop, and pastor. The high school had been discontinued in May 1969, and the school had an enrollment of 240 students in grades one through eight. Grades seven and eight would probably be dropped at the end of the school term.

The school was highly respected, and without exception the parishioners that she interviewed were opposed to closing it even though they recognized that the building was deteriorating. They told her that the school was vital to the Jackson Negro and his prestige, and they planned to build a new one as soon as the church, which was in the process of being built, was completed and the mortgage paid. They expressed a fear that if the school closed and children transferred to other Catholic schools, their parents would soon follow them to the church where the school was located, and Holy Ghost parish would suffer. They objected to merging with any of the white parishes in the area for fear they would lose their identity and all that they had worked and sacrificed for. Father Bourges, the pastor, maintained that the school was not segregated since he would accept any qualified student who applied, white or black.

When asked how else the sisters could serve the people in the area, they pointed out to her that the school was located in a poverty area and many families were on welfare or low income. As soon as families reached a certain level financially, they moved away to the more affluent neighborhoods in Jackson. Hence, the area could use a community center run by a team of sisters dedicated to solving problems rather than emphasizing service.[11]

By the time Sister Engratia had completed her research in Jackson and moved on to Meridian, the Natchez-Jackson diocese had a new superintendent of schools. Msgr. Koury had retired and Father James K. Gilbert, a 38-year old teacher who had been the first white instructor at Jackson State College, was appointed as diocesan superintendent of schools to fill the vacancy.[12] A fearless man, willing to stand up for his convictions in the face of opposition and hostility, he devoted his first weeks in office to visiting schools, checking files and studying each situation, much as Sister Engratia was doing for the Holy Spirit Missionary Sisters.[13]

On November 21 he issued a statement to the principals of the 57 Catholic schools in Mississippi, noting that integration was soon coming to all the public schools in the state and that they, too, should prepare for full integration of their students and faculties. He said that they should be looking for black teachers for the next school term. He was also aware, he said, that many white parents in Mississippi were withdrawing their children from integrated public schools and hastily establishing private schools for them. Some would turn to the all-white Catholic schools as well, and he reminded the principals that the diocesan schools were not to become havens of segregation for students who were running from integration in the public schools.[14]

On December 12 at a meeting with the principals held in Jackson, Father Gilbert passed out a paper that went even further than his first communication. It contained suggestions for consolidating and integrating the diocesan schools.

Except for Sacred Heart School in Greenville, which was to pair with Our Lady of Lourdes School, the position paper recommended that all the other schools staffed by the Holy Spirit Missionary Sisters be closed and the students absorbed by the all-white schools in the area.

These suggestions are made to stimulate serious

*thinking and to underscore the urgency and the neces-
sity for planning,*

he told the principals, adding that he did not think it
right to pull out of every black school. He acknowledged that the proposals would upset and anger
some people, but he thought that the school boards
had to start somewhere.[15]

The principals reaffirmed the diocesan policy of
full integration of student bodies and faculties in the
Mississippi Catholic school system and resolved to
back and encourage consolidation and integration of
racially-imbalanced schools where this was feasible
and advantageous following dialogue between the
boards, principals, and pastors.[16]

Bishop Brunini also spoke out in favor of integration in the Catholic schools in a pastoral letter to the
people of the diocese in the early part of January
1970:

*There should be no mistake concerning the Catholic
Church's attitude towards school integration. Every
Catholic school in Mississippi is obligated to admit
applicants without regard to race. In our policy and in
our teaching, including our school curriculum, we
proclaim that racial segregation is an affront to the
informed conscience. While this should be obvious to
all with any knowledge of the Catholic Church, we
repeat it now in order to make it perfectly clear that the
Catholic school system does not offer a refuge from
integration.*[17]

On January 3, 1970, Mississippi Governor John
Bell Williams went on statewide television to an-
nounce that the fight over school freedom of choice
was lost and that parents should

decide for themselves what type of school their child

would attend.

That moment that we have resisted for fifteen years, that we have fought hopefully to avoid, at least to delay, is finally at hand. The children of Mississippi, white and black, have been denied the right to attend the school of their choice by an arbitrary edict of the United States Supreme Court.

The arsenal of legal and legislative weapons have been exhausted. [18]

Thus the decade of the 70's began with the superintendent and principals of the Mississippi Catholic schools, the bishop and the governor all speaking out for integration or at least accepting the fact of its being forced upon them. Pro-integration groups naively assumed that it was simply a matter of the races sitting down together and working out the minor details. That the diocese at last had an aggressive spokesman for integration in the person of Father Gilbert, who had demonstrated that he was not afraid to express his Christian convictions even when they were unfashionable or unpopular, pleased the Holy Spirit Missionary Sisters, who thought such a champion was long overdue.

But even as the sisters were rejoicing in their good fortune, Father Gilbert was preparing to resign and return to his teaching post at Jackson State College. Word had passed through the diocese that the school board of St. Richard's School in a northeast affluent neighborhood of Jackson was accepting white students fleeing from integration. [19] At the same time, a controversy had arisen in Vicksburg in which events appeared to be different from what they really were. The two elementary school principals, Sister Priscilla Burke (St. Mary's) and Sister Ancilla Harkins (St.

Francis Xavier) were members of St. Aloysius High School board and both were committed to integration, as was the entire board. There was a spirit of openness coupled with a genuine Christian attitude toward integration among the Catholic schools in town,[20] and the board was taken aback when Sister Virginia, the principal of St. Aloysius, asked the board to make a public proclamation that it wouldn't accept any students at midterm in compliance with diocesan policy. Instead, the board preferred to make a strong statement for integration of the schools, knowing that any parents not wanting to place their children in an integrated school would be kept away, and it passed a resolution to that effect.

Sister Virginia refused to accept the board's resolution, demanding that her own be passed. When the board refused, she resigned.

On the surface the controversy between the school board and the principal appeared to place the board in an unfavorable position since it was refusing to make a public proclamation not to accept students in midterm, and something of this had reached Father Gilbert.[21] When he approached Bishop Brunini about these apparent violations of the diocesan school policies, the Bishop gave him no assurance that he would intervene and stop them. Bishop Brunini was of the opinion that he had exercised his pastoral duty in teaching justice in the present circumstances in his January pastoral letter, and now he expected the pastors and parish school boards to weigh each situation and act in the best interests of all concerned.

Father Gilbert became so disturbed over what seemed to him to be a total disregard for diocesan school policies and Bishop Brunini's unwillingness to intervene that he made a decision to resign in protest. Sister Kathleen learned of this, and in a conversation with Sister Priscilla she suggested that the Vicksburg principal talk to him and try to persuade him to remain in office.[22] Sister Priscilla perceived the situation in Vicksburg as more of a power struggle between the board and the principal rather than a racial dispute. She drove to Jackson and spent some time with the frustrated priest, trying to persuade him to change his mind, reminding him how much his leadership meant to the sisters in the black apostolate.[23] But he was convinced that his resignation would do more good for integration than his staying on the job, and in a letter dated January 20, he notified the principals of the diocesan schools that he was resigning. He wrote that he was doing so on principle because the diocesan school board, which had voted total and full integration of student bodies and faculties, was not upholding the principle, not even over his protest, that schools not accept students during the year for fear that parochial schools would become havens for segregationists.

His resignation was a real disappointment to the Holy Spirit Missionary Sisters, who had regarded him as a courageous leader in the complex struggle to integrate the Mississippi Catholic school system.[24] But before they had recovered from this blow, they were shocked to read a statement from Bishop Brunini in the Jackson *Daily News* in which he accused Father Gilbert of having established a "one-man policy" while calling it a diocesan policy. He said:

We have a diocesan school board which we have had now for some eight to ten years, but Father Gilbert

362

wasn't willing to abide by the decisions of this board.
The official policy of the school board was a simple
suggestion that there be no registration of transferees
in the middle of the year, unless they were Catholic
children who had been in Catholic schools in another
town.[25]

The missionaries were stunned. Not only had they
lost a courageous spokesman, but they judged the
bishop's public attack on Father Gilbert to be grossly
unfair and unwarranted. They believed that the
priest had stood for his convictions and had acted
within his competence. On the other hand, the bishop appeared to be very inconsistent, enunciating
theories and principles in letters, then hedging and
refusing to take a stand, even contradicting himself
when it came down to practical applications.[26]

Saddened and distressed by this tragic turn of
events, a group of Holy Spirit Missionary Sisters met
at Holy Ghost Convent, Jackson, to discuss the problems regarding the implementation of the diocesan
policies on integrating the schools and to determine
the action they should take. Besides the situations in
Jackson and Vicksburg that induced Father Gilbert to
resign as superintendent of Mississippi's Catholic
school system, they knew of other instances where
diocesan school policies were being flaunted, apparently with the bishop's approval. In the wake of
integration, white parents throughout the state were
withdrawing their children from the public schools
and establishing private schools for them in any
buildings they could find. Two Holy Spirit Missionary Sisters from Sacred Heart School were teaching Sunday religion classes that year in Indianola,
about 25 miles from Greenville. They had found the

atmosphere of the parish a very closed one on the question of integration, but had continued teaching the children with the hope that they might have some salutary influence upon them and their parents. However, as the weeks went by it became increasingly clear to them that the people were resisting any change of attitude on racial issues. They had looked in vain for some encouragement from the pastor to turn his people's thoughts toward the basic tenet of Christianity, that of love of neighbor regardless of race, creed, or color. Since everyone in the town of about 9,000 knew that they working in the black apostolate in Greenville, for the sisters not to see any results from their teaching was becoming an embarrassment to them. The same week that Father Gilbert resigned, Sister Ann Therese Miller, the principal of Sacred Heart, learned that the pastor had sold the old Immaculate Conception church building and classrooms to an individual, knowing that this person was going to turn it into a private school for white children fleeing segregated public schools. This was the ultimate affront to the missionaries' integrity. Sister Ann Therese and the other members of her religious community concluded that they could no longer teach religion at a parish where racism was openly encouraged. After informing the pastor of their decision, she, Sister Janet, and Sister Andre Peil joined about thirty black Catholics on the picket line to protest the sale.[27]

Clarksdale near Merigold was another trouble spot. Here St. Elizabeth Church had received approval from the bishop to reopen its seventh and eighth grades for Catholics, supposedly to accept students who were fleeing integration in the public schools.[28]

After discussing these and other distressing situations in the diocese, the sisters who represented the five schools in Mississippi decided to review the problems with their respective communities and incorporate their sisters' views in a letter to Bishop Brunini. Sister Kathleen would also contact the president of the Jackson Sisters' Organization and ask her to call a meeting of all the Jackson sisters to discuss the issues, and, if appropriate, formulate their concerns to the bishop.[29]

Within a few days all of the convents but St. Joseph's in Meridian had sent off letters to Bishop Brunini.

The reason given for Father Gilbert's resignation was, indeed, a sad commentary on the Christianity of the school board which voted to accept students who were fleeing integration in public schools,

the letter from the sisters at Holy Ghost Convent began. Then quoting from the bishop's letter in which he wrote that racial segregation was an affront to the informed conscience, the sisters continued:

We can only conclude that what you agree to in theory, you do not agree to in practice when following through on principles would cost something in the way of conflict with certain vested interests. This grieves us very much as we were proud of your enunciation of Christian principles and were hopeful that you would take a stand for the right in the name of the Church in Mississippi even when this was not popular.

Unless you can find the courage to do this, we are doubtful that we personally could continue to work in your diocese.[30]

From Vicksburg, the sisters of St. Mary's wrote:

We received the news of Father Gilbert's resignation with a real sense of loss for we appreciated the strong voice for Christian social justice with which he has so courageously spoken.

Then they reviewed the events in the diocese which seemed contrary to diocesan policy on integration, adding:

*If leaders of the Catholic Church in our diocese do not take a positive, **specific** stand for the principles of social justice, then perhaps the Negro Catholics and the Mississippi Negroes are right when they say (as was said by a thinking member of our parish council at our September meeting), "The Negro means nothing to the Catholic Church in Mississippi." This parishioner added as part of the reason for this statement: "If it weren't for missionary priests and sisters, the Negro would not be part of the Church . . .." We implore you to clarify the stand of the Catholic Church in the Diocese of Natchez-Jackson by a public, **specific** statement which makes occurrences of incidents of segregationalistic momentum within the framework of the Catholic Church in Mississippi impossible, and says to the Mississippi Negro and, in particular, to the Catholic Mississippi Negro as well as to the Catholic Mississippi white: You are important to the Catholic Church and to the Diocese of Natchez-Jackson.[31]*

After quoting from the bishop's pastoral letter of early January, the sisters of St. Rose Convent wrote:

We are repulsed and horrified by the thought of repercussions resulting from this seeming retraction, not only among the black Christians with whom we have daily contact, but also within the larger body of Christians for whom "racial segregation is an affront to their informed consciences.''

*Black men understand our refusal to abandon the white racist. But to paraphrase John H. Griffin, they do not see much concern over the alienation of **their** souls, because while loving the afflicted white racist, the Church gives the unfortunate appearance of at least condoning his racism. We must face not only the questioning attitude of our people; but even among ourselves, the dichotomy between your beautiful pastoral letter of January 12 and your alarming interpretation of the diocesan school board resolution puzzles and frightens us.[32]*

Finally, from the Sisters of Sacred Heart Convent, who also expressed deep sorrow over Father Gilbert's resignation and the developments in the diocese which led to it, the letter concluded:

It is a sad commentary that the unchristian stand of a number of our Catholics in Mississippi and the wavering position of the leaders of the Church in Mississippi in regard to the practice of affirmed principles placed Father Gilbert in a position where he had no other choice but to resign .... We have hoped for a much stronger support of the principles and practice of social justice on the part of our bishop, our clergy, and lay leaders ....[33]

On January 29 a number of priests were in Jackson for a workshop on the new liturgy, and a biracial group of about fourteen took the opportunity to visit the bishop in the chancery and protest the opening of the seventh and eighth grades in Clarksdale. Early the next morning Bishop Brunini left the city for an ecumenical meeting in Chicago, but he wired back to the chancery rescinding his permission to the Clarksdale group to open the two grades. He delegated

Msgr. Paul Canonici, who had been appointed as diocesan school superintendent to fill the vacancy left by Father Gilbert, to deliver the message to the school board.[34]

On the same day that the delegation of priests met with the bishop, about thirty sisters teaching in the Jackson area met at Holy Ghost Convent. There were School Sisters of Notre Dame, Ursulines, School Sisters of St. Francis, a Dominican, a Holy Cross Sister, and a Pax Christi lady, representing teachers from Holy Family, Christ the King, St. Mary's, St. Therese, Holy Ghost, St. Joseph High School, and Jackson State College. No Mercy Sisters were represented, nor was anyone from St. Richard's School, where the trouble lay and where the Sisters of Mercy taught. The purpose of the meeting was to provide a forum for addressing the problems in the Mississippi Catholic schools regarding integration. Sister Kathleen, who hosted the meeting, was impressed by the sincerity and goodness of the sisters, who wanted to be fair to all the students, the parents, the pastors, and the bishop.

They resolved to invite the bishop to meet with them and discuss the Mississippi Catholic schools as a unitary school system. They also decided to offer positive assistance in preparing the white community for pairing and/or consolidation with black schools by developing adult education programs. Sister Kathleen was named to a committee to work on these materials.[35]

As a follow-up to his telegram to the school board of St. Elizabeth Church in Clarksdale, Bishop Brunini sent a letter to the pastor on February 3, acknowledging that the problem of division had reached beyond the boundaries of Clarksdale to encompass the whole diocese, and, indeed, the nation. He reminded him that his approval for reopening the seventh and eighth grades had been granted on the condition that black teachers and black students be made to feel welcome. He praised them for the efforts they had made to do this, but added that the black community hadn't been able to really feel welcome under the present circumstances.

I was approached by significant numbers of dedicated priests, religious, and laity who saw the situation as a contradiction of my pastoral letter and who told me, in effect, that it was creating for them a crisis of conscience. I could see serious divisions developing within the diocese as a whole and these are factors no bishop can easily dismiss. The whole situation was fast developing into something that could tear our diocese apart. Consequently it called for serious and thoughtful re-evaluation and for a difficult response in faith. In view of the overall situation it became evident to me that St. Elizabeth parish and school, the Church in our diocese, and the Church nationwide would suffer if the designed plan continued. I felt there was no alternative but to withdraw my approval of reopening the seventh and eighth grades.[36]

In his reply to the Holy Spirit Missionary Sisters, Bishop Brunini said that he hoped they would accept a joint letter since the letters he had received from them were similar. In it he praised Father Gilbert as a man of strong convictions and greatly interested in social justice. He added:

However, the statement of the Diocesan School Board that no transferee be accepted was merely a suggestion, and he felt that the local school boards should have some ability to consider local situations . . . . Father Gilbert's attitude was that if one child were admitted as a transferee at midterm this would label the school a haven for segregation. He wouldn't consider that there might be other factors involved, such as transportation.

With his letter the bishop enclosed a copy of the one he had sent to the pastor in Clarksdale. He also wrote that the proposed sale of property in Indianola had not been terminated, and he was holding the property in the name of the diocese. He said that he would like to see the whole church building in Indianola turn from a symbol of division to a symbol of unity. Then he pointed out that the predominantly-black Immaculate Conception School in Clarksdale had also accepted some transferees at midterm, but no one had complained about that. He continued:

A bishop has to listen a good deal these days. That's what I'm trying to do. Let the local people work out their answers. If there is anything against faith and morals, then the bishop must step in and veto the situation.[37]

At the invitation of the newly-appointed diocesan superintendent of schools, fifteen Holy Spirit Missionary Sisters, representing the five schools in Mississippi, met with him on February 1 at the Sun and Sand Motel in Jackson. Msgr. Canonici was not entirely unknown to some of the sisters since he had been principal of St. Joseph High School in Jackson, and those who knew him expected him to take a fair and firm stand on issues. The sisters were grateful for the opportunity to sit down with him informally and share their fears and frustrations of the present and the expectations and visions of the future.[38]

The five schools were at various stages of dialoguing with members of the predominantly white schools in their areas, but each had its own unique set of problems and goals. St. Mary's School was waiting for the bishop's approval to close its doors and send its students from grades one through six to St. Francis Xavier School. The people of Holy Ghost and Sacred Heart schools wouldn't hear of the word "merge," and St. Joseph and St. Rose of Lima schools wanted pairing, but were open to merging if it came to that.[39]

There was a general consensus among the sisters that a blanket statement from the bishop regarding the closing of schools and parishes would not be good, would be even harmful because of the diversity of factors to be taken into consideration in each local parish and school situation. However, they wanted the bishop to emphasize more strongly the major premises that had already been established as diocesan policy, support dialogue and a local community's efforts when they were clearly in line with the principles and policies of the Church and the diocese. All agreed that there was a need to educate the people throughout the diocese to improve race relations and give direction to the parishes and schools. They told him that they saw their apostolate to be one to the total Church in Mississippi and not strictly restricted to the blacks. In the transition period they were going through, they saw themselves as a bridge between the whites and blacks in the Christian community.[40]

The meeting of the sisters with Bishop Brunini requested by the Jackson Sisters' Organization was scheduled for February 28 and was open to all of the sisters in the diocese. They presented the bishop with a set of questions that concerned them, and he did not flinch from answering them, although he clearly expressed his opinion on what a bishop ought to do. He stressed the point that to impose one moral solution where there were many moral alternatives was contrary to the role of the bishop as described by the Vatican Council and was unjust because it denied the laity freedom and room for action. In the context of American society, he told the sisters, dictatorial methods do not work. One has to respect the uniqueness, interiority, and freedom of every person. Leadership in American society, if it is to be effective, particularly in context of Church today, had to involve shared responsibility in both formulation and the execution of policies. On the point of a unitary school system for parochial schools in the diocese, he said that the word "dual" in this context had its origin in civil law where black students were forbidden to attend white schools and vice versa. He went on:

> *If by unitary, you mean that there are, in fact, predominantly black schools and predominantly white schools, you must recognize that these have their origin in history, sociology, and freedom, rather than Church teaching or Church law. I have inherited this situation. I have not imposed it. I do not feel I can start closing down parishes and schools contrary to the wishes of the people involved when faith and morality are not being violated. Neither can I impose busing or pairing when there are obvious moral alternatives.*

The bishop's candidness in facing the problems, his willingness to listen to all sides of a question, his wisdom in holding back in order to bring as many as possible along together were his special gifts to the diocese in its most difficult years.[41]

Bishop Brunini admitted in an interview that year:

I know a lot of my priests are affected with racism. But how much pressure do you use and how do you bring people along? Am I supposed to call a Catholic in, give him a rigorous examination, and, if he doesn't measure up, throw him out of the Church? I'm affected, too.[42]

Like so many other white Mississippians he had to learn how to accept the black man and woman as brother and sister in the Lord. But he was willing to learn and in so doing would be an example to the entire Mississippi church.

In the meantime, each of the five schools in Mississippi and the two in Arkansas staffed by the Holy Spirit Missionary Sisters was struggling through its own integration problems.

Sr. Curmella, after May Crowning, Bay St. Louis, MS, 1979

Chapter XIX Footnotes: Septembers of Confrontation

1. SVD, Sister Marilyn Dobberstein to Rev. John Bowman, carbon to Most Rev. Joseph Brunini, October 18, 1966.

2. SVD, Minutes of the Meeting with the Missionary Sisters of the Holy Spirit and the Fathers of the Society of the Divine Word (November 10, 1966).

3. Marilyn to Bowman, op. cit.

4. NJ, Brunini to Marilyn, October 31, 1966.

5. This and following paragraphs from Minutes, op cit.

6. Minutes of the Meeting held by the Provincial Councilors and the Sisters Engaged in the Southern Apostolate (March 15, 1969).

7. Sister Kathleen, *Report on Negro Apostolate in Mississippi*, December 26, 1967.

8. Ibid., December 27-January 1.

9. Minutes of Sisters' Meeting, op. cit.

10. Interview with Sister Engratia Gales, April 2, 1983.

11. Sister Engratia's Report from Jackson to the Provincial Council, November 7, 1969.

12. Interview with Sister Ann Therese Miller, January 1, 1971; JDN, January 23, 1970.

13. Sister Ann Therese, op. cit.

14. Rev. James Gilbert to Principals, November 11, 1969.

15. Gilbert to Principals, December 12, 1969; Minutes of December 12 meeting.

16. Resolutions before Principals and Diocesan School Board, December 6, 1969.

17. Brunini Pastoral Letter, January 9, 1970; evidently read on different days in churches.

18. *Clarion-Ledger Jackson Daily News*, Vol. XVI, No. 13, (January 4, 1970).

19. Kathleen to Marilyn, January 6, 1970.

20. Priscilla to Brunini, February 7, 1970.

21. Interview with Sister Priscilla Burke, June 16, 1970.

22. Kathleen to Marilyn, January 15, 1970.

23. Interview with Sister Priscilla Burke, April, 1983; Priscilla to Marilyn, January 28, 1970.

24. Gilbert to Principals, op. cit.

25. JDN, January 23, 1970.

26. Kathleen to Marilyn, January 24, 1970.

27. Interview with Ann Therese, op. cit.; Ann Therese to Marilyn, February 1, 1970; newspaper clippings, undated.

28. Priscilla to Marilyn, op. cit.

29. Kathleen to Marilyn, op. cit.

30. Jackson Sisters to Brunini, January 26, 1970.

31. Vicksburg Sisters to Brunini, January 28, 1970.

32. Bay St. Louis Sisters to Brunini, January 30, 1970.

33. Greenville Sisters to Brunini, February 1, 1970.

34. Kathleen to Marilyn, February 2, 1970.

35. Ibid.

36. Brunini to pastor of Clarksdale, February 3, 1970.

37. Brunini to the four convents, February 4, 1970.

38. Minutes of Meeting of the Holy Spirit Missionary Sisters from Mississippi with Monsignor Paul Canonici (February 10, 1970).

39. Ibid.

40. Ibid.

41. Responses to Agenda Submitted to Bishop Brunini by Sister Evelyn Garrity, February 28, 1970.

42. Interview with Bishop Brunini, op. cit.

CHAPTER XX
Septembers in the Seventies

After completing her research for the sisters in Jackson, Sister Engratia went to St. Joseph's Convent in Meridian, where she learned that a meeting to discuss the integration of St. Joseph's School and the St. Patrick's all-white school had already been scheduled by the school boards for January 15. The Holy Spirit Missionary Sisters were not anticipating any major difficulties, and Sister Mary Angelica Miessen, the principal, told the community emissary that she was confident that the two school boards could draw up a plan that would be acceptable to most of the parents. Both schools were teaching grades one through six and were duplicating grades, staff, classrooms, and equipment in buildings that could accommodate additional students. While the parents of the children enrolled in St. Joseph's wanted integration, they did not want to merge their school with St. Patrick's for fear they would lose their identity and voice in the formulation of school policies. Instead, they were prepared to suggest pairing with the lower grades in one building, the higher grades in the other.[1]

With great expectations, the St. Joseph representatives, Sisters Engratia, Mary Angelica, Xavier Ann Schwacha, and Mary Eileen Vallimont, eighteen parishioners, not all of them members of the school board, and the pastor assembled at St. Patrick's, where the meeting was to be held. It was a day the black parents had long awaited, the day when they would sit down as equals with the white people and devise an educational system that would benefit all of their children.[2]

Representing St. Patrick's were Sister Marian, the principal, Msgr. John Scanlon, the pastor, and the members of the board. Before any discussion could begin, Msgr. Scanlon shattered the black parents' expectations of equal bargaining power by flatly announcing that not for a moment would he entertain the idea of pairing the schools, rezoning, or busing. His solution was clear and simple. Send your children to our school. We will welcome them.[3]

Disappointed and offended by this one-sided approach, the black parents expressed their disapproval, but to no avail. When they realized they could not move Msgr. Scanlon from his position, they asked for some assurance that their children would be made to feel welcome at St. Patrick's and that they themselves would be permitted to serve on the school board and be treated as equals by the white parents. Sister Marian promised them that all the children would be treated alike and would be given equal chances, but she said that she could not speak for the white parents and what their attitude toward the black parents would be.[4]

As the discussion progressed, it became clear to some of St. Joseph's representatives that the other school had ulterior motives for wanting their students: it hoped the sisters would follow them to St. Patrick's and replace the white school's higher-salaried lay teachers. Msgr. Scanlon said that he would like to have at least three Holy Spirit Missionary Sisters teach at St. Patrick's in September even if no black children came; but Sister Engratia replied emphatically that the sisters would never teach in an all-white parish school in the South. The sisters would be willing to teach in an integrated school in order to help their students make a smoother adjustment, but the number of sisters would depend upon the number of black children attending the school.[5]

By the end of the evening those present were satisfied that they had honestly faced the real stumbling block to integration, which was racism, but decisions were left for future meetings. When April came the boards were still at the discussion stage, St. Patrick's not budging from its stand against pairing, and St. Joseph's being forced to look ahead to the coming September.[6]

At a meeting in the parish hall on April 19, 1970, attended by the St. Joseph parish school board and parish council, the pastor and sisters, and interested parents, Sister Mary Angelica explained the school situation in detail. For some time, they had been operating the school with double grades, a teaching principal, inadequate equipment, and outdated books. Rather than going to the expense of hiring additional lay teachers and buying new materials, she thought it would be better to integrate the

379

schools even if it meant sending their children to St. Patrick's. By the end of the evening most of the parents agreed with the principal's assessment of their dilemma, and before the meeting adjourned the school board voted to close the school.[7]

Sister Engratia visited Msgr. Scanlon the following day to acquaint him with the board's decision. He said he was very anxious to understand the black mentality and admitted that he was scared because he didn't know it. When she told him that Sister Martin Williams, a black Holy Spirit Missionary Sister and a native of Vicksburg who had been teaching at St. Joseph's, would transfer to St. Patrick's in September, integrating the faculty and assisting the students of St. Joseph's to make the adjustment to an integrated school, he was very pleased and proposed giving her a salary of $4,000 a year. Of this, the community would receive $1,700, more than double Sister Martin's stipend at the mission school, and the remainder would be used as scholarships for the students coming from St. Joseph's who could not afford the $40 a month tuition at St. Patrick's. The money would be given to the sisters, who would distribute it to the parents according to their needs; thus allowing every child to pay the tuition fully, without anyone but the sisters and the parents knowing who were receiving help. The sisters readily accepted this plan.[8]

St. Joseph's Elementary School was leased to STAR, an antipoverty program sponsored by the Office of Economic Opportunity and the U. S. Department of Labor in cooperation with the diocese. Administered by qualified local leadership, it provided basic education to illiterate adults and helped them find gainful employment after they had completed their internship.[9] Sister Xavier Ann joined the staff of STAR in September and Sister Bernice Fenske accepted a position as Latin instructor in a public high school during the week and also served the parish as religious education coordinator on the weekends.[10] The parish, which numbered two hundred members, would not consider merging with the white parish. They preferred to worship in their own church until the time came when the blacks experienced equality in an integrated church.

Eventually, the three Holy Spirit Missionary Sisters in Meridian moved into a smaller building on the premises, renting the 20-room convent, which had also served as a boarding school, to a family.[11]

While the two Catholic schools in Meridian were working through their integration problems, Sister Engratia had visited the other schools in Mississippi, returning to St. Joseph's for all of the important meetings of the two school boards. When she came to Greenville on February 11, Father Gilbert had resigned as diocesan superintendent of schools; three sisters from Sacred Heart Convent had joined the picket line in Indianola; the bishop had stopped the sale of the church building and rescinded the permission for opening seventh and eighth grades in Clarksdale, and in Greenville the rapport between the school boards of Sacred Heart and St. Joseph schools was in shambles.

In 1964 a new elementary school and convent had been built for whites in the southeast sector of the city.[12] The school, named Our Lady of Lourdes and staffed by Irish Sisters of Mercy, was governed by the St. Joseph School board, which also governed the high school by that name, located in the southwest part of the city. St. Joseph Church was in the downtown area in the extreme west section of Greenville and one block south of the street that divides the north and south sectors.

Sacred Heart Parish comprised the highly industrialized northeast sector of the city where lived more than half of Greenville's 24,000 blacks. It included some of the poorest areas as well as the modest homes of most of the middle-income black families.[13]

The parish had a debt of $13,000, which the finance committee hoped to have paid by the end of the school term. The school, built in 1957, was staffed by five sisters and two lay teachers. It housed a kindergarten and grades one through six, and had an enrollment of 192 pupils, of whom 46 were Catholic. The children paid ten dollars monthly tuition with about twelve exceptions in whole or in part.[14]

Lourdes had a total of 292 students and was staffed by five sisters and five lay teachers. Tuition was paid according to a rating scale. The school board was planning to build four new classrooms, and the Sacred Heart parents hoped, instead, to utilize their classrooms through pairing. To discuss this possibility, they had initiated a meeting of the two school boards, which had taken place two days before Sister Engratia arrived. In preparation for the meeting the Sacred Heart School board had prepared a position paper which reviewed the situation of the two schools, the proposal of pairing and the Christian and educational reasons for doing so.[15]

The board was disappointed when it arrived for the meeting and found only three officers of St. Joseph's School board—the pastor, who delegated full autonomy to his board, not taking part in its deliberations or decisions—and the sisters teaching at Our Lady of Lourdes.[16]

After presenting their position paper, the black representatives were appalled when the president of St. Joseph's School board took it amiss and lashed at Sister Ann Therese, the principal, accusing her of not preparing him adequately for the purpose of the meeting. Sister said that she saw no reason to tell him more: the paper discussed the situation of the schools which the black people wanted out in the open. The meeting lasted scarcely an hour, ending with St. Joseph's School board tersely requesting a report on the financial status of Sacred Heart School although the position paper had already made this quite clear.[17]

Hurt and disappointed, the members of the Sacred Heart School board called a meeting of the parents of the school children to ask for their opinion on the pairing of the schools and to find out how many of them would send their children back to Sacred Heart in September if the schools paired or if the school would continue as it was. A letter had been sent to the St. Joseph's School board, inviting them to be present to become better acquainted with the black parents and to be available to answer any questions or to ask any questions they might have. Instead of coming, however, it sent a letter which arrived only minutes before the meeting.[18] It again attacked the principal as if the question of pairing Our Lady of Lourdes and Sacred Heart schools were her idea alone. It offered the usual complaint of white people: that they were being forced to move too quickly in making a decision about the schools.[19]

They then proceeded with eight points that disregarded all that had been explained in the paper presented by the Sacred Heart School board at the earlier meeting, questioning the academic abilities of the children and the financial status of the school and parish, condemning the condition of the buildings, and concluding that it was the board's unanimous opinion that the pairing of Our Lady of Lourdes and Sacred Heart schools was not feasible. Perhaps in the future they would reconsider the possibility of doing so. In the meantime, they would continue to accept any black Catholic child from Sacred Heart School without exception into their school system and non-Catholics up to the limits of their capacity. Finally, they said that they thought it unwise to go into any joint meetings of the school boards at this time as had been suggested in the position paper.[20]

This cold rebuff stung the parents of the children at Sacred Heart. In replying to the letter, the board refuted the charges that had been made, explaining that the urgency was due to the need for making plans for the new school term; that the buildings were adequate and not in need of repairs; that the parents were able and willing to pay more in order to give their children quality education in a Catholic school. They did not want to close their school and merge with Our Lady of Lourdes. They wanted to be treated equally and given a share in administering the schools, and pairing seemed to be the only fair way to do this.[21]

When a letter of explanation from the Sacred Heart School board to Bishop Brunini brought no further action, the board voted to retain their autonomy and keep their doors open in September.[22]

In her report on Greenville to her superiors, Sister Engratia quoted some of the remarks she had heard from disappointed black parents.

We want to maintain our dignity.

The white man will only do something for the black man if he is forced. He will not do it because it is right.

The Catholic clergy does not support civil rights.

We will not merge.[23]

It was clear that the black parents in Greenville were determined to keep their own school open until they were accepted as equals in an integrated school system.

In Vicksburg and Bay St. Louis, the dialoguing between the school boards was more cordial than those going on in Meridian and Greenville, but similar problems had to be faced.

St. Mary's students from grades seven through twelve had already integrated with St. Aloysius High School. Since St. Mary's Elementary School facilities were in poor condition, there was no thought of pairing with St. Francis Xavier, the other elementary school in Vicksburg, which educated the children from St. Paul and St. Michael parishes. It was simply a matter of closing St. Mary's School and sending the children to St. Francis Xavier. To make the acceptance of St. Mary's students easier for St. Francis Xavier, Sister Marilyn promised the school board two Holy Spirit Missionary Sisters if the black Catholics, at least, were made to feel welcome.[24]

Tuition at St. Mary's was $75 for a single child and $144 for family tuition. Compared to the tuition at St. Francis Xavier, which was $180 per child and $700 for family, this was a formidable increase for the black parents.[25] When Sister Priscilla brought up the idea of using part of the sisters' salaries as scholarships for the black transferees, similar to the plan later adopted by St. Joseph's in Meridian, the white parents were incensed, complaining that the black children were getting in for nothing. They forgot that they were often the ones who underpaid the black parents for their work. But to keep peace, the sisters withdrew their proposal, confident that they would obtain the money elsewhere.[26] On several occasions, Bishop Brunini had indicated that the annual mission funds which were formerly channeled into school and church buildings would be better used in the 1970's as scholarships for black students who wanted a Catholic school education but who couldn't afford the ever spiraling tuition costs.[27]

On Christmas day the bishop was in Vicksburg to visit his brother and invited himself to St. Mary's for 9 a.m. Mass, coming over to the convent for rolls and coffee afterwards.[28] The sisters were living in a new convent completed in May, 1968.[29] An award-winner for its Greenville architect and designer, Robert Sferruzza, the $78,000 convent was located on the site of the former Geiger home which had been demolished by the wrecking crew. It contained eight private rooms, each having its own porch, screened from the street by louvres permitting ventilation while allowing for privacy. There were two parlors for visitors, a chapel, a combination dining room, common room and library, a kitchen and laundry facilities. The outside walls of the two-story building were of redwood with at least one wall in each room of the same material. The wood on the exterior walls was treated to achieve a silver-gray weathered patina, while the interior was a natural red finish.[30]

During the nine months of its construction, the Holy Spirit Missionary Sisters had been guests of the Mercy Sisters in Vicksburg and were given an especially warm welcome by Sister Mary Hildegarde Schumann, who as a child had played on the back porch of the original convent predating the Geiger home and who had later become a Mercy nun and the provincial superior of her community and was now retired and living in Vicksburg.[31]

When it came time for the Missionary Sisters to move into their new St. Mary's convent, the Sisters of Mercy showered them with linens, table service, lamps, and money for furniture. The same Christian spirit that had been present 62 years before when the Mercy Sisters offered the mission the furnishings of an unused chapel was visible again in their generous gifts for the new convent.[32]

As the bishop enjoyed his coffee and rolls amidst the convent's beautiful Christmas decor, Sister Priscilla seized the opportunity to speak to him about scholarships for their Catholic students who wanted to transfer to St. Francis Xavier, but were unable to pay the higher tuition cost. He assured her that mission money would be available for the purpose and that he was interested in making the schools in his hometown an example for all the others in the diocese.[33]

With this information to support them, St. Mary's School board met on January 27, 1970, and voted unanimously to discontinue the elementary school.[34]

Msgr. Mullen commented:

At long last the Catholic Church in Vicksburg is establishing a unitary school system. I feel that the people from all three Vicksburg parishes will work cooperatively to provide the best possible Catholic education for all Catholic children of Vicksburg.[35]

Father Frank Corcoran, pastor of St. Michael's Church, wrote to Sister Marilyn:

We are very sorry to see St. Mary's School close. But the priests and sisters who worked there for over 60 years were looking forward to the day when black and white children could go to school together, especially in our Catholic schools. We pray that the day of their dream has arrived and that the children will play with one another, not taking much notice of the difference in the color of their skin.[36]

When September came, seventy-six former students of St. Mary's, sixty-four of whom were Catholic,[37] enrolled in St. Aloysius and St. Francis Xavier. Sister Edwardine Stinn and Sister Ann Martin were on the faculty of St. Francis Xavier to facilitate the move of the elementary school children to the integrated school. Sister Priscilla became a student counsellor at St. Aloysius and taught classes in Home Economics and Remedial Reading. St. Mary's retained its kindergarten, taught by Sister Joan Liebhauser, and a nurse, Sister Canisilde Hesse, came to Vicksburg to work at Kuhn Memorial State Hospital about two blocks from the convent.[38]

St. Rose High School in Bay St. Louis had closed its doors in May 1968.[39] In 1970 Sister Mary Pardy was principal of the elementary school and some fruitful dialogue had taken place between the two elementary school boards of St. Rose and Our Lady of the Gulf.[40] The greatest anxiety among the black parents about integrating the two schools was the same expressed by the black parents of the other schools: they feared they would not be treated as equals. They had a tremendous pride in having built their school and in having successfully managed it over the years. They were quick to point out that the ratio of teachers to pupils at St. Rose was lower than at Our Lady of the Gulf; that grades one through eight had a fine academic program with a non-graded reading lab equipped with pacers, ear phones, overheads, tape recorders, and other helpful devices and materials. They valued highly the excellent education their children were receiving at St. Rose and were not sure they wanted to exchange all of this for integration.[41]

In addition, the parish had a substantial debt to pay off before it could seriously consider integrating the schools.[42] For its part, Our Lady of the Gulf School, operating with an annual parish subsidy close to $50,000, had its share of financial problems and could hardly absorb more students.[43] Realizing that the blocks to integration were more financial than racial, both school boards agreed to have a year of mutual preparation, meanwhile pairing the schools for various scholastic and athletic events during the year.[44]

In the meantime exciting events were taking place in Holy Ghost Parish in Jackson. On April 12, 1970, the parish dedicated its new church, a beautiful modern circular building costing $84,000.[45] At the same time, it was thinking about building a new elementary school or remodeling the former high school for the elementary grades. The 65-year-old building that Father Heick had put up as the first Catholic church and school for blacks in the capital of the state had become a fire trap and its plumbing had all but collapsed. Nevertheless, the parents were determined to keep the school open at all costs because of the excellent education their children were receiving from the Holy Spirit Missionary Sisters and because they did not feel welcome in the white parishes of the city nor, they were convinced, would their children feel welcome in the white schools. In her interviews with the people of Jackson, Sister Engratia had seen this fierce love that the people had for the school. Even Protestants would not hear of closing it. It had done so much for them, they had told her, uplifting them educationally and culturally, and it was a symbol to which black Catholics could turn with pride.[46]

The Holy Ghost School board had promised Sister Agnes Marie Crabb, Provincial of the Holy Spirit Missionary Sisters, that they would either remodel or begin building a new school by 1972, but when the 1971-72 term ended and nothing was in sight for the coming September, she and her councillors, unwilling to have the sisters teach in classrooms that were unworthy of the name, withdrew them from the school although not from Jackson.[47]

The people in the parish were furious. They hired lay teachers and opened the school in September with ninety pupils in kindergarten and grades one through three and housed them in the former high school building. Necessary repairs were made and the classrooms were carpeted and paneled, transforming them into safe, modern, pleasing study areas.[48] Since the reasons for withdrawing the sisters from the school no longer existed, Sister Agnes Marie and her councillors reconsidered their earlier decision, and on February 16, 1973, Sister Leonette Kaluzny was appointed principal and the fourth grade was added.[49]

On May 26, 1974, after the liturgy celebration, surrounded by the alumni of the school, the pastor, Father Malcolm O'Leary, himself an alumnus, burned the mortgage on the church.[50] Two weeks later the 65-year-old elementary school building that had cradled and nurtured the first black Catholics of Jackson was demolished.[51]

Across the Mississippi River in Pine Bluff, Arkansas, St. Peter's School had reached its capacity with a registration of 217 children in September 1970 and was turning others away for lack of room.[52] Beginning on January 26, 1971, several meetings were held between St. Peter's and the all-white St. Joseph's faculty to speak about integrating the schools, but nothing serious ever came out of them.[53] However, in May 1971 the Sisters of Nazareth left the white parish. The school was placed in the care of lay teachers, and that September, thirty-nine white children from St. Joseph's registered at the sisters' school.[54] In order to accommodate this new influx of students, Sister Carissima Zelenak, the principal, received permission from Bishop Albert Fletcher to purchase two mobile classrooms,[55] but before the plan was carried out, he retired, and Bishop Andrew J. McDonald was consecrated bishop of Little Rock.[56] He took a different view of the situation in Pine Bluff. By using both school buildings there would be no need for mobile classrooms, and he ordered the two school boards to appoint committees and address the problems of the merger, the school to be named the Pine Bluff Catholic School.[57] On April 15, 1973, the sisters received word from the bishop that the merger would take place that September.[58] Since St. Peter's had an excellent gym, grades five through eight were assigned to its campus and grades one

391

through four to St. Joseph's.[59] Sister Carissima was named principal.[60]

It was clear that the white people vehemently opposed the merger and were going through the motions only because the bishop had told them they had to do it. Consequently, the combined school boards had some very stormy meetings during the summer.[61] When September came, only 318 children enrolled out of a possible 450. The blacks weren't able to pay the higher tuition, and the whites refused to come.[62] The situation worsened when two lay teachers resigned in October,[63] followed by parents withdrawing twelve of the white students in November.[64]

In September 1974 only 206 pupils registered, less than the number at St. Peter's before the two schools had merged.[65] To reduce expenses the school board agreed to locate on one campus—St. Peters's—which meant that the school was in a less favorable position than before the merger since it had lost some of its black students due to a tuition hike.[66]

Sister Agnes Marie and her councillors decided that they had had enough, and in a surprise move they withdrew the sisters from Pine Bluff entirely.[67]

An article in the Pine Bluff *Commercial* on February 2, 1975, read:

> *The news that Pine Bluff's Catholic School board had made a decision to close the Catholic School system here comes as a shock . . . . Some have traced the declining enrollment in the Catholic schools to their admirable decision to integrate in the most complete and sincere fashion, just as the public schools have.*
>
> *If the only way to save these parochial schools would be to maintain racial segregation, of course that would*

392

be unworthy. To run a religious institution as a School of the Holy Evasion would not only be unworthy; it would be an abomination.[68]

It's interesting to see that in Pine Bluff Bishop McDonald had tried to exercise leadership by pushing for integration, but the people's attitudes were not changed and in the end they were able to destroy everything he had tried to accomplish.

St. Bartholomew's School in Little Rock had closed its doors in May 1973, its 25 Catholic children placed in the predominantly white schools.[69]

As early as April 1952 Msgr. Koury, superintendent of the Mississippi Catholic schools, had requested a Holy Spirit Missionary Sister for the diocesan Department of Education,[70] but the provincial superiors, already finding it difficult to staff the community's schools in the South, believed that their first commitment was to them.[71] In 1966 a dynamic, personable nun, Sister Betty Tranel, who was teaching at St. Joseph's School in Meridian, became involved with the youth religious education program in the city, later expanding it to include adults. Msgr. Scanlon was so impressed with her teaching methods that he spoke about her to Msgr. Koury, who visited her classroom and was likewise impressed and asked her to work in the Diocesan Office of Religious Education.[72] This time the superiors said yes, and in 1968 Sister Betty became religious education coordinator for the northern half of the state; in 1970 she took charge of the entire state, working through the religious coordinator in each of the 108 parishes in the diocese, teaching religion teachers content and methodology, and instructing parents on how to prepare their children for the sacraments of the Eucharist, reconciliation, and confirmation.[73]

The three film strips that she found in the office when she arrived in 1968 grew to $20,000 worth of material by 1971, and included not only film strips, but movies and music records which were loaned to the diocesan schools around the state as books are loaned through libraries.[74]

When Holy Ghost High School closed in Jackson, Msgr. Canonici, who had worked closely with Sister Kathleen in her role as the liaison person between the Diocesan Office of Education and the Holy Spirit Missionary Sisters, offered her the position of Curriculum Coordinator for the Mississippi Catholic Schools. Her duties included planning and supervising curriculum and personnel for grades seven through twelve; developing inservice teacher-training programs and coordinating education programs for these grades.[75] She also represented the diocese on the Mississippi State Advisory Council for Titles I and III of the Elementary and Secondary Educational Act.[76]

Both sisters held positions through which they could influence the instructional materials passed on to both children and adults in Mississippi and show in their day-to-day contacts with the parishes and schools a respect for both races that would be conducive to lessening race-related prejudices.

For some time the Holy Spirit Missionary Sisters had discussed the possibility of having a state-wide conference on human relations as a means of bringing both races together for dialogue. There had been several such conferences in the past, the last probably in September of 1967, which was sparsely attended.[77] When Sister Ann Therese proposed having the conference through the Social Peace and Justice Committee of the Sisters' Senate, the idea was accepted, and she was named the chairperson of the steering committee.[78] Backed by the Priests' Senate[79] and laity who were active in regional Peace and Justice Task Forces set up around the diocese to work for improving race relations,[80] it was not difficult to persuade Bishop Brunini to support the conference, especially when he learned that the steering committee was not composed of outside agitators, but were members of his own flock, people who sincerely wanted to face the issues of racial inequality in the Mississippi Catholic Church. He seemed even grateful that the Sisters' Senate was helping him in his effort to educate the Catholics of the diocese and offered them his full support.[81]

At the urging of members in the Priests' Senate, Bishop Brunini sent a strong letter to each of the priests in the diocese inviting them to attend the conference and to bring with them some of their interested parishioners.[82] The laity were also invited through the Regional Task Forces for Peace and Justice.[83]

The bishop, except for his opening and closing remarks at the conference, which was held at the Hotel Heidelberg, Jackson, on January 29 and 30, 1971, sat in the audience with his priests and laity as a listener, a learner.[84] The speakers—blacks, whites, Hispanics and American Indians—were all well-known Mississippians, products of their time and culture, who understood better than others ever could the problems facing their people, and they spoke forcibly, candidly, and sincerely. Not even the bishop was spared, but to all unpleasant observa-

395

tions he meekly turned his other cheek, not excusing, not flinching. He had given his people an opportunity to speak, and he would listen to what they had to say. His presence at the conference was probably the key to its success in healing many race-related scars that had been marring the beauty of the Mississippi Catholic Church over the years. It was a Church pulling together, trying to understand itself, trying to love itself.[85]

As a follow-up of the conference, tri-ethnic materials—on blacks, Hispanics, and Indians—were sent to all the diocesan schools, and plans were made to follow this up with a training program for eighth grade teachers.[86]

In September 1975, seventy years after Father Heick had tried to open a school for blacks in Merigold, black and white Catholics were taking their first giant steps in dialoguing with one another as equals. For seventy years the sisters had worked quietly, humbly, but consistently within the system, slowly forming a black Catholic Church in Mississippi and Arkansas that *could* dialogue and confront the Church with its racism.

That September St. Rose of Lima School in Bay St. Louis paired with Our Lady of the Gulf, the combined schools given the name the Bay St. Louis Catholic Schools. Holy Ghost School remained open with kindergarten and grades one through four. The Holy Spirit Missionary Sisters had left the other parishes in Mississippi and Arkansas. It was the age of the laity, and thanks to the sisters' seventy years in Mississippi and fifty years in Arkansas, there were communities of black Catholic men and women who could carry on the faith.

Chapter XX Footnotes: Septembers in the Seventies

1. Sister Engratia Gales, Report to Superiors, November 8-December 5; Meridian House and School Chronicles.

2. Ibid.

3. Ibid.

4. Ibid.

5. Ibid.

6. Ibid.

7. MHC, March 21, 1970, and April 28, 1970; Engratia to Marilyn Dobberstein, Provincial Superior, April 20, 1970.

8. Engratia to Marilyn, April 20, 1970, and April 21, 1970.

9. *Mississippi Register*, Supplement, Vol. XIII, No. 11, January 27, 1967; MHC, January 15, 1966; MSC, February 23, 1964.

10. School Reports, Meeting held by Holy Spirit Missionary Sisters in Jackson on November 28, 1970.

11. Ibid.

12. GHC, October 25, 1964.

13. Greenville Rectory Files, Benoit to Brunini, February 3, 1970.

14. Proposal of Sacred Heart School Board to St. Joseph School Board, presented February 9, 1970.

15. Ibid.

16. Interview with Sister Ann Therese Miller, January 1, 1970.

17. Ibid.

18. Ann Therese to Bishop Brunini and Msgr. Canonici, May 3, 1970; Ann Therese to Marilyn, May 11, 1970; Report on Greenville by Sister Engratia (February 11-March 11, 1970).

19. Engratia's Report; Copy of St. Joseph School Board Letter, March 3, 1970.

20. Ibid.

21. Sacred Heart School Board to St. Joseph Board, April 17, 1970.

22. Engratia's Report, op. cit.

23. Ibid.

24. Engratia's Report of St. Mary's (December 9-23, 1969).

25. Interview with Sister Priscilla Burke, June 16, 1970.

26. Ibid.; Priscilla to Brunini, March 5, 1970.

27. Interview with Priscilla, June 16, 1970.

28. Ibid.

29. VHC, May 2, 1969.

30. Ibid.

31. VHC, May 2, 1968.

32. Sister Ancilla Harkins, RSM, to Marilyn, August 24, 1967; VHC, August 18, 1967.

33. Priscilla to Msgr. George L. Broussard, January 29, 1970; Brunini to Priscilla, April 6, 1970.

34. St. Mary's School Board to Brunini, January 29, 1970.

35. VSC, date not noted.

36. Rev. Frank Corcoran to Marilyn, February 23, 1970.

37. Priscilla to Brunini, April 4, 1970.

38. Holy Spirit Sisters' Meeting in Jackson, op. cit.

39. Sister Mary Pardy to parents, May 3, 1968; Mrs. Lionell Bradley, Secretary, to parents, not dated.

40. Holy Spirit Sisters' Meeting, op. cit.

41. Interview with Sister Mary Pardy, February 7, 1970; Bay House Chronicle, undated (hereafter cited BHC).

42. Mary, op. cit.

43. Meeting, op. cit.

44. Mary, op. cit.

45. MHC, April 11, 1970.

46. Interview with Rev. Anthony Bourges, June 14, 1971.

47. Sister Agnes Marie Crabb, Provincial, to Sisters, April 17, 1972.

48. Interview with Parish, September 27, 1974.

49. Agnes Marie to Sisters, February 14, 1973.

50. Sister Anacleta Kaiser, paper undated.

51. Ibid.

52. Pine Bluff School Chronicle (hereafter cited PBSC), August 1, 1970.

53. Ibid., January 26, 1971, and January 27.

54. Ibid., April 16 and August 30, 1971.

55. Ibid., November 1, 1971.

56. Ibid., February 25, 1972.

57. Ibid., April 15, 1973.

58. Ibid.

59. Interview with Sister Carissima Zelenak, March 12, 1983.

60. PBSC, 1973-74 summer.

61. Ibid.

62. Ibid.

63. Ibid., October 18, 1973.

64. Ibid., November 2, 1973.

65. Ibid., August 21 and 22, 1974.

66. Ibid.

67. Sister Carissima Zelenak, op. cit.

68. Newspaper clipping in chronicle.

69. Little Rock School Chronicle, June 3, 1973.

70. Paper in Diocesan School Archives, School Board Meeting, April 29, 1952.

71. Diocesan Education Office, folder School Board Meeting, April 29, 1952.

72. MHC, November 13, 1966; August 22, 1967; Interview with Sister Betty, June 9, 1971, op. cit.

73. Betty, February, 1974.

74. Ibid.

75. PP, Agnes Marie to Sisters, July 20, 1970.

76. Interview with Sister Kathleen Kane, December 10, 1974.

77. Greenville Convent files, Koury to Clergy and Religious of the Diocese, September 12, 1967; MHC, September 23, 1967; Interview with Ann Therese, January 1, 1971.

78. Meeting of the Peace and Social Justice Committee of the Sisters' Senate, undated; Interview with Sister Ann Therese Miller, January 1, 1971.

79. Ibid.

80. Ibid.

81. Ann Therese, December 22, 1970.

82. Ibid.

83. Ibid.

84. Author's observations.

85. Ibid.

86. Interview with Sisters Kathleen and Ann Therese, April 24, 1971.

Cottonfield . . .just outside Memphis, TN

Going Home . . .a scene almost forgotten in the new south

Bales of cotton . . .ready for market, with cotton gin in the background

Sr. Dolores Marie and Neighborhood Kids, Greenville, MS